From Vendor To Adviser

DAVID STELZL

For information about this title or other books and/or electronic media, contact the publisher at: SVLC, PO 628 Waxhaw, NC 28173

Printed in the United States of America

Cover Photography by Hannah Stelzl

Edited by Lynn Bowen

ISBN-13: 978-1466319462

DEDICATION

To my family members who inspire me to reach higher toward the goal. Your prayers, encouragement, and undying support for all that I do give me purpose and energy to keep going every day. My thanks goes to my wife Tina, and children, Hannah, Sarah, David, Bethany, Jonathan, Josiah, and Timothy who encourage me daily to press on toward the goal of helping others. Also, to my father Henry who continues to provide much support, always there answering questions and encouraging me.

CONTENTS

ACKNOWLEDGMENTS

This book is a product of years of trial and error, study and brainstorming. People have mentored me, supported me, hired me, and encouraged me to step out from the safety of big company employment to pursue those things I am passionate about. There is no way to mention or thank everyone, so I extend my heartfelt gratitude to all who have helped make it possible.

I am grateful to my wife Tina and our seven children who have sacrificed much time with me as I have traveled the world working with clients to build this businesses. A special thanks goes to my wife who ends up carrying the load for homeschooling, running the home, and taking care of all of those things that seem to break when I am out of town, and for those in my family who labor with me to make this business run: Sarah my office manager, Hannah my Creative Director, Bethany who maintains my office, and David my Sales Manager.

I am thankful to Lynn Bowen and my wife Tina, for their hours of effort and dedication while editing this book and keeping me on schedule.

For the great ideas, feedback, and encouragement along to way to think outside the box, I would like to thank: Landy Chase, Fred Deluca, Dr. Bill Gothard, Jim Guido, Jay Haller, Randy Sklar, Chris Squier, Henry Stelzl, Bill Whitley, Mark Wilkes & his sons, and my friends at the North Carolina National Speakers Association.

INTRODUCTION

I started my journey sitting on the client side of the sales table, working in the Information Technology (IT) organization, listening to hundreds of presentations. From there I made my way into meetings with Andersen and PricewaterhouseCoopers; taking notes as these high-level consultants led the projects, interfaced with the business leaders, and made the strategic decisions for my employers. As a custodian of systems and applications, my vision was to one day move from maintenance to strategy, but it soon became clear this wouldn't happen while sitting with the IT group.

From there, I joined various consulting companies, helped start one, developed practices for others, and worked my way through systems engineering, project management, presales, selling, marketing, management, and ownership; finally emerging from IT solutions to speaking, training, and consulting. This book is not about theory, but is instead a collection of stories and experiences, strategies and skills; that have been painstakingly learned through many trials, failures, and successes.

This manuscript is for those who really want to be the trusted adviser – people who are tired of vending and spitting out one proposal after another; only to have them scrutinized, picked over, torn apart, and shopped for better pricing. It's not for those who want to continue down the product quotation route of the average sales person, or those who might occasionally sell a project or call on a C-level prospect, but rather for those who are ready to move out of their comfort zone and truly help business leaders solve problems, overcome challenges, and face the roadblocks of growing their businesses amidst heavy competition.

What If?

What if sales were different? What if my clients called me whenever they were working on new initiatives, or when their company was acquiring another company, or when anything was about to change in a way that affected or required or involved technology? As I think back to those days when I was working with, and observing, those high-end consultants, I recall that they didn't have to sell hard, close hard, or make endless cold calls, only to be directed to voicemail, ignored, or even hung up on. Why? Because they presented undeniable value.

Isn't that what this business of selling technology is supposed to be about, enabling companies to do more with less and giving them greater access to information, but without exposing them to danger? Isn't it about building better applications and leveraging the internet, and creating ways to bring new products to market, serving customers globally, and manage it all centrally? Why then is it so hard to get a meeting, or convince people to attend a free event, or make a sale without extending discounts into the 30, 40, and sometimes 60% range? Why don't buyers appreciate what we do? What if companies actually valued what we sold, and sought out the counsel we are able to give, rather than having us chasing deals and pushing to get the attention of decision makers?

The Problem

I believe it is a question of value. As I write this, I have just left a meeting where I was actually paid to present to business decision makers; delivering a talk on technology and strategy. A talk every one of them need in their business, but not unlike a talk I might give for free in a conference room to a group of prospects.

It was a sales call of sorts, but in this case, given to over thirty economic buyers. They attended because it didn't feel like a sales call. Why can't every call be like this one, where over 75% of the prospects made a decision to move to a discovery phase of the sales process? A process that will likely close 90% of the deals to either buy a product, a service, or a managed service. Is this repeatable or predictable? I believe it is.

Changing the Game

Meeting with one of my clients the other day, the first words out of his mouth, when he saw me, were, "Game changer!" Somewhere marketing and sales got on different tracks. Marketing came in one morning to their office and the sales people went out to sell. Somehow they stopped talking, and while marketing developed messaging, sales went out selling, and they just didn't see each other anymore. The messages became stale and calculated, while the sales people worked harder and harder to sell something; but without regard to the things that cause people to buy. For years I have studied this phenomenon, working with sales teams all over the world, looking at their messaging, studying their approach, and watching them present. This book is about the solutions I found that will make you a *game changer!*

Have you ever been to a great seminar? If you have, you know that the exceptional ones build an excitement and motivation that makes the attendees want more. They tell their friends, "You have to see this guy." They pay money to attend. There is value in the message, and perhaps a coaching program or audio series they are willing to pay for, in order to hear the presentation again and again.

How often do your prospects leave a sales meeting feeling that way? Do they want you back, do they encourage you to speak at their next board meeting, or ask if they can record your message? Probably not, but why not? Again, I think it's a question of value.

I want to change that. They may not record you, or pay to hear you speak, but I do believe sales people can become great at communicating with their clients, discovering their needs like a paid consultant, and making recommendations that move their audiences to action. I believe we can build a compelling value proposition that people do want to hear again, and do recommend their managers sit in on. And I do believe that salespeople can grow into an advisory capacity that demands we are invited to strategy meetings and product discussions. Developing a message that matters to business people, and delivering it in such a way as to actually help them build the business they are shaping, will make that happen.

Mastering the Boardroom

This book is about mastery. Perhaps you can look back on your years in school and see tremendous investments in time and money to get an education. Perhaps you pulled "all nighters" to pass your exams, or researched for hours in order to write a paper on something you found extremely boring. With all that effort behind you, why did your first boss, the only employer that really asked about your education, hire you for a small wage, with little regard for all of your investments?

But now, learning has become a passive exercise that only occurs as you accidently stumble across facts that interest you. And now is when it really counts! As a sales person, marketing professional, or manager of a team charged with driving business, your potential is great. This book is meant for the person who wants to learn – who wants to harness the power of effective messaging and value proposition; a person with a vision for mastery and success.

Hard work does pay off, but that alone won't allow you to reach your full potential. By becoming proficient at the skills of presenting, discovery, assessment, proposal writing, fee setting, and positioning, you will find that sales doesn't have to be a process where you push people to buy. These skills can put you in the respectable role of advising those who are running divisions and companies, and need your input to keep it going, improve its efficiency, and maintain an acceptable level of risk, as they deploy technology to get it done. With this will come much greater sales potential, as you point them to the right products and services to build their business.

Going from Vendor to Adviser is the vision. It is about moving away from haggling, and manipulating, to advising and helping. Walking into the board room, welcomed by those waiting to see you, sensing their expectation that you will be delivering value that will somehow make their businesses better, their lives easier, and their risk lessened, is the result. This is the role of the adviser and as we go through the book, I will give you the tools to attain it!

1. REDEFINING YOUR VALUE PROPOSITION

I met Phil a couple of years ago. He worked for a small reseller that was based in a rural town in South Carolina. Middle-aged and tired, he was working hard to get back on track. Phil was passionate about his business, at least that's what he told me when I first met him. He had been with the company for about a year and his anniversary date was just around the corner. Since I had been working as a mentor for the owner of his firm, I was asked to talk with Phil and assess whether or not he was going to make it. The business owner wanted to keep him, but every month he saw lucrative deals in the pipeline that never materialized, and then was subjected to a long list of reasons why next month would be the "big month."

As Phil and I talked, he boasted of his past. "I've worked on very large accounts, traveled the world, and sold multi-hundred thousand dollar deals," he said. Still, it was evident he was exhausted and that no longer described his present situation. I looked at him, wondering how to help. "I'm dying Dave," he said in a moment of clarity. He didn't mean physically. His business was dying. Oh, he had a few deals coming in, but mostly low margin product sales that produced very little commission. His hope was running out. He could sense something was about to change in his world, and he dreaded going home to his wife with the bad news that he could no longer provide in the way he once did.

You see, years ago Phil sold for several large companies, including competitors of IBM. He had managed global accounts, worked with presales engineers and been recognized by his management for impressive sales achievements. But then things started changing. The world became different. Something happened around the turn of the century, that caused him to lose a bit of his momentum, and in the wake of downsizing, Phil found himself on the street. At first, things seemed to go well. He landed a small reseller sales position, selling to mid-size companies, working with networks and servers. Business was going well for the small town reseller, but for some reason Phil wasn't making money. He had grown accustom to a big staff, marketing momentum, and people calling in from accounts he already managed. This situation was indeed different. His management wanted him to go out and find new business, but it seemed like people weren't buying. At least not enough companies to make a reasonable living. Months later came the bad news – they were cutting back. It seemed like only a few months, but in reality, he had been there almost a year.

Down, but not out, Phil quickly found another job selling similar products and services. "I was determined to make this work," he told me sadly. "I thought, with a better understanding of the reseller business and better sales literature, this would be it. But history repeated itself and I was again looking for employment. I don't understand it," he said as he twirled his pen between his fingers. "My resume still sounded good, and before long, I landed this job. I had a friend here who was familiar with my past and knew of my successes. He promised this would be a great job for me, and soon I found myself sitting right here in this office, a new computer on my desk, and a phone just waiting to be used. That was almost twelve months ago. I haven't really sold anything this year. The quotas aren't that high in this small business, but my numbers don't pay me enough to live. I'll never retire at this rate," he mumbled, looking at the floor worn from years of chair wheels running back and forth. "I hate selling computers," he said almost angrily.

"Phil, what is it you sell?" I asked quietly. "Computers," he responded with a certain impatience. "Everyone in your business sells computers, Phil. What problem do you solve? What do you bring your clients that no one else can bring them? And who would want to buy that thing?" He looked at me with a puzzled expression. I could see the wheels turning. Phil was about to have an epiphany; a paradigm shift in his thinking. I began to relate experiences in the small business world that I had, after conducting dozens of events with small business owners. "It's not about the product," I said shaking my head. "Everyone has products and they all look the same – at least on the surface." Phil pondered these ideas. Suddenly it clicked and he started to get excited again. Could this work in his new market? Phil thought it might, but he needed a new approach.

It's the Economy...

> Only those who are able to create business...can experience long-term success

It really doesn't matter whether you sell to small or large businesses, or work for the hardware manufacturer, or the resellers, when the economy is weak. Companies cut back, decision-making moves higher up the ladder, and sales cycles lengthen. But even when things are bouncing back, and they are in certain sectors, the products are getting more efficient and cheaper. Only those who are able to create business with greater business value, and thus higher margin, can experience long-term success in this market. As technology continually moves toward the commodity side of the market, and mass distribution gravitates to online e-tailors, your ability to create new business will determine whether you survive.

Phil is not alone. I've met dozens like him in classes and mentor programs with a similar story. Some of them own reseller businesses, others run regional sales offices, and still others work as front line sales representatives for large and small manufacturers. They come from unparalleled achievement, but for some reason, as the market trends have shifted, they are no longer highly successful sales reps with big incomes. They are no longer getting calls, and those they call on seem slow to buy and far more cost conscious. As time goes on, they lose hope. If something doesn't change, they'll find themselves working twice as many hours and making less than half of what they earned ten years ago. For some, the end of the line will come and they'll find themselves "on plan", moved to sales agent status with no base or benefits, or worse, on the street, looking for their next gig; even if they've reached what they once thought to be retirement age.

Re-Engineering Your Position

Remember Michael Hammer, author of *Re-engineering the Corporation*? Back in the early nineties, Hammer had it made. His theory went something like this:

Companies have grown quickly, become bloated and inefficient. Hammer believed the solution was to strip things down to nothing and redesign everything, as though the company were starting from scratch. His ideas were well received and consultants made a lot of money with this approach. Of course, at some point, companies started realizing how expensive the re-engineering was and soon Hammer's star began to fade.

But wait. There is something worth hanging onto here. Remember, Phil's business is in trouble because his approach relies on trends from the eighties – old processes, habits, and product trends. He's jumping from company to company because he doesn't understand how to deal in a highly commoditized world, crowded with competition and choices that all look alike. He has nothing to offer in terms of differentiation, not because he has none, but because he doesn't really know what he has. He can't articulate his value to those overseeing the budgets. However, the good news is that there is an opportunity here. In order to re-engineer the business, Phil must change a few things. "Phil, you can't live in the eighties," I said. "It's a new millennium, and you must embrace the tools, methods, and trends of today. You have to take a step into the consulting world; the world of the adviser."

Phil nodded. He had been living in his fantasy of yesterday. It was time to make a change – time to re-engineer Phil's business.

Novell and the Heyday of Networking

In my early years as a computer scientist, the Novell CNE designation was coveted by my peers as the ultimate status symbol. Remember LAN Times, the paper every IT department lived by? With a CNE certificate in hand, and a few years of installation experience, one could write their own ticket to success. Novell's system, the gorilla in the network operating system market, was fairly complex, proprietary and in demand. Then it happened. I was just three years out of college with my B.S degree in one hand, my CNE certificate in the other, and a great job as a network engineer working for a large bank, when Novell produced a new version of Netware that installed in minutes (4 minutes to be exact). It was at that very moment that something hit me like a ton of bricks. As I watched this proprietary, complex system go from days (or at least hours) to minutes, I mumbled to myself, "I don't want to be the Novell guy anymore," and that very same day I rebranded myself as the Router Guy (wide area network design).

Most of my peers missed this moment. Routers were new and no one really understood what they did. TCP/IP (the basic language or protocol of the internet) was something only government ARPANET (the early version of what we now call the Internet) people knew because traditional businesses ran on mainframes with low bandwidth, multi-drop technology. The CNE was suddenly worthless and no one really knew what to do about it. But I did. It was clear to me that wide area connectivity was the new Novell.

Many of my colleagues continued doing what they always did; riding out their career on a product that would one day mean very little on a technology expert's resume. The same fate followed those who specialized in selling it. Not that Novell was suddenly out of business, but those companies who concentrated on this one offering, were forced to compete for a few accounts as the rest of the world began adopting Microsoft's Windows platform for both server and desktop. I still know sales people, almost twenty years after that fateful day, who have yet to recover or reengineer their go-to-market strategy. Phil was just one more example.

What's the solution? Computer products constantly commoditize. Focusing on any one so strongly that you lose the ability to see over the horizon, where products fade away and new products come to life, is certain death to the salesman. Learning to discover needs and develop creative, technology-based solutions, is the answer. Creativity and innovation always win over the certified, product ready, sales person who has memorized the data sheets and takes pride in recalling almost any function or feature. Selling is not about memorizing product specs, it's about discovering needs and designing creative solutions to the problems common among business decision makers. This is the difference between the vendor and the adviser. The adviser is the sales person who is willing to take the next step and be a consultant.

The 5% Rule

Michael Bosworth, back in 1995, told his readers to assume only 5% of the people you might call on are in the market for some new thing (in our case, new technology); the remaining 95% don't perceive they have a need. But they do have needs. They just don't know what they are, or feel they are impossible to solve right now. To further illustrate his point, he gives the example of a balding man. The assumption for most of us, who have lost more than our share up top, is that there really is no solution. We are not interested in those ugly plugs, and going the "rug" route is not a solution, since it is far too obvious. While 5% of the men may be looking at these options, 95% of us are not. If someone suddenly came up with a painless solution and had proof that it worked, we would do it. In the technology space, the average sales person is going after that 5% group, and it is crowded! The competition is fierce. RFPs (Requests for Proposal), purchasing group involvement, and ridiculous discounts (at times greater than 50% off), abound. Selling has lost some of its appeal, and many reps are bringing home far less compensation than they should. One of my clients recently closed a million dollar deal and his cut was about ten thousand dollars. Something isn't right here!

Creating Business

Creating business means going after the 95%. The resourceful sales person gains access to buyers who don't know they have a need, and then demonstrates that need with compelling justification; backed up by a track record to prove they can fulfill their promise. Security is just one area that is predictably essential in every account. Most companies are doing the wrong things, and security issues are going unaddressed. Similar things can be said about operational efficiency areas that might include mobility, wireless, and cloud computing. But how do you, the sales person, find these decision makers, and what does it take to move them forward?

The Value Proposition

We've been lied to. We've been lulled into thinking everyone wants great technology features and the latest gadget. But, this isn't true. Most decision makers want strong businesses, profitable businesses, efficient businesses, and secure businesses. The *value proposition* must focus on real business value, and that means you the sales person, are addressing real business issues. As you are planning for the next quarter, start thinking through your message, your selling strategy, and what you will say in your meetings; especially those early meetings where you position yourself and your company. Is your message unique? Compelling? Interesting? Are you getting in front of people who can make a decision or are you getting demoted back down to non-decision makers after the first meeting? Be honest with yourself. You need a plan that provides access to people usually inaccessible to the majority of your competition. Events, social networking, educational presentations....there are numerous ways to do it, but done incorrectly, they are sure to fail. So, here's the bottom line. First, you must have a message built to stimulate action, then a means to take it to market. The adviser has the right ingredients and knows how to use them.

Old School Selling

Product knowledge used to be a key part of the sales role. "Tell me what you have, how it works, features, benefits, etc." Google has changed all of that and replaced many of your technical experts. Today the purchase starts with Google. Since most high-tech sales are done by referral and lead follow-up, the prospects tend to be people who are already in the research process. They are googling to learn what they can about technologies under consideration, and likely spending more time reading and researching the bits and bytes than you do. Sales has become a commodity and the basic sales person is no longer worth their wages. An electronic chat person can perform almost as well, and the prices online can't be beat. The more your products become commoditized, the sooner your entire company will be replaced by an e-tailor operating in some low-rent district, selling through a beautiful website. The high-involvement sales rep's life will come to an end if he doesn't change the way technology sales are approached. So what's the answer?

Reaching Back to the 70's

In the 1970's, Mack Hanan wrote *Consultative Selling*, a book that is probably more relevant today than it was the day he completed it. He described a process of measuring return on investment (ROI) over various clients, creating a database of norms from which the sales person can now draw justification, based on ROI and predicted hurdle rates, to sell the product. While I tend to steer away from ROI with most sales (given our inability to face CFOs with confidence), I do wholeheartedly embrace the idea of focusing on value (in this case, financial justification) to improve the client's position. The sales person must become enough of a consultant to figure out what those values are, and then demonstrate a connection between the proposed sale and the client's business needs. If you want to beat the online e-tailors, you will have to change your value proposition and become the valued consultant.

So What is a Consultant?

When I hear someone say they are a doctor, I get it. I have the same reaction to anyone who tells me they are an insurance rep, teacher, police officer, etc. But, when I hear consultant, I have no idea what they really mean. They might be anything from a PWC partner to unemployed. I would actually rather hear what they do, than what they call themselves. If they tell me they work with manufacturing companies, helping them improve efficiencies in the widget manufacturing process, I understand. I see that they work toward improvement in the client's situation, taking them from current to future state, with improvement, cost reduction, efficiency gains, or risk reduction (you can fill in yours), in mind. They provide the analysis/discovery, make recommendations, and point the client in the right direction with practical, specific information. In the end, it may be a product sale, but the real sale is in helping the client achieve something specific. Note: the later you are in the sales cycle, the less likely it is that you actually do this.

Let me offer a more specific example. When the guy comes by to cut my lawn, he's a vendor. If he suddenly becomes an expert on soil conditions, timing of treatments, pros and cons of various products including organic options that build the soil over time, then he's on his way to a bigger payday; he's becoming an adviser. A few years ago I contracted with a national lawn care company. My lawn was a disaster, full of weeds, large patches of dirt, erosion on the hill beside my driveway, and generally out of control. Now, I don't mind telling you, I am not big on outdoor landscaping projects. There are other things I'd rather do with my time, and between homeschooling seven children alongside my wife, and running a business, I don't have much free time for that sort of thing. For some reason, the lawn care company wasn't making the kinds of improvements I would expect, and when I had questions, they didn't have answers. Then one day I received a call from a guy who used to work for a lawn care company, but now runs his own. He was familiar with my lawn and recommended I take a different course. He claimed the company I had contracted only uses chemicals, and by continuing with my current program I would never actually improve my yard. I would just keep pouring in chemicals to make up for the bad soil conditions. Instead, he recommended a series of treatments that would, over time, create looser soil, build nutrients back into the soil, and hold water so that the grass would have a chance to get established before the hot summer weather rolls in. Lawn care companies, that act like vendors, are selling seed, fertilizer, weed killer, and other soil products. The advisor is selling me a green lawn.

It is important to understand that not every consultant bills time. Some make their money through the sale of products or other services. They consult with the client to bring this value, delivering it through the product or service they then sell, and others will do the follow-through work themselves with an associated fee. So, as you build your business, consider this: What problems do you specialize in solving? What business benefits or gains do you specialize in giving? Can the value you bring be provided through Google and e-tailors, or are you unique in some way that requires your presence? Is your value worth the additional price of the product or is the client better off buying it from a major distributor? These are the questions we all need to be asking as Google grows.

The Andersen Alternative

My first two high-tech jobs were IT positions. I started at a large pharmaceutical company, and then later took a job with one of our nation's largest banks. I distinctly remember the day a small army of well-dressed, polished strangers descended on my cubicle. They politely requested network diagrams, server names, and access to "my" wiring closets and server rooms. My first reaction was to ask, "Who are you?" "Who gave you permission?" "Are you authorized?" I didn't recognize these guys, but they began spouting off names I did recognize. Names of executives holding offices on floors I would only see after hours, when cables are being installed or systems upgraded. I soon learned these men were *the Andersen guys*. They had offices upstairs, worked with our executives, conducted studies, developed strategies, recommended applications, and advised the leaders of our company on just about everything, including IT. It was that encounter that birthed the vision for my next career move. I saw the need to move out of the "cost centered" job and into something profit producing, something respectable; a position that would allow me to actually have input into the decisions budget-creators were making.

Years later, I had the opportunity to team up with a small group of like minded entrepreneurs, to help build a company that would resell high-tech equipment and provide technology to companies around the Charlotte, North

Carolina area. I referred to our new company as the *Andersen Alternative*. Having bought from value added resellers (VARs) over the past six years, I knew that I did not want to be in the product install business, but rather in a position to drive technology decisions, then resell the product as part of a project, with an end goal of providing support with recurring revenue potential. Having watched the Andersen team, and later working alongside Price Waterhouse, I had seen consultants in action, studied their meeting skills and observed their selling style. They were pros. They didn't act like the resellers I was used to, and they had no problem submitting proposals to study and assess; even quoting fees that ranged from tens to hundreds of thousands of dollars (and sometimes millions). This was definitely the business I wanted to be in. I believed we could offer this type of assistance to the mid-market for less, do it faster, and locally staff higher-end technical expertise (they frequently had people flying in from all over the country whenever something complicated had to be done). In the end, we sold more product, out produced our competition, and I believe, put more on the bottom line than many of our competitors. The manufacturers we represented loved us. We had figured out the secret to creating value through intellectual capital, and were not dependent on the brand or lead generation capabilities of the vendors we resold.

Twelve Things I Learned from Andersen

1. They improve their client's position – a business level improvement.
2. Product is never the business driver; it is simply a tool being used in the improvement process.
3. Money is not at the center of negotiations, the likelihood of successful improvement is.
4. Discovery is an integral part of the selling process; fees are not quoted until the project is understood.
5. The discovery process involves both technical and business people, and the sales person is intimately involved with each business discovery meeting.
6. The primary targets involve people who have predictable needs, not those shopping for widgets.
7. The projects show specific improvements in operational efficiency, risk levels, competitive advantage, or return on investment. They are measureable and understood before the project is sold.
8. High-end consultants and engineers are part of the delivery process – and the sales person is usually one of them.

9. Projects are sold with a scope of work, not quoted as a line item with an associated discount.
10. They consider business people to be their peers, not the IT department.
11. They are continually learning, investing time in reading and attending educational offerings and often there is an internal program to provide mentorship to new-hires.
12. They differentiate their offerings with intellectual capital, not discounts.

Understanding What is Not Consultative Selling

Selling installation services along with your product is not consultative. Neither is training, RFP responses, fulfilling orders, or selling to those who already know what they need. Most of these things are sold on price alone. There may be a hint of existing customer loyalty, but in today's economy don't expect that to last. If you are primarily dealing with purchasing, IT, or other procurement functions, consider yourself a transactional product sales person. But, understand that this role is destined to be replaced by Google.

Death of a Product Salesman

Remember Arthur Miller's 1949 play, *Death of a Salesman*? Loman's downfall is directly tied to his continued misconception of himself...not so different from today's product sales rep. The product sales rep who continually studies the features through the company's online training resources and WebEx meetings, walks into sales situations confident that his product will do the job. Little does he know that Google has already been there. For weeks or even months, the technical team has been pouring over data sheets, customer reviews, technical blog notes, and competitive solutions. With a few key search words, it's all right there, at their finger tips. Lists of bugs, future release promises, user forums, and independent developers talking about what will come next and where this product fits best. In some cases that may kill the sale, in others, the product is named number one by some respectable E-zine.

In Jeff Jarvis' book, *What Would Google Do?*, he writes, "Google has changed everything," and he is right. If your company growth strategy is to be the go-to for some particular technology, expect two disastrous things to occur. First, expect your clients to be on Google, and likely ahead of you in product knowledge. Second, expect your product to be one of many commoditized offerings. The misconception of being there to deliver inspiring slideware on product features will be the demise of next year's sales team.

Google Changes Everything

I learned about Cobol programming, Fortran, 8-inch floppy drives, and outdated architectures at college. I also learned how to cram for tests, gain the teacher's favor, and correctly fill in Scantron test sheets with a #2 pencil. Eventually I graduated and needed a brain dump of essential information concerning pertinent technology, which at the time included Novell operating systems, ArcNet and Ethernet, PCs, and mainframe/PC connectivity. The first part of my education came when I realized that my professors lacked any relevant field experience. Sales people educated me, kept me up to date on product road maps, and even taught me how to address TCP/IP back when network engineers addressed everything manually. There was value in product knowledge, and other than some outdated bulletins our company subscribed to (at a very high price), I had few resources to turn to. Even books were out of date by the time they hit the market, and the current on-demand publishing didn't exist.

Enter Google. Need to know how to cook something, understand a math formula, fix an engine problem, find a verse in the Bible, or learn about a technology? Google it! I used to be the central resource of knowledge when teaching my kids at home. No more. Now I just have one answer…google it. Just about every question that comes at me during the day can be answered on Google (well almost every question). We may be close to the point where I don't have to ask my wife what's for dinner! Chances are it's on our family blog and all I have to do is Google the question.

So what is the sales person's value? It was about product knowledge, coming features, and compatibility. Not anymore. It's all on Google. So where is your value? It comes back to "improving the client's position." What Google doesn't have is your expertise and customer interaction skills – it can't listen and understand. You can find a million articles addressing someone else's situation, but not one that exactly fits your client's current situation right now, with the current market conditions, partners, employees, plans, and technology deployments. This must become central to your value proposition and you must be able to communicate it with confidence.

Re-engineering Your Job with Intellectual Capital – Your Next Step

In 2003 I was looking for something new. My wife recommended I sit down and figure out what I really love about the work I have done in the past, what I don't like, where my passion is (making sure it won't commoditize in the next year), and create the perfect job. Then, taking a note from Jim Collins, author of Good to Great, I added the economic engine concept. (Notice this type of decision process is not in Google). Speaking, writing, teaching, mentoring; these are the things I love. I do them in our homeschool program, I do them at church, so why not do them for a living? Therefore, on December 17, 2003, Stelzl Visionary Learning Concepts was formed. I found my niche and have never looked back. In fact, in the early days whenever difficult times would come, I would simply call up one of my buddies in product sales and ask him how things were going. His answer always validated my choice. Whether or not I sold a product didn't matter. What did matter was that I offered something based on intellectual capital, something uniquely mine. I don't sell hours, skews, or discounts. I sell IP (Intellectual Property). This is at the heart of every adviser's offering.

In sales, you must pick something you believe in, are passionate about, and accordingly can excel in; in that field. Then it must have an economic engine that works. Take inventory of your intellectual capital. What value can you provide which cannot be commoditized through Google or filled through your prospect's everyday social contacts? Hopefully, you can come up with something your company can offer and support. Then become the expert in it, and figure out how to take it to market. Remember, don't stop the learning process or the market will quickly bypass you.

2. COMMODITIES, PROFITS & THE
FOUR THINGS BUYERS BUY

When I first entered the technology consulting business, my new manager referred to our firm as a VAR (value added reseller). "VAR!" He said it with pride as though it meant something special. Coming from a large bank where we referred to our technology providers as vendors, I knew this was no compliment. Yet our manager seemed to take pride in a label we were already viewing as a commodity. I soon learned that, on the provider side, VARs were partnered with vendors and supposedly adding value, but in my heart, I knew the client perceived us all as one thing – the vendor! Simply put, as an IT manager I didn't see any value in those we called vendors and there was no such thing as "Value-Add." Vendors provided people and products at the lowest possible price, and free lunches on occasion. Being viewed as a vendor or a VAR, is not the right fit for your company if you are looking to build a profitable business.

In 1995 Geoffrey Moore brought us ground-breaking information in a book entitled, *Inside the Tornado*. This book was required reading for many technology manufacturers, including HP; a strategic partner of my employer at the time. Using a standard marketing normal distribution curve, Moore showed us how market adoption changes when you start talking about technology. It takes years, for what he refers to as *discontinuous innovation*, to catch on when talking about cars, traditional telephones, or modes of travel. But when speaking of today's hot technology innovations, suddenly adoption is taking place in months. Why is that important?

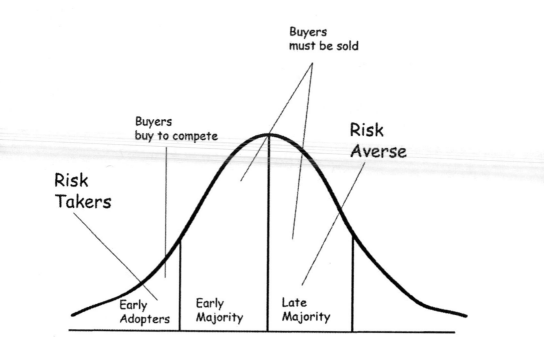

Technology Adoption Curve

In Moore's book, he is writing to the technology manufacturers such as HP, Cisco Systems, IBM and others. Working through pages of computer history, Moore explains how products that met the first inflection point of his model were early-adopters, then transitioned to early majority and finally, all buyers in the majority market segments. However this audience is a bit more conservative than the first, and unwilling to work with technology that is bleeding edge! This group represents people who might be risk averse or, like many information technology professionals, goaled and paid on up-time, not innovation. The first group, however, representing those who will take a risk with new technology, is likely in the camp of profit center managers, looking for technology that puts them out in front of the competition. This is further explained in Bosworth's book, *Customer Centric Selling*, as he applies the model in a slightly different way to various kinds of buyers. In it, he breaks down buyers as those who will take a risk and require very little selling, as compared to those who manage functions such as IT, and require lots of selling.

Manufacturers study these models with profit and adoption in mind. Moore's point was that manufacturers needed a way to enter the larger markets of early majority and late majority (possibly representing 33% and

33% of the possible market for each), as soon as possible. The first one there, would be given the greatest opportunity to become the market's de facto standard. Once there, the channel was established to meet the accelerating demand for their products, which Moore termed, the Tornado, thus the title, *Inside the Tornado*. This is where the manufacturer views the channel, but is not necessarily where the profits are for the channel partner. The problem is, most resellers (VARs) are positioned exactly in the middle of Moore's Model; perhaps the most unprofitable position possible for a reseller.

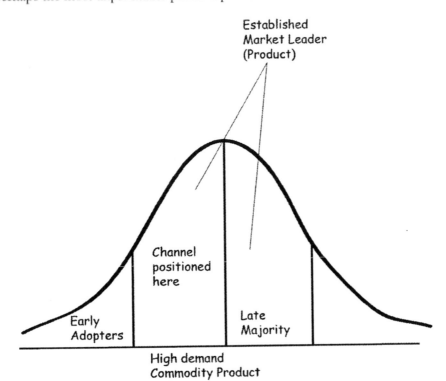

Reseller's Position – High Volume Sales

Manufacturers Who Made It!

Those who understood this model, or perhaps were just lucky, managed to get through the Moore Chasm (a point in the model where many technologies die for lack of adoption among the larger majority markets) and make their way into the early majority market. Those who didn't understand the model or have the power to break through, lost out. For example, look at Wellfleet and Cisco; two companies with similar products back in the late eighties.

It was during that time period, that I was just beginning my career as a network administrator in a national bank. I was working on a large project that promised faster turnaround time for corporate loan approval. Our goal was to reduce the multi-week process down to a few days by allowing our lenders to collaborate through email and share applications, as well as mainframe access through a national network. Believe it or not, the proposed solution, which I learned about when I was assigned later to the project team, was to use IBM desktop computers running DOS or OS/2 with a Windows-like interface and some type of word processor. The loan officer would write up the contract and send it around via mainframe email application, which meant converting the documents to mainframe language (EBCDIC - I'll spare you the details), and routing it through multi-drop SNA (IBM's proprietary network protocol – System Network Architecture) networks. Talk about cumbersome!

When I saw the plan, I knew we were in trouble and so I contacted Wellfleet and Cisco, as well as a few other up and coming router companies. Wellfleet and Cisco were both in the two billion dollar stage of their business. Competing head to head over router technology using TCP/IP, they were fighting it out for market dominance. Still, at this point in computer history, there was no clear winner. I guess everyone has their own opinion, but mine at the time was that Wellfleet had the better technology. In fact, we chose them over Cisco to build our nationwide network!

Fast forward a few years, and look what happened. Cisco had the marketing genius to move through Moore's Chasm. Wellfleet, on the other hand, was a purely technical company with little in the way of marketing. They failed to convince people to move in their direction, while Cisco made their way into the early majority; the coveted 33% of the market. Meanwhile, Wellfleet, seeing they were behind (just my outsider view here), merged with Synoptics, the market leader in intelligent hub technology. Synoptics had already made it into the early majority, so this seemed like a good move for Wellfleet. However, for some reason, they could not get their act together quickly enough. The new Wellfleet / Synoptics company, now called Bay Networks, fought to gain favor in the router market, but Cisco moved ahead, becoming the de facto standard for routing and then switching (taking Synoptics completely out of the race). When this kind of situation occurs, the leader often picks up 75% of the market. (Today Cisco owns about 85% of the router/switch market).

As an interesting side note, look at Apple with the Ipad. They owned 90% of the market in one short year! Who can challenge that? Also look at how fast they made it from product launch to early majority. They are quickly commoditizing this market and are able to control the application side of this platform so far. This is an amazing business case study on marketing savvy.

Once a company holds this position it is nearly impossible to unseat them. Another example of others who made it is Oracle, when they competed against Sybase and Informix. Their fight occurred during the same timeframe as Cisco's, and they had similar success. Oracle took most of the market and held it. They dominated then, and continue to dominate now, the database market along with adjacent markets they've built.

Novell, another interesting business case study, lost what was nearly a monopoly in the NOS (Network Operating System) market. For some reason they thought buying WordPerfect would help them beat Microsoft. They were wrong. Today, the Novell NOS market share is nothing to write home about, while just about everyone is using Microsoft despite all of its ills. The only remaining question now is, will Apple steal the majority market by moving people from PCs to iPads and iPhones?

The point of this information is that the manufacturer makes most of its money in the early majority and late majority markets, and so getting to these targets is the objective of the senior leadership level. These goals represent about 66% of the market share, so getting there quickly and becoming the de facto standard is critical to the success of any product company. Once accomplished, the company will work to hang onto their edge by developing new features and perfecting their current product. They will also continue to simplify the system, making it easier for more conservative buyers to adopt.

The innovative company will always continue to improve their product and therefore their product share. Those who don't, will lose. Look at the cell phone market. How many of us had Motorola phones years ago? We all did. The Motorola flip phone was the standard, and everyone had them. Now take a poll in your office. What are the popular choices? You will find Apple iPhones, Androids, and perhaps a strong following of Blackberry users, are the winners.

Innovation is key! How about Microsoft office? Is the market growing or shrinking? It is hard to believe people will continue down the Windows laptop road with Microsoft applications at $500/ seat. With Google apps, Apple's mail applications, social media, cloud applications, and all of the other ground-breaking products, Microsoft might be in trouble. Poor customer service, lack of pioneering product improvements, and a fat company are harbingers of a difficult road ahead. Have you read Jeff Jarvis' book, *What Would Google Do?* There you will find some interesting thoughts about the direction technology companies must take, as well as insights regarding how businesses might use technology in the future.

Let's revisit Cisco Systems who, historically, did well with their adoption strategy. They led the pack early on with routers, then picked up a switching company, and passed Wellfleet/Synoptics (which became Bay Networks, and was later acquired by Nortel, which was then acquired by Avaya) in the adoption race. Holding somewhere in the neighborhood of 85% of the world's router/switch market, they then came out with a compelling IP-Telephony offering around the year 2000. Their latest efforts are now focused on data centers, as they broaden their portfolio

Innovation and crossing the chasm into the majority market, are hallmarks of the companies that execute well and win the race as they establish their position and become the de facto standard. From there, they work to hold their position through improvement and great customer service, while going back to innovate and repeat the process. Along the way, mistakes in this strategy will create set-backs, such as Cisco's move into the security space with MARS and the SAFE architecture, only to then pull back with a focus on consumer electronics which resulted in some significant losses. However, a recent acquisition of Ironport brought them back into the race with a chance to address new challenges emerging around the world in cybercrime.

Earlier, I mentioned Apple's recent successes with the iPad. This company continues to surprise the market with innovation; even some novelties that have already been tried by others in the past, with little success. Apple entered the education market early in the 80s, putting desktop Mac workstations in the hands of students through school programs. I was one of them! If I remember correctly, the strategy, at least the word on the street, was if they could influence the students and get them to favor the Apple brand while in school, these future graduates would eventually become decision makers and bring Apple into the corporate world. Though it has taken much longer than I expected, we are finally seeing the desired results. I don't know anyone who is really excited about the next Dell, but Apple's stock is in the $350 range right now, having just completed a year's worth of iPad sales – first generation. The Wall Street Journal recently featured Apple's CEO, Steve Jobs, on the front page reporting Apple's 90% tablet market share. They have generated over 9 billion in revenue, with 14 million iPads on the street and a presence in 200 million accounts or businesses. Another great lesson in marketing. By marketing a mindset, and attracting a group of people that think differently than the average PC user, Apple has created a following that is more than a client base. People want to be part of this club – part of the innovative crowd that somehow promises to outperform the average worker. It's a paradigm shift in business – the iPhone, iPad, iLife and a whole host of tools that make computers more friendly and interactive.

Why This is Important?

It's important, because, as companies like Apple and Google perfect the art of simplicity and speed up the adoption rate, the value of the seller diminishes.

The manufacturers must innovate with greater simplicity, and must find ways to accelerate the pace of adoption, while also holding onto whatever market share they already have.

Commodity Sales and Margin Erosion

I recall early on, selling firewall projects that required a quote of $100K in products and services to get them up, running and secure. It involved engineering, testing, and third-party products to create a security scenario that worked. Often, TCP/IP addressing had to be designed, and addresses applied for in order to connect to the world. We would attend seminars featuring new products coming to market, no longer as servers and software, but rather as an appliance. The complexity was gone along with high margin design/installation services. Older firewalls were actually installed on Sun's (or some competitor's) UNIX workstation, and eventually some were ported to Windows machines, which were thought to be unsecure. But, with the appliance came the phrase, installs in minutes! Minutes? Wait! That was our source of profit. We were counting on complex integration issues and testing to boost profits as gross profit margins eroded.

If the manufacturer is going to hit that early majority market first, they must commoditize the product. It has to become simple, easy, and low risk if it's to be adopted by the risk-averse buyer. And then to be chosen as the de facto standard and picked up by the late majority, the cost must come down. It must be even more simple, over distributed (perhaps online), and proven. Otherwise, the product will die.

The iPad fits this description, with the exception of being over distributed. It's easy to get, simple to set up, simple to use. There really is no risk in buying and using an iPad as far as the user is concerned, and compared with laptops that require at least some set up, iPad is changing the way application developers write, and business people compute. It's like buying an iPhone, and a little easier than the MacBook Pro, which I am currently writing on. Note, all of this is far easier than the Dell Desktop that sits in my office to run my accounting software. With both in the office, I can tell you which one requires more maintenance. And until the Windows 7 operating system came out, Microsoft's Vista was driving me closer and closer to finding a whole new way to handle the applications running on that desktop.

The point is, the consumer wants things that work out of the box, require little maintenance, and have a longer lifespan with an easy upgrade path. Apple and cloud applications are both headed in the right direction. The manufacturer who wants to beat the competition, must comply. This is putting Google and Apple in the forefront and driving their stock values to unbelievable heights in what most see as a flat, difficult economy.

But all of this goes against the principles that, in the past, have made the solution provider/reseller profitable. Let's take a look.

The History of the VAR

Historically the value-added reseller was introduced to fill in the gaps as the manufacturer's product hit hyper-growth (Remember Moore's Tornado?). Staffing large sales teams to cover small, medium, and large enterprise companies was expensive, not to mention the integration and support services needed. Somewhere along the line, manufactures moved from the independent manufacturer's rep, to hiring an entire company to resell their product; complementing their internal sales organization.

Given the manufacturer's demand for high-involvement sales people, VARs sprouted up everywhere, latching on to new innovations and riding them into the larger majority markets. Starting with the left of the adoption life cycle, manufacturers controlled product distribution, added reseller's certification programs, and worked to bring their product through Moore's Chasm…even if they didn't really understand, that's what they were doing. Once established, more feet were needed on the street. In some cases it was all product fulfillment. In others, project work and design were sold, front-ending the product sale. In all cases, high-tech sales people were generating large sales, and demanding strong salaries.

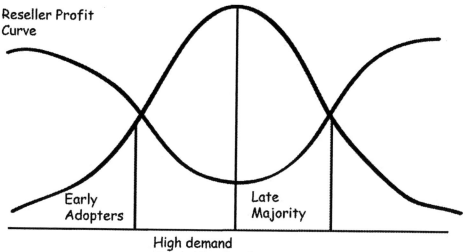

Reseller Value Curve

The tension came as resellers saw the acceleration of commoditization. As long ago as 1996, I heard resellers talking about the need to move away from product, focusing their efforts on selling services with higher margins. The manufacturer's view was, "Installation services will make up for the margin loss," but they didn't. Sun Microsystems wanted their new mainframe sales process to be led by a complementary assessment; something resellers could probably sell for fifty thousand dollars, given the option. Sun was insistent on not charging in order to drive more product deals, but the margin pressure on the reseller was significant.

Over the past fifteen years this pressure has continued to grow as products like the iPad move through the first half of Moore's model faster than ever. There are no installation services to speak of, and support is likely a simple replacement. New innovation has been replaced largely with technology advancements that bring us less complexity, and lower margin. Not only does this affect the VAR sales team, it reduces the need for high-involvement sellers across the board; at least those who are simply function-feature literate sales people.

Does the high-involvement model still make sense? The smart seller continues to reinvent, looking for new, discontinuous innovation to fuel their pipeline, and learning how to apply whatever technology they sell to solving business problems. This has worked for some, simply because new discontinuous products tend to require some level of integration. Even the iPhone and iPad have some application integration and security challenges out of the box.

Virtualization and Unified Communications or VOIP (Voice over IP) are two areas where discontinuous innovation created new markets for these high-touch, sales efforts. VOIP was big enough in the year 2000 to convince many resellers to start up or retool, almost entirely focusing on one technology. This was not much different than a host of resellers that established themselves around PCs in the eighties, then Novell in the early nineties, UNIX in the mid nineties, and networking (routers and switches) on the heels of that. It seems, about every five to eight years, there's been a new innovation offering, a chance to retool and go after higher margins with more complex sales – at least until recently. The astute sales people have reinvented themselves for each one, leaving those less observant product specialists in a wake of rusty hard drives and outdated floppy disks.

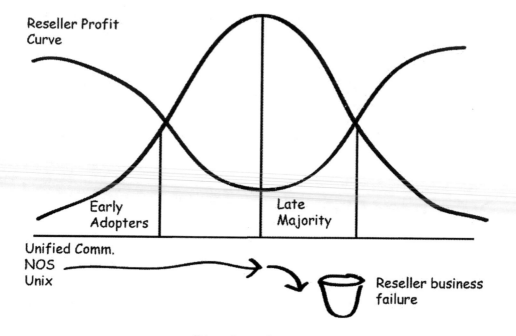

Discontinuous Innovation

The point is, the high-priced sales model which relies on high-end sales people, is clearly in the early market segments. The value message is one of integration, but with commoditization, less integration is needed. So what does the seller do?

Enter managed services and annuity revenue. We have not had a strong discontinuous innovation to build on since the turn of the century. In response, software companies are looking for 40% of their business to be license renewal. Hardware companies are taking back some of the level-1 support services and paying less on renewals. Meanwhile, companies like Nable are developing tools akin to "Managed Services in a Box", a way to provide ongoing support services on a monthly contract, that target the small business arena. This is a great idea for resellers as it allows them to generate support revenue, like a Perot Systems or EDS (now a part of Hewlett-Packard). The problem is, with so little margin in the overall equation, both hardware and services companies are looking for ways to increase profits, while coming to the inevitable conclusion that, high-end sales people are not needed to renew support services or keep the managed service contract going. So why would I pay out full commissions on this type of business? As the trend continues, it is my feeling that Google will take over more of the sales process, leaving many sales people out on the streets. How will you, as the seller, protect your role in high-tech sales, with a move toward greater simplicity prevailing?

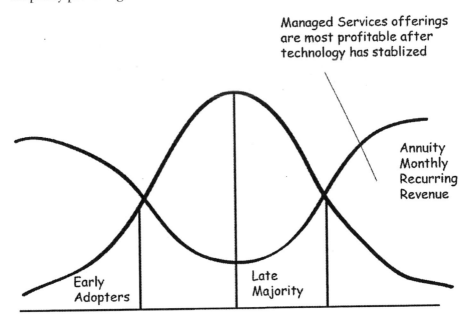

Recurring Revenue

4 Things Buyers Buy

Some would dismiss these ideas, saying sales are strong right now, but across the board, I disagree. Margins are getting thinner, and volume can't continue to grow enough to maintain the type of income we once knew in this business. Also, I am not advocating the dismissal of product vendors or resellers (moving toward all services), or asking vendors to eliminate the VAR to save money – moving to e-tailor models; quite the opposite. This isn't the first time channel partners have faced financial struggles, but as always, a change is needed. A change in the message and a change in the solution strategy. Marketing, sales and delivery must all be involved, whether direct or channel. High-involvement sales people must change their focus on sustaining value – moving away from product feature selling.

As I've worked with both vendors and VARS, I've observed customers buying four things. Just four things in almost every case. Perhaps a fifth in the consumer market. They are not products, and they are not services. All four impact business.

The Four Things Buyers Buy...

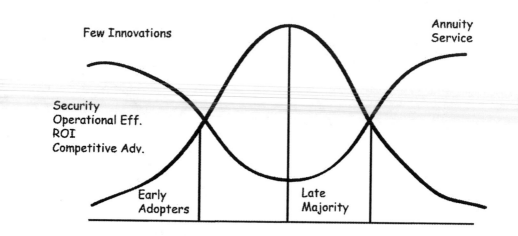

Few Innovations

Annuity
Service

Security
Operational Eff.
ROI
Competitive Adv.

Early
Adopters

Late
Majority

Four Things Buyers Buy

- ROI (Return on Investment)
- Competitive Advantage
- Operational Efficiency
- Risk Mitigation

The fifth consumer related area would be – Experience (such as a special vacation or the thrill of skydiving). I won't spend time on this one simply because it isn't relevant when talking about business to business sales.

Influencers may be buying features and managing budgets, but budgets are being approved based on one of the four things above. In fact, whenever there is a budget to be spent at the IT level, someone above has approved it based on some consideration that involves one of the four things.

When sales training programs urge sales people to call high, they are asking them to talk about business, to business people, and these four things should be central to the discussion. When they're not, the discussion is short, often hijacked by a technical influencer, and leads to repositioning you and your sales team at the influencer level, long term. It's simply a demotion.

All four work, but not all four are alike. And while you, the salesperson, can choose any of the four to focus on, the average person is not going to be successful in all four – it requires considerable focus. In my workshops I recommend sales people major on one. So, regardless of what your company offers, I am advocating that you pick one and become fluent in its language. Let's look at all four and see how this changes your message, your positioning with the client, and the value you bring to the client.

1. Return on Investment

ROI is likely the oldest method of justification, and the one most written about in sales books. People are always talking about ROI on the selling side, trying to talk customers into seeing that a product will deliver ROI and therefore should not be constrained by budget. In theory, this is correct thinking. The problem here is, ROI is demonstrated with math, not emotion, and when it comes to really proving there is an ROI, a certain depth in financial experience is needed.

Most sales people I know have never analyzed profit & loss balance sheets or income statement reports. They don't understand the real meaning and effects of capital expense vs. operational expense, or how full-time W-2 employees differ from contractors, when valuations, stock prices and other financial metrics are reported. How can they? If you've not worked as a CFO at some point in your life, what is the likelihood you can really show the CFO true bottom line returns on their financials? It would be nearly impossible. So while I hear sales methodologies calling for ROI, I strongly disagree and recommend sales people pick a different tact for demonstrating value, unless their financial experience is considerable.

To be clear, I am not saying it can't be done. I am simply saying it requires some very special training, not something you would learn in a one-day class. Car leasing sales people are trained to talk about ROI and do a good job of it, but in most cases they are talking to people who don't know better. They might get away with it, but you probably won't. Plus, it's always a bad idea to base your value on a pitch rather than your ability to actually meet a real need. The first is deceptive and manipulative, the second is honest value.

2. Competitive Advantage

In similar fashion, I don't recommend choosing competitive advantage. Of course, the question might be asked, "Why not?" This one is better than ROI because it's easier to see physically how companies can use technology to compete. However, this type of advantage is often short lived unless the company deploys some type of unique patented technology; something their competition can't go out and buy tomorrow. More often than not, technology driven competitive advantage is really an operational efficiency, gained by the perfection or automation of their internal processes. So in the end, it's really an operational efficiency sale, not a competitive advantage sale.

True competitive advantages are seen when a larger company has more buying power, putting others out of business by squeezing their margins, such as in the case of Home Depot stores competing with smaller hardware stores. Walmart does this by putting highly efficient distribution processes in place that are unaffordable by the average mom and pop store in your local area. While Walmart may have some unique applications in place, their infrastructure isn't so unique that it can't be copied. It's just unaffordable to smaller companies. The process itself is key and cost prohibitive to the smaller company.

Operational efficiency in itself may offer competitive advantage, as seen above, and the seller can use this to gain momentum in the sales process, but the efficiency is more easily articulated by the buyer. To go down the competitive advantage road with technology sales, may require a deep understanding of vertical market pressures. Perhaps, if the salesperson has come out of that industry, they'll have success with this technique. I often use competitive advantage in my own marketing. This works simply because of my experience (over 20 years in the reseller and IT business) in the technology market.

Competitive advantage may also come in the form of location such as the best corner owned by McDonalds, exclusive distribution of a product, or patented technology such as the iPad and Mac OS. These advantages are not easily matched. Will Dell come out with a better laptop than Mac? Probably not, in my opinion. However, they certainly have a less expensive one. Note again how first to market has earned Apple 90% of the market on tablet computers! This won't be easy to steal. On the other hand, Microsoft's hold on the Desktop market has grown with little competition, having leveraged the existing hardware platforms that have dominated corporate offices since the mid 80s.

I was recently proposing a training class for a large hardware manufacturer. My main point of contact wanted the training and had money approved for it. However, they required a certain multiplier as a return on investment. Is this an ROI sale? No, it's a competitive advantage sale. The request for numbers was purely red-tape, in this case, and was submitted using the client's ROI model. The same could be said for TCO (Total Cost of Ownership) requests. If the client already wants what you provide and has access to money, but requires some internal financial documents be filled out, don't think of this as an ROI sale. In this case we were simply using the client's model and we made my numbers work. Can I prove there will be a certain return on training? No. However, bureaucrats upstairs required the paper, so my client worked out the math and submitted it. My value proposition remains, competitive advantage – I let him know there is no way to prove these numbers will work prior to class.

3. Operational Efficiency

The third area is operational efficiency. I consider this area highly profitable, and a strong motivator for clients when considering new technology. The key here is in the second word, efficiency. When sales people talk about operational efficiency or the related topic total cost of ownership (TCO), they often have no idea what they mean. They are parroting empty words created by marketing people, without the vertical industry knowledge to actually help clients achieve this goal. So it may sound good, but in the end, it is just another sales pitch.

Instead, if you are going to head down this path, become an efficiency expert. I often recall, from sales training classes, the story of Cheaper by the Dozen (which is a true account). In the original movie, the father is known internationally for his time-in-motion studies. People from other countries would call on him, willing to pay all his travel expenses for a month (which at that time **This kind of wisdom is worth paying for and is certain to put you ahead of your competition** required crossing oceans by boat), just to present at an upcoming conference. The fees here were justified by the great wisdom he brought, wisdom that would greatly enhance productivity in the manufacturing process. This kind of wisdom is worth paying for and is certain to put you ahead of your competition.

The problem comes in when the product or service does not directly relate to a business issue. This is common with efficiency gains when considering products that relate more to infrastructure (such as routers and switches or disk). However, TCO numbers can play a strong supporting role here; where product doesn't necessarily require a tight connection to a business function. Virtualization and data center consolidation are good examples, where a true ROI might be hard to prove, but TCO may be more readily apparent. If you're going down this road, make sure your numbers make sense. It is always best to get numbers from the client - at a level above those charged with system administration. If the client has a TCO model they use, by all means, use it.

A question frequently asked is, "What is the difference between TCO and ROI? Our company uses these terms interchangeably." I use the term TCO specifically to mean, it will cost you less to produce the same or better results. By focusing more on business results and less on cost, the seller has a chance to avoid a true ROI study; which may be analogous to asking the CFO to audit your proposal. The last person I want to sell this to is a CFO (or anyone in the purchasing department). Once the focus on business moves to finances, value is compared only to the cost of other options, and not on the value you bring to the business.

You might think of ROI as purely mathematical. One way to describe it is:

$$ROI = (Financial\ Gain - Cost\ of\ the\ Investment)\ /\ Cost\ of\ the\ Investment.$$

True ROI calculations involve a deal's net present value (taking into consideration a proposal's future cash flow estimate and the cost of capital), payback period or hurdle rate, and internal rate of return. In other words, ROI at its core, is a math problem dealing with investments, returns, and the cost of capital. The average sales person's ability to compute these numbers, or even review them with a financial officer is limited in most cases, and for that reason I won't go into the details on this. The bottom line – avoid it.

TCO might be defined as the cost of acquisition, installation, and operation. In this case, we look at only the current solution (whatever is in use at that time, or under consideration). Gartner Group often reports TCO numbers for various technologies, taking into consideration the above as well as long-term operations and future replacement of decommissioning of a technology solution. When TCO is fairly evident, meaning one solution might involve many smaller servers or appliances that require data center real estate, cooling, and possibly additional staff, it makes sense to use this as justification for your solution.

As I mentioned earlier, when someone requires you to deliver ROI or TCO numbers as part of the red-tape process, the sale really isn't based on ROI or TCO, but rather this is just a protocol that company has for vetting possible providers. In most cases they will have a format or model for doing this, and your best bet is to work with them, using their models to make your case. However, don't fall into the trap of believing numbers are the deciding factor. They rarely are. The lowest price only wins when offerings are equal. So what are you doing to set yourself apart? Anything that can be productized can be commoditized. And anything that can be commoditized can be computerized. And anything that can be computerized can eventually be done on an appliance or smart phone. Creativity and perspective are yours uniquely. But make sure they are uniquely great.

True operational efficiency, on the other hand, can be easily shown if certain criteria exist. First, you absolutely need to be in touch with your customer's business. Second, your offering has to affect the business process somehow. Business opportunities can be created when both of these are true, as long as you can get an audience with someone who cares.

Case Study:

I was recently talking with an account manager responsible for breaking into a large fast food chain. He could have brought in his Power Point slide deck riddled with company statistics, product offerings, roadmaps, and perhaps a list of customers currently using his product. If he had, he would have looked just like everyone else calling on that account. Instead, he did the unthinkable…

Reaching out to the local fast food franchise, he explained his role as an account manager to the store manager and offered to come down to their location and work for free. His assigned task the first morning was to help unload the eighteen-wheeler that arrives around 6:00 AM each morning. It took about an hour to unload that truck, along with half of the store's workforce. But look what happened.

After working there for a couple of weeks, this rep was able to compile a compelling list of operational inefficiencies, from which he laid out a roadmap for improvement. Calling the headquarters was now an easy task, as he was armed with all kinds of data and recommendations that could turn around any fast food restaurant. He had bestseller material in hand. He requested a short twenty minute meeting, citing his observations of cars leaving the restaurant simply because a truck was in the way. He offered software and hardware solutions that would turn this truck around in about fifteen minutes, freeing up parking space, making it easier to get in and out of the lot, and allowing an army of people to go serve customers! This is what executives want to hear, and this led to a multi-million dollar sale that put him ahead of quota after one short twenty minute meeting. What are you doing to improve your customer's business?

4. Risk Mitigation

The final area, and the one I consider most compelling, is risk mitigation. Risk is a broad topic, but in the data world, think – confidentiality, integrity, and availability. If a system must be up and running 24 hours, 7 days a week, that's a security or risk issue. If quality of service (QoS) on routing must be perfect to handle phone calls, that's a voice integrity issue, which is also a security or risk issue. Disaster recovery, business continuity, access control, high availability; these are all security issues. The power here is, security is urgent. If something has a high likelihood of failing, the issue must be addressed soon. If something is actually failing, it must be addressed right now. There is no waiting on a budget cycle. But the best part of risk and security is this; no one has a thirty year advantage. When you approach a company with operational efficiencies, and that decision maker's thirty year tenure is compared to your zero years of manufacturing experience, it's hard to stand there calling yourself an adviser. In the security world, only the last few years are relevant. No one really has more than a few years of experience that actually matter — it's always changing and it's always new. The likelihood of their executives understanding security issues in the data world is probably nil. So become an expert in the next few months and start advising.

Asset Focused

In my first book, *The House & the Cloud*, I continually chant, "Forget products, focus on the assets, find the asset owner." This advice bears repeating. When you sell one of the four things, you are selling to improve the client's position around assets. Your discovery process will center around assets as you ask questions that relate to the prospect's business. You'll find yourself talking with their top performers about success and failure, and looking at how they use technology, data, and processes to achieve results. In later chapters, I will be addressing in detail how these questions get formulated, how to access the people you need to talk to, and how to interpret the results in a way that builds justification. Too many deals have been lost simply because the seller was focused on product features and offered the wrong value to someone with no liability.

Vendors focus on products, advisers help manage assets. Vendors will lead with products, using fear, uncertainly, and doubt to build their justification. Advisers will study the business and find ways to improve it. Successful people surround themselves with advisers, admitting that they cannot know everything. They use legal counselors for legal advice, doctors for health advice, perhaps a nutritionist, a financial adviser, and investment advisers may even be used for special investment strategies. At home they may look to others for spiritual input, help with resolving marriage conflict, and working out issues with sons and daughters. But who counsels them on technology use? In most cases they are getting product knowledge and some technical help from IT, but no real advice about how to leverage technology for improving their business. There is a disconnect here in so many businesses.

The asset focused adviser will seek out the asset owners. They will then learn their business, find out what is important to them, and find ways to improve what they are doing, while providing ways to manage their risk. This is worth money and should be the strategic goal of every high-tech sales person.

The goal moves from selling a product to achieving results. This is at the heart of being the trusted adviser, and will be central to any consultant's value proposition. The more you specialize, the easier this will be as you learn the language, study the problems, figure out the solutions, and become the hub of information every company in your focus area turns to when trying to build their business.

Profit and Process

McDonalds was probably the first significant fast food franchise, starting with one small store. From that genesis, an amazing number of look-a-likes have popped up on just about every highway exit. While most will not argue that McDonalds has the best hamburger in town, McDonald's has accomplished their mission to build stores in just about every part of the world, with a product that looks and tastes the same no matter where you go – and it's almost always delivered quickly. When I was growing up in New York, I learned that we were the only state where McDonalds did not put mustard on the hamburger; though I understand that has changed. Now everyone gets mustard, unless you're like me, "Ketchup only!"

Consistency has been their success. No matter where you go, graduates of Hamburger University are working behind the scenes to prepare the same burger at the same time. You can count on it. If the order is wrong, they replace it. While customer service may vary, the process works, is profitable and is teachable to just about anyone willing to learn.

The owners stopped "making hamburgers" long ago, and instead decided to build a program that works – a systematized program. Then, they sold that program to millions of franchise owners around the world to create a network of restaurants that have produced more profit than any other fast food restaurant in history.

Your success as a seller and adviser is largely dependent on a couple of key things; your character and your process. If you want to be the adviser, you'll need to be the trusted adviser, and while this term is way over used and cliché, the root of the phrase does **Trusted advisers** mean something. To be trusted demands **are trustworthy** tremendous character in the wake of so many **and able to** dysfunctional, greedy sales people, and to advise **advise.** means having counsel that people actually need. Being that trusted adviser allows you to prospect, market, position, discover and deliver in a way that leaves time for your family; while producing enough income to support your lifestyle.

I've heard it said, the $100 business requires $100 people, $100 products, $100 processes and $100 clients. The $100,000 business requires $100,000 people, $100,000 products, $100,000 processes and $100,000 clients. And, the $1,000,000 business requires $1,000,000 people, $1,000,000 products, $1,000,000 processes and $1,000,000 clients. Your processes will have a lot to do with the success you see in the next twelve to eighteen months of selling, and the value you bring through your message and intellectual capital will be your responsibility. Your marketing department, CRM system, and managers will try to help, but don't expect to succeed because of them.

There are several processes to consider here:

☐ Your positioning process – how do you position your value? Is it online, in meetings, by phone, in writing, or something else? Are you worth $100 or $1,000,000 to your clients?

☐ Marketing Strategy – you probably have a marketing group, but my experience is that you must market yourself. You can do this online through social media, book writing, article writing, speaking, and through every contact and relationship in your CRM database.

☐ Your Sales Process – your company may have a sales process, but chances are, few are using it the way it was intended. It might be good or it might be outdated. For smaller companies, it won't exist. The more you can refine a repeatable prospecting process, sales process, and proposal process, the better off you will be.

☐ Account Management Strategy – Todd Duncan, in his book *Time Traps*, does a great job explaining how he watches over his accounts. Much time is wasted watching over the wrong accounts, or finding new clients when existing ones leave. I recommend reading his book to develop a process to balance your time between those that buy and those who could be buying.

☐ Personal Time Management – related to the above is your time management process. How you plan your day, prioritize tasks, vet urgent and non-urgent calls is important. Todd Duncan claims that sales people spend about 90 minutes each day selling. Imagine what would happen if you doubled your time selling!

☐ Personal Growth Strategy – your company probably won't provide training – at least not sales and marketing training, and certainly not business training. They will give you product training and perhaps some surface type sales training. Having a process to learn is important to anyone who aspires to be the adviser. Time to read and a way to catalogue new information is critical.

☐ Refinement Process – Finally, a way to refine all of the above over time will help you make improvements daily. As one author puts it, if you improve 1% each day, it takes about 75 days to improve 100%.

Systems produce consistent results by following the same process over and over. Most sales people continually change their approach, thrashing about as they look for new business. Develop a routine that works, use the same illustrations, lead with the same programs, and become great at it. Successful sales people sell all kinds of useless things, so you can't blame the product. Instead, perfect the process and learn the intellectual capital around that product area. Then move from vending to advising. (Note: If your product truly is useless, you should change jobs as soon as possible).

Selling the Program

The program is what I call a series of offerings that create a path from initial introductory offerings through to recurring revenue or annuity business. For example, in the information security world, I recommend leading with an assessment, providing remediation and driving through to managed security. It looks like this:

1. Educational Marketing Events: Invite asset owners who have no apparent needs, and uncover a whole world of disaster through today's cyber crime trends. This leads to an urgent need for discovery and assessment. I'll go into more detail on this later in the book.
2. Assess: Discover the urgent issues, gaining access to key decision makers, top performers, and other key influencers. I'll cover this in greater detail later as this provides an important aspect, which is moving from pure vending to becoming an adviser.
3. Remediation Projects: The assessment discovers urgent matters that demand your attention. They create immediate justification for moving ahead, perhaps even that afternoon!
4. New Projects: In the course of making corrections, there are likely new tasks that should be carried out; creating longer-term project work.
5. Managed Services Contracts: Once done, there is a need to maintain an acceptable level of risk. The managed contract is much easier to sell at this point in the process.

This process starts with a marketing effort that has produced thousands of leads for clients I have worked with around the world. It has proven to be efficient at getting the attention of upper level management, and moving them to buy. By perfecting this process, companies have been able to largely eliminate the cold calling process that focuses on product, call blitzes and other ineffective calling campaigns. The problem is, many companies try doing this one time, do it poorly, and then abandon it. This is a mistake. Perfect the program and then work it to success. The end goal is to produce recurring revenue which should make any sales person or business owner happy.

What Clients are Looking For

I can tell you what clients are not looking for – another vendor. This book focuses on making the transition. No one needs another vendor. Google has taken care of vending for us. If you need a product, search for it and buy it. In fact, products that are not available online create an irritation for customers like me. If I can't buy it online, I want to know there is a good reason for working with someone live. Since there is always a cost in time or hard-dollars, when dealing with high-involvement sales people, there must be a reason for it. A great example brought out by Jeff Jarvis, in his book, *What Would Google Do?*, is real-estate sales people. If the MLS (multiple listing service) books were available online, would we really need to give up three to six percent of our profit for their services? Jarvis concludes, in most cases, we would not.

Recently I changed my property casualty company. I did my research online, but eventually had to talk with some people, which of course required me to leave email, and then wait for a call back. Why should I have to do that when the policies are nearly the same? Then, when it was time to run a comparison, I set up a meeting to review my policy before buying. We set a time, I sent an email giving them my contact info, and at the appointed time, waited for a call. Finally, I called the sales person to find out what was going on. They had expected me to come by the office! Why would I do that? What a waste of time! Ultimately, it took ten minutes to review my information by phone and I made the purchase with a credit card. I would have been just as happy doing this on a website, if it saved me more money.

Sound advice is what clients want. They want someone they can trust, who is business savvy, who has considerable business acumen and who has a vested interest in the success of their company. Advising is not an easy task, however, with the few who are actually working on it, the competition won't be great. Become a learner, demonstrate integrity, and discover how to communicate with those who need advice. You'll stand out as one of the few.

The Natural Evolution of Clients

As you move from vendor to adviser, your value goes up. As you apply the principles in this book you should find yourself working on larger more profitable deals. Don't be afraid to lose clients. Looking across your client base, you should find that there are old clients who are not willing to pay for the new you. They still want the cheap stuff at great discounts. Drop them. You can't manage a million one-dollar clients. As you build the million dollar process, look to upgrade.

Attributes of Great Consultants

Great consultants have great attributes. Those with million dollar products and processes, must have the attributes to go with it. Some say that sales people are born winners, and there is a big debate over who can become great and who can't. In the end, I believe great consultants and sales people are made. Some were made earlier than others, as they learned social skills and self confidence, or developed creativity while at home in the early years.

I am not questioning that some of my children are more outgoing than others, but this is not like sports where some have the right genes to be great runners. Most people can develop great character, learn to speak publicly, and develop a solid sense of self worth and servitude. At the core of great sales people I find a strong sense of self worth – not proud, just confident; followed by some key character traits including discipline and ambition.

Next Steps

How do vendors and advisers differ? In the way they present themselves, brand themselves, conduct first meetings, go through a discovery meeting, conduct marketing activities, set fees and deliver results. It's a different mindset; a way of life. It's not for the faint in heart. One author writes, "Self acceptance is the number one defeating factor among consultants." I believe this is a key contributor – if you believe you are worth $10/ hour, you'll act like it, price like it, and deliver like it. If you believe you are worth a million dollars an hour, you'll act like it, etc. But if you don't deliver, you'll be knocked back into reality before you know it.

Summary

☐ Executives driving the product business depend on making cheaper products, faster than their competition. This erodes the value of the sales person, yet is necessary to compete effectively in the product world. Don't build your value on product knowledge – it's short lived.

☐ The high-tech market is on a 5-8 year cycle. Stay on top of product trends and learn to apply innovation to the business process.

☐ Buyers buy four things – operational efficiency, ROI, competitive advantage, and risk mitigation. Specialize in one of these four and learn to consult in your area of choice. Competitive advantage and risk mitigation are the two most effective choices; risk mitigation generally commands greater budget, sooner.

☐ Focus on assets and find the asset owner. This means focusing on mission critical data and working with those liable for data and company profitability. Generally you will find these people in executive positions or running key business profit centers.

☐ Systematize your process. Develop a process to educate potential buyers on predictable issues, providing solutions to the problems common among prospects at the asset owner level. Then perfect the process to build your business.

☐ Sell a program – starting with education, discovery, implementation, and ongoing management or support.

☐ Build personal character in areas of time usage, customer interaction, and continuous improvement to reposition yourself and out sell your competition.

☐ More buyers are looking to save money and time by buying online. The serious seller will actively work to be an adviser in areas that demand consultative involvement, avoiding those areas of commoditization.

3. YOUR PERSONAL BRAND

There's been a raging debate in one of the forums I follow. They are asking if anyone can be a great sales person?" It's a loaded question with no clear answer, and the back and forth comments show a split among numerous contributors. The problem with the question is, it leaves too much to the imagination. There is no context. What type of people are already in sales? Do they have trainers and coaches, and how much time do they have to become great? (The list goes on.)

While reading some analogies given about athletes, it occurred to me that great athletes do possess a genetic advantage. However, they also spend their life training. The average high school varsity player (far from professional) spends all week training in order to play one two-hour game! Many professional athletes practice even more and play less. But, in sales, the average player spends 1 day training to compete the other 365 days/year. That is, minus whatever weekends and holidays/vacations you actually completely disconnect from your Blackberry or iPhone – which is rare these days. How can sales managers expect their team to win with this kind of regiment?

You and the Sale

Add to this the thousands of sales techniques out there and different approaches to selling. But when you boil it all down, people buy from you (or don't) because you are you. So what value do you bring to the sale? You've heard it said, "People like to buy, but hate to be sold." I've heard this for years, so whoever claims it is their unique tagline is probably lying...but the statement is true. The question is, "Do they like to buy from you?"

41

Your character, your motives, your personality, and idiosyncrasies define a unique person. You might be high-maintenance, bored with your job, angry or bitter from years of abuse at home or at work, or perhaps frazzled from stress that doesn't easily go away. You can't hide this – at least not for long. You might be angry or arrogant, greedy or self-serving. None of these character flaws can remain concealed and they will ultimately destroy your business. But, none of them are unchangeable.

You might be truly interested in the improvement of your client's business or position. You might be hard working, ambitious, diligent, reliable, and on time. These traits describe superior character, and as Jim Collins rightly points out in his best seller, *Good to Great,* character has a lot to do with the making of a quality employee, or in our case, salesperson. Great companies have great people, great processes, and great products. However, great process and products do not compensate for people without great character.

Positioning is how you present yourself. It's not a mask or deceit, but rather the real you. You can become someone who is highly technical and peers with IT people, or you can move yourself into a high-level position, associating with the decision makers. The question is, what are you willing to do to get there? While I don't recommend moving up at any price (many have sacrificed their families and friends to get there), I do encourage sales people to picture themselves working with executives as advisors, and begin partnering with other business people. It is a learned process that requires time and commitment.

If you find yourself being reintroduced to the technical group after each high-level meeting, you have a positioning problem. If your clients don't call you before they begin new initiatives, this too is a positioning problem. Trusted adviser may be a cliché, but there is normally a person who is considered trustworthy and able to advise at the executive level. Positioning is likely the most important thing you can study as you take your products to market.

7 Secrets of Positioning

1. Choose a Niche

PeopleSoft chose to start in HR software, and then branched out. Oracle dominated the relational database market before moving into all kinds of applications. JD Edwards did the same with financial institutions. Companies and people who understand the need for a niche have a much higher likelihood of succeeding. I've offered up the four things buyers buy –

operational efficiency, competitive advantage, return on investment, and risk mitigation, as a place to start or a focus for your value proposition. However, there are many areas where you can create a niche. One example of that is Michael Jordan's niche. When you hear the name Michael Jordan, you think basketball, even though he has played many different sports. It's his brand, or should we say, niche?

When I hear large resellers calling themselves the Walmart of technology sales, I cringe. That is bad marketing. Walmart's niche is providing the cheapest prices across the broadest spectrum and tends to appeal to the lower income market. This is clearly not the place for high-involvement selling. Open up a low income PC online e-tailor and you might make it; if you can find a way to sell for less than Dell. Good luck. But don't hire any high-end sales people or you'll find yourself out of business. Sales people cannot afford to go after this market. Call on clients that require input and advice. Walmart customers are not paying for advice.

It's tempting to go after the largest market, but in that market you will find many competitors with the lowest prices; Walmart, Target, Lowes, Home Depot, etc. They all call on the masses and staff little in the way of high-end expertise. Our local Lowes has about two people on staff that really comprehend what they are doing. I know who they are and seek them out when attempting a home improvement project. Unfortunately, for me and Lowes, if a better job offer came along for these guys, they would likely quit.

Specialize according to your personal talents and abilities, your mission and focus, your passion, your product area, the type of customer you call on, and perhaps your geography. Become the thought leader in these areas, and begin marketing it through social media, article writing, and perhaps even putting out a book.

Twelve years ago, the company I worked for was acquired by a mammoth corporation. I went from having an executive role to being a number. Recognizing the need to create a place in this new company, I began to rebrand myself as the "executive level security adviser ". I knew I could not compete with the very technical security people, however, I did have big company consulting and project management experience, so I refocused all of this energy into security trends. I went out and got my CISSP certification on my own time, using my own money. I developed high end presentation materials and began studying international news stories about the security discipline. My thought was, if the Wall Street Journal headlines stories about security, it must be interesting to senior managers. I was right. Before long I became known as, "the guy with the house", as people saw my House & the Cloud presentation (also the title of my first book, *The House & the Cloud*). It won the test of attracting new opportunities at the CXO level.

2. Be the Best

One aspect of Jim Collins' three part hedgehog model in the book, *Good to Great*, is be the best. It sits beside the need for passion and an economic engine that works. Executives want expert advice. No one likes to make a decision in a vacuum, however there are few who can be trusted when dealing with sensitive corporate information. As you are positioning yourself in your niche, determine to be the best. Build a plan to get you there. You goal is to become a thought leader. This means having an opinion, knowing the opposing opinions, and standing up for your opinion with solid justification.

When Rush Limbaugh comes on the radio, millions tune in all over the country. He begins at 12:00PM, eastern standard time, and for three hours, holds captive an enormous audience nationwide. Everyone listening in the U.S. is tuning in during business hours. Why? They want to know Rush's opinion on politics. Some oppose him while others love him. The more the liberals oppose him, the more the conservatives love him. He doesn't waver on any issue – his opinion is made known in uncompromising fashion (often to the point of being arrogant) and people love it on both sides. He is obviously committed to being the best at his niche.

Study. Become known as someone who has the facts at his fingertips. Make a statement. Take a leadership position, and gather together the crowd that supports your view. Form alliances with those who support or add to what you are doing. And as Jim Collins recommends, do it with great passion.

3. Share Your Story

When I speak, I often talk about my seven children building businesses and homeschooling. There are some who hate the fact that I do this. They think I am somehow abusing my children by keeping them out of the world's education system. There is another group who loves this, and observe us as we go along; waiting to see how everything will turn out. They are hopeful, but would never educate their children themselves. Then there is a third group, who either also home school, or desire to do so. This is part of my brand

On many occasions, people have approached me after a speech to ask me if I really have seven kids. Of course I do! But some people just think it's part of my shtick, like I made it up to be funny. Talking about entrepreneurship and using examples from my twelve and thirteen year old children is the real David Stelzl. The more open and authentic I am, the more real I become with my peers and clients. No one wants to work with a Teflon person who has no issues, no stress, and has never had a bad day in his life.

Some won't like your story. They may not do business with you because of it. However, your story will make your brand real with others and will propel your business much faster than anything else. I recently met Chuck Gallager, an ethics motivational speaker from the National Speakers Association. He was indicted for fraud years ago and sentenced to federal prison. Today he speaks about ethics at company meetings. He could try to hide his past, but instead, he shows up in an orange jump suit with handcuffs on. Some companies won't hire him simply because he has a record. Others repeatedly hire him and refer him because he is real. And when he tells his story, people listen because he has been there and understands the consequences of poor decisions. Who better to talk to your staff than Chuck, a repentant thief?

> Intellectual capital is the key to profitability and differentiation.

4. Be Unique

Intellectual capital is the key to profitability and differentiation. Your company must have it, but you should also have it. Creativity is one of the most important areas of development, and yet our school systems have taken this from us. You can't be creative on tests and pass. Start working on creativity. Set aside time to create. I used to schedule a day at the start of every quarter just to go away and think about my business – to create new ideas. Now I spend three! Three days, three times each year, I take off and head out for a personal retreat, a time of renewal, and a time to think creatively about my mission, vision, and direction for work, family and life. While your management probably won't give you this time off, at least find some chunks of time to brainstorm with yourself, or with colleagues, about how to improve your business.

5. Be Everywhere

Social networking makes this possible. Be everywhere. Build your profiles, comment on blogs, tweet useful information – things your clients care about. Start your own blog. Write articles. Use instant messaging. Do whatever you can to be in communication with the people you call on and work with. People often say to me, "You're everywhere." That is my goal. I will deal with this subject at the end of the book in greater detail, providing insights about how to take advantage of the free online tools available to all of us.

6. Be Persistent

One call doesn't do it. But don't pester. Instead surround people with value. One of my favorite sales people won my loyalty years ago by showing up at the bank I was working at, ready to do whatever he could to help. He invested in us. He wasn't begging for a sale, instead he was helping us. He spent time learning about our problems, offering free solutions, and within six months he was making a fortune as we adopted him for our go-to provider. It takes work and value.

7. Be Passionate

When I finish delivering a keynote speech, people often say, "You love what you do, don't you?" I do. I'm passionate about my topics and I give them all I can because I love sharing these ideas. If you don't feel passion for the business you are in and the people you work with, move on. Life is too short to waste it. And if you're not zealous about what you do, you probably won't be successful long term either. When people sense your energy, it excites them, too. Find something you are ardent about and go to work on it. Be the best, and persist. The diligent worker, passionate about his business, will prosper.

I have a story that will illustrate what I am talking about. The brother of a friend of mine was in business installing alarm systems. The job didn't pay well, but he was a man of character and passionate about his work. One day, he was in a store picking up parts (something he did almost daily). A man pulled him aside and asked him if he would like to be in business for himself. He said he would. Long story short, an opportunity was given to him to install a nationwide network of alarm systems in nursing homes, with a three-year contract to monitor and maintain. He took the opportunity and started making "big money". In the process, another man at one of the nursing homes came up with an idea to use the security technology to control medication abuse. This resulted in the creative use of some of his security technology and a contract to monitor it –for far more than he made as an installer. A diligent person, with great character, passionate about his work and a bit of creativity can go a long way.

Trusted – Character Does Matter

One of my favorite sales calls was one by a gentleman from Electrolux Vacuums. I actually initiated the meeting by contacting the local sales office when I arrived in Charlotte, North Carolina, with my new bride. We were looking for our first vacuum. If you grew up in an "Electrolux home" you may understand what I am talking about when I say, "What other option is there?" At the time, I was convinced this was it – one vacuum would last us a lifetime.

I explained to the guy on the phone that I wanted his top of the line model, refurbished (The new ones were way out of my price range as a newlywed). This is how my family had bought one, and my father had passed on this bit of wisdom to me as I was starting my new family.

When the salesperson showed up, he had some pamphlets and a box. As he began reviewing the models with us, I stopped him. "All I need to see is your refurbished, top of the line vacuum," I said. The salesman apologized because he did not have one with him, but assured us he could get it within a week. Still, he wanted to show us the next model down and demonstrate it. He told us this was about the same price, and really a better choice. Again I stopped him. He was all set to demonstrate, but I really didn't want to see it. In fact, he had promised to bring the vacuum I had requested with him, and as I shared this with him, all he could do was apologize and try to convince me that this was really a good choice. Refusing to continue, I sent him on his way.

The next morning I called another dealer across town and told him what I was looking for. I explained that I was prepared to buy now. All he had to do was show up with the refurbished top of the line system. That evening he arrived on time, vacuum in hand. My wife and I took it out, tested it, liked it, and handed him a check.

The very next morning the first sales person called us to let us know he had located a refurbished top of the line vacuum. "Too late," I told him. "We bought one last night." He couldn't believe it. In fact he was irritable on the phone with me about this. I explained, "All you had to do was show up with the vacuum you claimed you had, and I would have bought it. Alternatively, you could have told me the other day on the phone that you didn't have one, but would get one and schedule an appointment. I would have happily waited the few days and bought it from you. Instead, you told me you had one, and then came without it. It's just too late." A person with integrity would have checked first, and if a mistake were made, would have called before coming to let us know they didn't have what we needed.

Knowledge can only be received in proportion to a person's character. Knowledge without character develops into arrogance or pride – characteristics of many sales people that buyers find appalling. With this in mind, our homeschool program correctly emphasizes building a person's character across 49 different character traits, integrating this in with the discovery of knowledge. From these 49, I have identified several that I find essential for sales people to master. Like Ben Franklin's habit of selecting one of these each month, every sales person should be doing the same. In my opinion, companies cannot take the time to develop character in their people – its costly and time consuming. If employees don't have it already, that company should replace the employee in question with another who is a person of character. That said, you, the sales person, should be developing this on your own from whatever point you currently find yourself, in each one of the following areas (listed below). People are often hired for their skills, but just about every person fired, is fired for lack of character. Taking this a step further, behind just about every personnel issue or conflict is a deficiency in character. Character is central to true success. (The following essential traits are based on training I received from the Character Training Institute, Oklahoma City)

Character Qualities that Matter

1. Dependability vs. Inconsistency

Dependability is simply doing what I said I would do, even if it requires unexpected sacrifice. People who lack this character trait tend to be possessive, unable to delegate, presumptuous, and inflexible as described in our homeschool materials. You produce dependability by:

- Developing systems
- Studying time management skills and a time management system
- Developing a concern for those you work for or sell to

Evidence: Being dependable means that once you commit, the person you have committed to can assume the task will get done. When circumstances hinder you from completing the task, an appeal will be made to the proper authority or customer, as soon as you foresee a problem. A lack of dependability is rampant among today's company employees – this character trait will not go unnoticed.

2. Availability vs. Self-Centeredness

Availability means putting my own priorities aside and focusing on customers I am serving. People who lack this character trait tend to be pushy, intrusive, and selfish. Some ways to develop availability might be:

- Prioritizing your time through a structured personal planning session each morning
- Scheduling periodic times for personal activities
- Planning ahead to avoid urgent issues that lead to thrashing about and stress

Evidence: Availability is an attitude more than the ability to always be available. Companies today have reduced overhead by eliminating support staff, putting fewer people on projects, and asking people to work more hours and travel more often. The results are that requisitioning help is difficult without advanced notice. Yet, there is an attitude of availability that goes a long way.

Let people know you want to make room in your schedule, and get it done. Rather than immediately objecting to a sudden interruption in your agenda, agree to work on figuring out an alternative plan. At least try to comply. And when it just can't be done, be apologetic, and offer the next best solution.

3. Humility vs. Pride

Humility is recognizing those around me who have helped me get where I am today. By this I mean, most of us have benefited from the many friends and family members who have invested in our lives and we should take note of that. While people don't often talk about the positive qualities of humility, those who lack true humility tend to be self-rejecting, lack self confidence, and tend to be introspective. Most of the time, pride is a result of poor self image. Those who collect knowledge and show off are actually compensating. By building up and focusing on those aspects of yourself that are good, and by understanding your real value, you can rid yourself of the destructive elements of pride.

- Invest in personal improvement through coaching and training
- Learn more effective communication skills
- Understand your true worth to those you call on and work for

Evidence: Deflecting praise, giving credit to others, and promoting others around you is a great start. People notice this as a sign of leadership. Not talking about yourself, listening instead of dominating the discussion, and considering others' opinions and ideas.

4. Attentiveness vs. Unconcern

Showing the worth of a person by giving full concentration to his words is one definition of attentiveness.. A lack of this trait leads to awkward staring, invading of one's personal space, being gullible, or excluding others. This is another issue that is exacerbated by a lack of self confidence. People who want to be the center of attention find it hard to give others their full attention.

- Develop questions to ask during conversations
- Start taking an interest in what makes others tick
- Develop a concern for the needs of those around you

Evidence: Listening and reflecting back what your are hearing, using good eye contact, and not looking over someone's shoulder when others approach. Let your audience (in this case a client or manager, or peer) know you are sincerely interested in what they are telling you. Taking notes in a meeting is a sure sign you are listening. Drawing doodles in your margins; not so much.

5. Persuasiveness vs. Contentious

"Guiding vital truths around another's mental roadblocks" is how The Character Training Institute defines persuasiveness. People who lack this attribute will tend toward manipulation tactics, being pushy, using deception, smooth talking, and defrauding. Persuasion comes as you understand people's true needs, and are passionate about meeting them. If you are not passionate about the need for the services or products you sell, it would be better to move on to something else. If you are not convinced people really need what you do, or that you bring great value to your client, you can't honestly persuade them.

- Learn to identify people's needs
- Gain an understanding of how your products and services benefit others
- Become skilled at communicating success stories with emotional impact

Evidence: Closing business is a good sign, but there are others. Learning to identify mental road blocks and where people are having trouble connecting their needs with your justification. Learn to tell great stories that demonstrate success. Not all stories are told with persuasive power, but this is a learned skill that can be mastered.

6. Truthfulness vs. Deception

Truthfulness builds trust over time as one demonstrates accuracy in what they say and do. A lack of truth results in gossip, being tactless or blunt, showing disrespect, and being indiscreet.

- Commit to be honest
- Make sure you are selling something you can be honest about
- Greed often drives deception. Replace a focus on money with a focus on helping your clients
- Focus on relationships to the point that you must be honest

Evidence: Consistency, honesty, and accuracy in reporting facts and stories. Over time people will notice that what you say lines up with the truth. Commit today to be accurate in everything you say, and to disclose the truth without any deceit. Reporting a truth in a way that deceives the listener is not honesty and disqualifies you from becoming a trusted adviser.

7. Diligence vs. Slothfulness

Diligence can be seen as I put concentrated effort into the tasks that are assigned to me. A lack of diligence will lead to neglecting priorities, becoming overly zealous, inflexible and lazy.

- Track your time. Find out where time is being wasted.
- Plan ahead. Make it a habit to plan each day- daily, each month-monthly, each quarter-quarterly, and each year – annually.
- Develop a consistent system for conducting business. Like McDonalds, this will lead to using your time wisely.

Evidence: The person with a well planned, well prioritized schedule is seen as diligent. One who procrastinates is seen as a person who wastes time. There is a time to rest, and a time to work hard. People are watching, so let them know you have the right priorities. I always say, it's better to use work time wisely and plan your free time, than to waste work time and never have true free time or planned vacation.

8. Patience vs. Restlessness

Patience or forbearance is demonstrated when I continue on, not focusing on the end or demanding a change. A person without patience will tend toward restlessness, fidgeting, and uneasiness.

- See difficult situations as a time for personal development
- Focus on the process rather than the circumstance
- Go into situations with realistic expectations and a plan

Evidence: Not complaining under your breath when things are not going your way. For instance, sitting in a traffic jam complaining to yourself, does no one any good. Looking at the positive side of problems and delays, and finding creative alternatives when the current direction is not working out.

9. Flexibility vs. Resistance

Flexibility is a willingness to have my plans changed or interrupted by my authority or clients. Without flexibility a person will become indecisive, spineless and dependent on others.

- Expect plans to change
- Don't over commit before you understand the real situation
- Avoid commitments you can't control such as department payments.

Evidence: When clients and managers change direction, the flexible person continues to smile and make it happen.

10. Gratefulness vs. Lack of Thankfulness

Gratefulness lets others know, by my words or actions, how they have benefited my life. Without gratefulness, a person will use flattery, talk too much, be insincere, and feel obligated.

- Studies show that gratefulness is a key to health. Thanking the people around you reduces stress and other health issues.
- Create a system to follow up with those who help you
- Start looking for ways to help those you network with
- Start thanking people and the rewards.

Evidence: Letting people know you appreciate what they are doing. Writing notes of gratefulness. Recommending or drawing attention to those around you to bring them credit and praise from their peers and management.

Remember, clients choose their advisers. Building character is the first step to becoming a trusted adviser. Strong character is evident simply because it is severely lacking in today's workplace. The salesperson with exceptional countenance, a strong reputation, and a track record of delivering will have a page full of references, and a list of long-term clients.

Proverbs tells us "your eyes are the window to the soul." A person of discernment can tell just by looking at you if you possess strong character. Keep this in mind as you meet people.

Adviser – One Who Can Actually Provide Advice When Asked.

Becoming the Adviser

Great leaders surround themselves with advisers. Get to know any executive and you'll find that they have an inner circle of people advising them on all kinds of issues. Only through their advisers can they keep tabs on all aspects of their business, covering a wide range of topics for which they claim no expertise.

How do you become an adviser candidate? Many have said, "The friends you keep and the books you read will determine who you become over the next five years." Perhaps if this were written today the speaker would add, "The videos you watch and the websites you visit." In any case, it makes sense that you read the right material, learning all you can to interact and advise executives.

On the other hand, several executives have shared with me that they like to choose those who advise and work with them. When people over perform to impress or gain access to the inner circle, it often comes off as self-serving. Bad character is hard to hide, and a person's real intentions will eventually emerge.

How Can You Improve Your Position?

1. Read Great Business Books

I constantly get asked, "What do you recommend I read?" Few of the sales people that attend my workshops read anything relevant to business any more. This is sad. Think about the effort you put into school. If you attended college, even if you did spend time partying, you probably studied hard for tests, stayed up all night to prepare for finals, worked on weekends and holidays, and spent a ton of money and time just getting through the four year program.

After that, perhaps you went on to get your masters. You spent more time, more money, and sacrificed more of your personal time, to get a piece of paper. Now you are in sales. Your income potential is probably limited only by your own efforts and market conditions. You could be studying things that actually matter. You could be learning about sales and marketing, negotiating, trends, public speaking, and presentation skills. But if you are like most, you are doing the minimum – learning about the products you sell, and expecting your hard work to bring in the accounts. Sales are strategic, making those who do not continue to learn how to improve their craft, somehow lacking. I have created a list of some of my favorite sales books at the end of this chapter. Consider getting yourself on a reading plan.

2. Coaching

Sports figures, and now even high school athletes, hire coaches. The executives you call on probably have business coaches (if you call high), and many executives have hired coaches to help them become great speakers. Mentoring is what I really mean. The coaching industry has altered some of the playbooks on us, turning business and life coaches away from giving advice; replacing it with reflective listening. My opinion is that you should have a coach who is similar to a sports coach. One who gives you advice as they watch and critique from the sidelines. Peer group input, like we see in the public school system, is largely a failure. On the other hand, personal mentorship and discipleship have been used successfully since the beginning of time.

3. Training

Training, while not as good as coaching, is important as well. There are many things you can learn online, such as news, product features, and methods. Like reading books, Google has become an invaluable resource, and blogs can provide laser focused insight on just about any topic. Soft skills, message delivery, and selling are better taught through interaction. Insist that your company keep you up to date and on track to improvement. Like an athlete, without training, you will slowly become less valuable, and eventually be replaced by someone younger and more energetic. Don't get caught at age 50 without the very things younger people don't have: years of experience and invaluable wisdom. Some areas I recommend for this focused training and learning are: selling, marketing, speaking, presenting, and time management.

How often have you spent your own time and money on some form of training? The company should pay for it, but how hard are you selling your need? Training is so important. You should do just about anything to get it.

A Plan for Personal Mastery

1. Renew Old Patterns With Right Responses. In a recent book I read, the author spoke about some old habits we pick up through life. They often develop into natural responses that can be bad reactions in certain situations. For instance, it could be a negative response you give when people block your goals, lash out at you, or tell you you're wrong. Left unchecked, they could have devastating effects when dealing with your customers.

2. Brand Yourself as a Thought Leader. I was meeting with a colleague the other day that specializes in social media marketing. He is fresh out of college, so his experience is somewhat limited. However, he has lots of great ideas and lots of energy. We were discussing ways to build his consulting practice and considering different directions to take. He agreed that the key to building this business would be establishing himself as an expert. The good news is social media is so new, no one can claim to have ten years of experience. However, his current marketing efforts have been focused around his company name, and not him personally. My advice – build a brand around your name. People want to know what you think. They want your opinion, not your business' position on something. If your opinions resonate with the market, the word will spread and your business will grow.

3. Make Connections by Delivering Value. Along with being a thought leader, learn to identify the needs and serve the people. Make connections, not for your benefit, but for the benefit of those with whom you connect. This means always being prepared to deliver value. Most people are just out for themselves, but I have found that people appreciate help when it's genuine, and that gratitude generally surfaces in time. Make the investment, it's worth it.

4. Invest in Training, Associations, and Conferences. In my early years of business I had to take time off for homeschool conferences. I had to pay for this myself of course, as they were not for business. But over the years, I saw so much business value in them that I began submitting requests to my managers to have the time off as training. For eight years straight this request was approved simply because I made the appeal – I wanted sound training! Four different companies and numerous managers, all signed off for me to go. The business value was clear to me, and so each year this was the first thing on my schedule. Either way, I was willing to pay for it and would have taken time off for vacation if necessary. As a business owner I continue to invest in coaching programs, associations, and personal development courses. I consider this a non-optional step to success.

Getting Your Message Out – Becoming an Adviser

Question I received in a recent online workshop:

"You gave some excellent information for what to say and do when you are in front of the executives/asset owner…when communicating by email and by other electronic means.

You mentioned that sound bites alone are ineffective and also how you throw away most of the marketing mail you get. I agree with both of those statements, so with that said, do you have any suggestions for what I can do to increase the chances of getting those messages heard/read?"

Answer:

Content is the key. When your goal is to sell, people feel sold. When your goal is to educate, people feel helped. The key is in finding things that are helpful to the buyer – the asset owner. Most asset owners are not technologists, so educating them on products, or anything technical, sounds like an opportunity for demotion. Expect to be delegated back down to IT.

Sound bites, or statistical data may be somewhat interesting, however it must be presented from a source they care about. If the Wall Street Journal publishes it, chances are it appeals to business people. However, statistics, as I often share in my workshops, lead to judgmental thinking, not emotional buying. So while, sound bites do build credibility, don't expect them to lead to a sale. Use them as attention grabbers only.

In my book, *The House & the Cloud*, I talk about "Idea Emails." These are ideas that I present to prospects to create knowledge gaps. "I have some ideas I'd like to share with you about how to make sure your employees are not stealing company secrets." Idea emails are one example of creating curiosity through a knowledge gap that will potentially help a client/prospect with something they would care about (we will cover this later in more detail). Other messaging might be "How to" posts on your blog – "How to educate the organization on safe data handling" or "Seven things your employees need to know before traveling with company laptops." This type of education can be written to appeal to asset owners in a non-technical, business format.

In summary, create content, use knowledge gaps to generate interest, and then educate with your content. This education should lead to action, using services your firm provides. As an example, my wife was reading a document on the harmful effects of amalgam fillings (dental). The document began describing all kinds of symptoms people complain of every day. The article went on to explain the importance of removing these fillings using a special process that prevents serious side effects including possible fatality from poisoning. The doctor writing the article included several case studies describing patients who had been improperly diagnosed and treated for major diseases including MS. He described the procedure for removal and then recommended using other synthetic metal-free materials. Of course, both my wife and I had the metal removed from our mouths.

What to Read

Study sales and marketing. Our industry encourages us to read the "technical stuff." If you sell technology, you know the speeds and feeds, and if you sell sewing machines, you know all about stitches, speeds, and parts. Personally, I detest the store we bought our vacuum cleaner from (Note: this is not the Electrolux – I should have remained loyal to the brand!), and are now a slave to, whenever there is a repair to be made. They lack that customer-facing polish! Knowing what makes sales work, and the science behind great marketing and messaging, allows the salesperson with some sound knowledge to bring the customer to a point of understanding and openness that the technician will never achieve. Understand customer service and you'll win a customer for life. This is why Cisco Systems far outsold the old Wellfleet, a company with sound technology, but run by engineers. Behind them stands a long line of broken companies with great technology and no message. Consider Control Data Systems, Digital Equipment Corporation, and 3 Com.

In a recent training class I was asked, "What should I be reading?" Here is a short list of some of my favorite books:

Reading List

The Wall Street Journal — I know, this is not a book, but it is important. In many presentations to technology company business owners, I will ask, "Who is reading the WSJ?" Only a few hands go up! Listen, every one of your executive level clients gets the Wall Street Journal. They may or may not read it, but they get it because they are supposed to read it. So read it!

Made to Stick, by Chip and Dan Heath — The Heath brothers do an excellent job of explaining what makes a message stick. If we could just apply a small portion of these ideas to our presentations, I would be a lot happier sitting through sales calls!

Let's Get Real or Let's Not Play, by Mahan Khalsa — I have listened to this in audio-book format dozens of times! Normally, once through is enough for me, but Khalsa's advice on how to answer executives, determine budgets, and move through "sales politics" is unparalleled.

Solution Selling, by Michael Bosworth — This book is older, and I'm not sure I really like the 9 box matrix Bosworth takes his readers through. However, the ideas behind his questioning and discovery process are right on, and his treatment of negotiations should be required reading for all sales reps!

E-Myth Revisited, by Michael Gerber — If you sell to small businesses, Gerber's book is a must! Again, I did this on audio book, and that is what I recommend. The book is wordy, and a little long for his subject matter. But, listening to the audio, I couldn't stop till I finished it. The way Gerber pronounces "pies", as he weaves his story of Sarah building her pie business, is like listening to old time radio. But the concepts are what make this book a winner. Talk to any small business owner, start sharing Gerber's truths, and they will be offering you a job. This comes from personal experience with a client of mine who has done this. Business owners constantly wish he would come work in their company at a strategic level — what more could you ask for?

Time Traps, by Todd Duncan — For the rep who does not have time to wade through Stephen Covey, this is the book. Short, simple, but very practical. My favorite part of this book is where Duncan explains that most reps spend about 90 minutes each day actually selling. What if they doubled that?!

Consultative Selling, by Mack Hanan — An old standby for anyone creating value. I had the opportunity to dine with Mack in NYC a few years ago. Hanan has a great deal of wisdom when it comes to demonstrating justification.

Good to Great, by Jim Collins — There is no excuse for not reading this book! Every executive has read it. There's just no excuse.

Permission Marketing, by Seth Godin — Did I say marketing is key? I did! Seth Godin has a lot of wisdom in this area, and seems to understand the steps we need to take in order to get past the noise. Thousands like you are calling on the same executives every week. How will you get permission to continue calling on them?

The New Rules of Marketing and PR, by David Meerman Scott — Yes, there are new rules. Scott has forever changed my view of marketing and social media. Every rep should take this book to heart and get moving on their marketing program. Waiting on your marketing department will kill your business.

Summary:

☐ Great sales people are made, not born. Experiences and training from one's childhood, along with natural personality traits, may give one an advantage over another. However, most of the behaviors we have and self confidence we exhibit, are learned patterns. Sales people are made, and it's not too late for you to be a great sales person; if your passion is to become one.

☐ Character is key. Jim Collins recommends getting together people of great character before deciding what to do with a new business. The people will make it successful. Be one of those people.

☐ If you find yourself being constantly introduced to IT, you are being demoted. Learn to be an adviser to business people to stop this process.

☐ Trusted adviser requires that you are trustworthy. In this section I listed 10 important character traits that must be demonstrated in order for people to really start trusting you as an adviser – inner circle person

☐ The ability to give advice is necessary to maintain this trusted adviser status. The one who gives advice is constantly learning and putting together important information that will help companies grow their business. This should be done in the context of one of the four areas where buyers buy.

☐ Personal growth requires regular business-relevant reading, coaching, training, and the discipline of being a student. You may be out of school, but learning is more important now than it ever has been.

☐ Choose a niche and be the best.

☐ Share your story – allow people into your life, building that trust relationship. Develop uniqueness and be a thought leader.

☐ Make sure you are passionate about what you do. If you're not, better to find that passion, and spend your remaining years doing something that really matters to you. Life is too short to waste this precious time.

4. MAKING THE MOST OF MEETINGS

I recall one high-level meeting I attended years ago. It was early in my solution provider career when I was serving as Vice President for a regional systems integrator. John, one of our sales reps, had managed to land a first meeting with the vice president of a local software firm. As he wanted to put his best foot forward, John invited me to join him on this exploratory venture. It was a big company, representing significant opportunities in several areas. Not knowing much about the company, I had asked to meet John beforehand to review the company's mission and objectives, and to glean whatever I could before facing our prospect. But, like many good intentions, that meeting never happened as several conflicts appeared that day. Therefore, I never even got the full name of the company from John.

On our drive over, John was on the phone talking to other clients, and so no planning took place before we arrived. We were running late and when we finally did arrive we went right into the conference room. I will never forget the first few minutes of this meeting. After a brief introduction, John's opening question was, "Now, what does your company do?" We had no idea what they did, and as they shared their story with us, I could see a look of concern on the vice president's face. Apparently, they were a big name in a specialty software application space that we should have known, yet we were completely ignorant. The meeting went downhill from there, and needless to say, it was our last meeting.

How did this happen? Why didn't John do his research before heading into the meeting, and why were we going right to the top on the first meeting without any preparation at all? Every sales methodology eventually encourages you, the seller, to make your way to the economic buyer; to get a meeting with a decision maker. However, most sales people will never do this (at least consistently do it) simply because they are afraid. In our case, John wasn't afraid, and that worked against us. His lack of fear and respect for the meeting led him into lackadaisical preparation, leaving us unprepared on the day of the meeting. The two extremes out there seem to be those without concern and no preparation, and those who avoid all contact with decision makers. Both result in failure.

Fear of Failure

In our case, John didn't fear failure, he thought he was so great he didn't need preparation. Most of the people that come through my mentor program admit they have exactly the opposite problem, what I call a fear of man.

Fear is a powerful thing. When you are meeting with IT influencers, you know you can continue to get together with them, even if they never buy from you; hence no fear. Furthermore, as long as you are able to schedule meetings with a given IT group, you see hope. You know you can have a bad meeting and still recover quickly; simply by taking them out to their favorite restaurant or for a round of golf. As long as they like you from the beginning, keeping the relationship is not that hard.

Heading into an executive's office is quite another thing. You have just one shot and you know it. If you do a great job, you'll be invited back. But if the executive feels you have wasted their time, your chances of future sales go down so fast you could lose your breath. It's a scary thing walking into this meeting. You don't really know what kind of day your prospect is having, what health issues, family problems, or financial stresses might be eating at them. And without some insider information from those who report up to that executive, you can only guess what will convince them of your value as an adviser.

In this chapter my goal is to share a few ideas that resulted from the successes and failures, both experienced by me and by those I have coached. Then, in later chapters I'll be going through specific areas or tools to equip you for setting up, conducting, and advising in these meetings.

Preparation

A few things to consider before meeting:

☐ Use Google and find out what they do. Are they in the news? Does their website explain their company's position on issues, their approach to the business they are in, their culture, goals, status with Wall Street, etc. Find out everything you can about their business.

☐ Some will tell you to go right to the top. I disagree. I personally think sales people should collect some information from influencers before heading to the boardroom. Establish coaches at the departmental level, and gather support from those who will eventually be asked if your recommendations and approaches make sense. This builds confidence and provides you, the seller, with ideas about where opportunities might be within this company.

☐ Know who will be attending future meetings and review their profiles on LinkedIn and possibly Facebook as well. I like the upgrade features of LinkedIn (which I talk about in the last chapter - Using Social Media) that allow me to view a person's profile without actually being linked to them. This is especially helpful for remembering who your prospects are and what they look like before heading into a meeting. Look at their groups, past positions and company experiences, the schools they may have attended, books under "Favorite Books", and any additional information they may have put in the video or slide deck areas of their profile.

☐ Their IT people will often tell you who else is providing services or products to their company, so find out as much as you can through them. I find that IT people will tell you just about anything if you spend some time with them, so why not make use of this? Later, they will be helpful in providing updates on proposals and setting future appointments.

End Goal

Every meeting should have an end-goal. In my opinion, there is no such thing as purely informational meetings. When sales people go in to give someone a company overview, with nothing else in mind, I find this to be a waste of time. This is also true of customer events that do not have an end goal. IT level meetings should be conducted with questions in mind, finding out everything you possibly can about the company you are calling on.

Picture a war room in a movie with white boards filled with information you have, information you need, your best guesses about the organization, and who will likely be your advocates, adversaries, blockers and key sources of information or decision makers. I recall my first exposure to this type of meeting. I was still working with the bank mentioned previously, but had my eye on a consulting role. One company I was contracting with would hold weekly meetings to strategize. They would meet together, filling in the blanks with anyone who could possibly contribute. At one point, I was acting as one of their coaches, which I didn't really understand, as I was an insider and working in IT. I was fascinated as they talked about how to expand their reach, asked me questions about the organization, politics, new beachheads to go after, and more. This was a long term initiative for them, and they took their job seriously.

With a strategy in hand, at some point it is time to move up. But move up with purpose. Move up because you have discovered something and have ideas that will help this client improve their situation. Move up because you now have pivotal information for that next manager or executive in your line of people to meet.

At the end of each meeting you should be able to look back and determine whether or not you have accomplished your goal. Each member from your team should have understood the meeting goal, and the role they were going to play. They should have known how the agenda was going to flow, how people were going to be introduced, and what subject areas might come up and who would address them. A team that does not know how to work together will end up stepping on each other's toes, short cutting the discovery process, and making everyone look bad. Don't let this happen – have a strategy in place.

Introductions

Introductions are my favorite part and perhaps the most important part of your meeting. In chapter three we talked about positioning – this is where positioning really counts. More meetings are blown right here simply because the introduction process is unrehearsed and treated with indifference. There may have been positioning done on the phone, and certainly on your website, blog, or other social media (LinkedIn, Facebook, Squidoo, etc.). However, now face to face, you have the opportunity to demonstrate character and professionalism. The impact you make here will last throughout your future relationship, and each member of the team will be remembered by their introduction. Don't forget, it's far more difficult to reposition if you don't leave a good impression at this first meeting.

☐ Take time to build up your team members. Let prospects know you feel privileged to have your manager along, or one of your top technical people. This does two things; it lets that company know your manager saw this meeting as important and took the time to attend. It also builds them up as someone your prospect should know. It doesn't matter whether you personally like your manager – this is a respect issue and a demonstration of true character. You want your client to see every person on your team as critical to his or her success. If your company is going to be their partner of choice, everyone must add value.

- ☐ Make sure each person gets an introduction; not too lengthy, but not so short that people see them as insignificant. Take time to establish value and memory recall of that person throughout the meeting. It should be obvious there is a reason for each person to be in attendance.

- ☐ Make sure your people have business cards and be certain you collect every attendee's card on the client's side. I appreciate the way cards are studied in Asian cultures. The card is offered with two hands and examined by the recipient. It is treated with respect like a gift. I like to make a note on the back of a card to refresh my memory regarding something important about that person. Note a person's title and ask a question if something is not clear. Determine who the real players are in the decision making process, but treat everyone sitting on the attendee side of the meeting with respect. You can't afford any blockers.

- ☐ I often draw a small table on my tablet and write in names as we go around. This way I can address people around the table by their proper name as the discussion begins. Sometimes I'll arrange the business cards in front of me, in the order of those seated at the table, to aid me during the discussion. Knowing everyone's name is a powerful indication that you care about the people you are meeting with.

- ☐ When it's your turn, don't arrogantly inflate your position, and make sure you give them straight answers as to who does what on your team. Avoid silly responses like "chief cook and bottle washer." Instead, provide functional descriptions so your prospects understand who does what and why they are attending this meeting.

Agendas

Every meeting should have an agenda. It communicates preparation and attention to the value of a client's time. In my first sales training class, years ago (one where I was the attendee and not the person doing the training), our instructor had each person walk to the front of the room and simply say:

"Thank you for meeting with us today. I understand your company is in the process of….(fill in with recent news or some insight you received while meeting with influencers – and comment on it)… Today I was hoping to cover…(and give three or four short points). From there we can see how it may make sense to work together. How does that sound to you?"

It sounded so simple, yet few actually did it well. In another situation, I remember one sales person called on me, when I was working in an IT department, assuming he could just go through his sixty minute slide show with me. I actually had some other ideas, and some specific questions to ask, and did not want to see his slides. I suggested we could skip his slides, but he insisted on going through them. After thirty minutes I let him know I was out of time and left the meeting. The client should not have to interrupt the meeting to change directions. The seller should offer the agenda and be willing to reset the course if the attendee has something else in mind.

The Message

Don't hide behind complex jargon. Written or verbal, business communication can be plagued with this unnecessary wording and convoluted messaging. Frequently we hear things, nod, and move on, knowing full well that we have no idea what that person just said. They have spoken in overly complex jargon. Why is this?

I think it goes back to fear. Fear that people will correct us or not like what we are saying. If the message is complex, people will just sit through it, not wanting to look silly if everyone else seems to be following along.

This book is about changing the game, changing the message and presenting clear, discernable value. Start speaking and writing clearly, and leave behind the complex meaningless language of made-up words and phrases that so many continue to hide behind. As we go though the next several chapters, I will be providing tools to help build the right message and deliver it. In some areas you may have a great toolset, in others you may find ideas for improvement. Whether you have a pretty full toolbox or not, you'll find challenging concepts here, built on real-life situations, providing a way to evaluate what you currently do. My hope is that you will come away with concrete steps to build a stronger value proposition, one that will allow you to truly transform from pure selling to advising. The latter offers a much stronger sales opportunity.

Dialogue vs. Discussion

These words sound similar, and are often used interchangeably, yet there is a distinct difference. Both are important to the sales call but serve a very different purpose. Dialogue calls for the exchange of ideas. It offers no resistance or debate. The participants exchange ideas, with the intent of understanding where the other is coming from, rather than waiting to make their own point. It provides a basis for learning and building rapport.

In the United States, and perhaps many other countries, the common method of brainstorming is to toss out a thought and have everyone in the room shoot it down. Objections come from all directions until there is just nothing left of the inspiration. Then another idea will come, and the same thing will happen. There is no looking for the bright spots in these suggestions. The winner must debate until others in the room succumb to his iron clad case. At some point, the winning suggestion will emerge.

Dialogue does not do this. Instead, dialogue offers a free flow of ideas to be brought forth for the group's consideration. This idea exchange builds understanding as it allows listeners and participants to view ideas and positions from each other's vantage point. As individuals gain new understanding they form new ideas, and the process builds as an exploratory exercise. People who do not normally feel creative begin to participate, putting away fears of rejection and failure.

Once done, a discussion can emerge. After all, you are in sales and you can't exchange ideas forever. Someone must make a decision, someone must lead the way to action. The decision comes as people review ideas from different angles, looking at positives, discussing improvements, cautions and perhaps new ideas to overcome those cautions. There are entire books written about what has been labeled lateral thinking and other forms of collaboration. This progression can totally change the sales meeting process as the consultant in you overtakes old vendor-like habits of pitching product. As an adviser, you must become excellent at opening the dialogue, encouraging the exchange of ideas, and then moving into discussion to draw conclusions. This is a wonderful use of boardroom meeting time and will be covered in much greater detail as we go along.

Presentations

The death of any meeting is the corporate slide show. With this in mind, I have dedicated an entire chapter to the process of presenting with various mediums. This is your chance to reposition everything you do and stand for; and it must be perfect. I'll talk about using PowerPoint, flip charts, white boards, and of course, just sitting around the table. Every presentation should be planned as a way to move your client forward, so master it!

Timing

You should not exceed thirty minutes. Less time is better. Your part of the sales meeting should be short, interactive, and pointed. Executives don't generally schedule long meetings and don't have time to socialize during the day. I'll give more attention later to how this time should be spent, how to transition to more productive discovery sessions, and how to move through various meetings from the initial influencers to those with tight schedules; but with ultimate authority over budgets.

Ending

End on time, and end with a purpose. High-level meetings generally take place in what I call Meeting Two – the Value Proposition Meeting. Again, I will be describing in detail later in the book the four meetings you must have, and how to accomplish each with a strategic objective in mind. We will cover ways to gain permission to build justification for projects and ongoing services, as well as maintain access at the executive level. This should all be part of your plan as you begin each meeting.

The point here is to make every meeting count by preparing. Have a goal in mind before beginning the meeting, and leverage the people there to position yourself, and your team, as important to the success of your client.

Begin With the End in Mind

If you've read Stephen Covey's classic on life management, *Seven Habits of Highly Successful People*, you may remember habit #2, *Begin with the end in mind*. This is key to any great sales call, marketing event, or any presentation you give. Having done many executive level presentations, I can assure you that it's not a numbers game, or a matter of giving so many presentations in a week. Instead, presentations should be well planned, and given to qualified audiences. Never give one, or take a meeting, you are not prepared to plan for and follow up.

When strategizing for a sales call, "the end" or meeting outcome, must be the first consideration! Doing otherwise wastes both the prospect's and your time. Given that you are presenting to highly qualified executives, a wasted presentation may be your last one with that audience. What should the outcome be? Almost every company I work with can tell me what leads to a sale. For instance, recently I was speaking at a software company's partner summit. They quoted a statistic showing that ninety percent of their "proof of concept" initiatives lead to a buying decision. In another national sales meeting I spoke at, an access assurance company presented a similar statistic.

A client I work with on quarterly marketing events, says that he closes follow-on projects for ninety percent of the complementary assessments he offers. With this in mind, they are generally able to quantify what qualifies their proof of concept effort, who should be involved, and how to run the program. Using this type of data, the goal should be obvious; to get to this leverage point in the sales process. Everything these companies do as far as meetings, presenting, and selling, should be focused on getting to that activity that leads them to a ninety percent close rate.

On the other hand, my non-scientific surveys show that companies are closing about ten percent of their proposals; even among companies who have shared their key to success as stated above, simply because they are not following their own formula. What that tells me is they are writing the proposals before getting to that predictable key point in the sales process, or they just have not identified it yet. If you don't know the end goal, you're just shooting in the dark. If you do know it, then start focusing your marketing and sales efforts around that one thing that creates the 90% success factor.

When I conduct *Data@Risk* seminars (One of the demand generation programs I offer), I am presenting educational material to business leaders; thus helping them establish better business practices, which in turn will better serve their customers and protect their company's intellectual capital. This has value in and of itself, but does not lead to many sales unless there is a follow up game plan. I've designed my keynote to guarantee three execute meetings, not just one. The first meeting comes through the educational event. My material is written to help business level people understand their risks and recognize that though they may not think they are experiencing security violations, they probably are. And, to agree that it is important to at least investigate whether they have some of the more surreptitious security violations in progress within their applications. I use marketing concepts to create urgency here, driving a certain reaction (something I'll cover in the chapter on presentations). Knowing what I do about today's cybercrime, this is easy to accomplish because I am confident that the need is real!

The next two meetings follow. Using *Habit # 2* thinking, I work with my client to develop a follow up assessment process that is designed to fit the opportunity. Some prospects are worth spending a great deal of time with; others not so much. The discovery process requires executive involvement. If they don't show up, I discontinue the process and continue the marketing effort until they do. Once they agree to involvement (which is minimal by design), I go through the process identifying urgent issues. Meeting Three comes when I deliver the findings. Again, if the executive does not show up, I withhold the information. Since it is complementary, I can do that (which I cover in the Discovery Chapter). Most often, those who agree to participate upfront will also avail themselves to the deliverable review. By knowing in advance how I intend to get people signed up, how the follow up discovery process will be conducted, and how the deliverable will be presented, I can predict some level of success that is commensurate with my effort. But it all starts with building the follow up program before the event ever begins.

Meetings can't just be meetings. They must be seen as a series of stepping stones, with well thought out objectives, targeting specific people, with specific information designed to gain the next level of access in the account. At each point along the way, we'll be able to evaluate if we really have buy-in, or if we need to stay at this level until we do have it. Then we can press on toward the goal.

Summary:

- [ ] Sales methodologies encourage high-level calling – I recommend working with influencers until you understand all you need to know before meeting with key executives.

- [ ] Spend the time to prepare – don't waste the time of high-level managers or it may be your last meeting.

- [ ] Consider the end before taking the meeting. Know where you are headed, and plan your agenda to accomplish specific goals. Every meeting must count.

- [ ] Introductions are where you position yourself. Be sure to introduce each team member, giving them credit for their accomplishments, and connecting them with an important role in your relationship with the client.

- [ ] Prepare a clearly planned agenda and review it with your clients - figure on 30 minutes for management level meetings.

- [ ] Leverage a balance of dialogue and discussion, understanding the role of each person in your meeting.

- [ ] Stick to your agenda and end on time.

5. PRESENTATIONS THAT SELL

Growing up I believed, like many young boys, that being a movie star meant you actually experienced the drama and excitement felt when watching exhilarating movies. For instance, the actors in war pictures had the thrill of "playing army" with real tanks and guns; something that appealed to my friends and I as we crawled on our bellies through the wooded park lands that surrounded my family's home. We were armed with gun-shaped sticks, pocket knives, canteens and camouflage outfits from the local Army-Navy store; ready for battle against the unseen enemy.

Have you ever had the opportunity to observe a motion picture in the making? If you've never done this, let me clue you in; it's incredibly boring and not exciting. The same simple scenes are shot over and over again. On a recent trip to Australia, I was given the chance to observe this process. I was on my way to the harbor area when I stopped to watch a scene depicting two businessmen greeting each other in front of an office building. An entire crew of extras sat on the sidewalks, waiting for the producer's call to action. Once summoned, the stars of this drama would walk toward each other and shake hands while dozens of extras crossed the brick patio in a seemly unarranged pattern. The truth was that everything was tightly choreographed as the scene had to be perfect.

The director knew what he was looking for and was willing to repeat the process over and over again until it was flawless. I watched for 45 minutes, and they still had not perfected the presentation. They only have one shot at profitability, and so the director took all the time he needed to make sure this movie would be great. In due time, it will begin playing for audiences, ratings will come out, and consumers will decide if the movie is worth their time and effort to head out to the theatres. Will it be profitable? Maybe, but only if it sells. The producer knows this, and so long before the film crew ever shows up, a lengthy process begins that includes writing the script, outside critique, actor selection and auditions, along with market research to make sure they have a winner.

Presentations are similar to movie making; you often get just one shot at success. If it's not great, you won't see a profit. So why are many presentations thrown together at the last minute, or prepared by a marketing department that has no selling experience? Where is the research, the director, stars, choreography, and the many cuts and critiques? Is there even a rehearsal for this thing?

I recently did a series of training classes for a large, global company. On day one we talked about the market, the opportunity, key decision criteria, and how to go through a predictable, educational marketing program that consistently fills your pipeline. On day two we analyzed messaging. We took that company's best messaging, tore it apart, reviewed the underlying principles of great marketing and messaging, and reengineered the sales team's approach. We looked at everything. Great attention was given to the way they introduced the company, how they positioned themselves, how they approached product and services sales, how proposals and assessments should be developed and delivered, and how to present the final solutions and pricing. Finally, day three was set aside to practice delivering the critical aspects of this material. But, to my surprise, on that day, the sales manager informed me that the team was not willing to present in front of each other. What? These are professional sales people calling on global accounts! They won't present in front of each other? The sales manager was somewhat annoyed by their response, but felt powerless to do anything about it. What a waste – to go to market without rehearsal, without practice; without the coach overseeing the team and helping them reach perfection before prime time.

The typical sales presentation is predictable. Colorful slides are delivered to the sales team by marketing. These same slides are then brought to stage without any real critique or practice, and the audience often recognizes that this team forgot to go through the refinement process. Where are the people who actually care if this presentation works or not? The results are predictable, but predictably poor. Oh, you might have a few natural stars on the team, or better yet, sales people who have honed their skills through education or hiring a coach. But most often, this seat-of-the-pants approach results in a mediocre sales team presentation.

Great Speakers

As an active member of the National Speakers Association and International Speakers Network, I meet quarterly with some very successful orators; people

I consider to be at the top of the speaker industry. Our topics vary as much as our style. Some are humorists without any concrete content, a few are professional storytellers delivering tales of the south, many speak to sales audiences as I do, and others have a religious, motivational, or health angle. But the one thing we all have in common is that we make our living speaking to audiences. Many of us share our experiences, hoping to motivate people to change, while providing encouragement in an area where our audiences need expertise and help.

So what makes a speaker great? I'm sure you've been to seminars, national sales meetings, or trade shows and have heard great speakers. You've probably also heard people who don't have the gift for speaking. What's the difference? Well, I have come to believe that it's not just in the DNA. There's a success formula. When someone says to me, "You're a talented speaker." I say, "No, I've given hundreds of speeches, then recorded them, listened to them, and had them critiqued. I've worked with coaches, and written, rewritten and written again, my speech content; in an effort to make it perfect."

When I first began my speaking career I needed a demo tape. I was discussing the needed recording with some of the veterans of our NSA chapter when our president asked me, "How many times have you given your primary keynote?" "Ten times," I boasted, "Although I have spoken to various audiences on other subjects over my career." He then encouraged me to hold off on filming. "Wait until you have given this talk at least one hundred times." "A hundred times?" I questioned. I couldn't image waiting that long. I needed it now. But he assured me I would be sorry.

Months later, a former World Champion Toastmasters humorist came to address our local chapter. He shared with us the story of how he entered the speaking industry and then played video clips of himself from his earlier days. His first clip was a routine he performed at a comedy club about twenty years before. It was awful. In fact, it was so bad, I was embarrassed for him. I felt pity as I watched him dying on the stage, facing a crowd of bored faces and people staring at their watches. I don't think I have ever seen such a bad act. Nothing was funny. In fact, he couldn't remember any of his lines, so he constantly looked down at crib notes to see what was next. It turns out, his friends had put him up to this. But that day, he determined to master the art of speaking! Our guest continued through the morning, playing samples from fifteen years ago, ten years, five, two, and then his present offering. It was amazing to watch the transformation and to learn that through coaching, practice, and self-recording, he had studied to improve his program and made

> Like the movie star, the great speakers you've heard, have practiced

it great. He had become an expert and achieved the number one position as a Toastmasters humorist.

Well, despite the advice I received from our chapter president, I went ahead and had my demo tape made. I was happy with it at the time, but a few years and several hundred speeches later, I was embarrassed to watch my own tape. In fact, I was reviewing my website one day, came across it, played it, and gulped – I had to get it off of there! I was humiliated. Suddenly I saw what our chapter president meant. It takes practice. It takes work. It takes someone who is an expert, looking over your shoulder, with a willingness to tell you the truth. But with practice and the right input, the talk can reach perfection. It can become great. It's not just DNA – it's work.

Like the movie star, the great speakers you've heard, have practiced. They've given the talk you just heard, hundreds of times. It's no wonder it is great. The speakers you don't like are probably not professional speakers. They probably did not have any coaching, and they probably speak infrequently. Most of all, they have almost certainly, never had to sit through their own presentation. Their lack of practice and input is evident.

Sales People

So you are in sales. You give the same information over and over. But, are you giving the same talk (or similar), and have you critiqued it, been coached on it, and put time into making the material great before going live? Or do you just wing it when you get "on stage"? Who do you want to be? The movie star, the great speaker or the guy that encourages his audience to spend the meeting reading email? I know you aren't necessarily giving a speech, but the concepts that apply to actors and good orators, apply here as well.

Consider How Professional Speakers Practice

Here is what the professionals focus on:

☐ *Stories*. This topic deserves more and I will cover it more thoroughly in a few pages from now. But, in short, stories are central to any impressive presentation. Recall your favorite conferences and I bet the speaker had great stories. Most likely, they were personal stories. Practice your own narratives, write them out, record them, listen to them, tighten them up, and make them perfect. An extraordinary speaker once told me to never make a point without telling a story, and never tell a story without a point.

- ☐ *The Alpha.* The alpha is the opening – the point in the meeting when your listeners either tune in or check out. Memorize it, rehearse it, know it, and speak it. Every sales call is different, but contrary to popular opinion, your opening can be memorized and modified slightly to meet different needs. Assume you have about six seconds to grab their attention.

- ☐ *Sound Bites.* Sound bites bring credibility, create interest, and build your case. Don't overdo it, but be armed with well-rehearsed sound bites from credible sources; sources your target audience will recognize and believe.

- ☐ *The Close.* The next steps are the key to moving the sales cycle forward. Make sure you know where you are going and that you have a compelling process which will move your client forward. Seth Godin, Author of *Permission Marketing*, writes about steps of permission that are gained along the way. What is the next step needed in the permission chain?

Almost every time I speak, I record it. Sometimes I have video and other times, just audio. Watching and listening to yourself will give you a whole new perspective. In fact, it's painful at first. Is your presentation style high-impact, emotionally charged, exciting,… enthusiastic? Is it credible and do you deliver concrete concepts that allow the listener to visualize the issues and proposed solutions? If not, head back to the lab to rebuild. Don't expect this to be easy. It's like golf since every move matters and lots of practice is required. It also pays to take a lesson from an expert. Like golf, practice does not "make perfect", but rather, practicing what is right, "makes perfect." Just imagine doubling your effectiveness and cutting your sales cycle in half. If there is one area that deserves some investment, it's your message and delivery.

I'm Not a Speaker or an Actor

The most frequent comment I get when talking about the need to memorize or practice sales calls is, "I'm not an actor." In fact, I received a *tweet* reply recently telling me that sales people who talk like androids irritate customers. The comment read, "Prospects don't like sales people that sound like robots!" This person was mocking my blog post. But the funny thing is, I totally agree. Let me explain.

The most irritating sales call experience comes from ill preparedness. When the sales person shows up without doing their homework, they end up stuttering through the first several minutes of their meeting and are seen as wasting everyone's time. They are also competing with those currently providing the service; those who already know the needs of the customer. Only in the wake of a previous provider's failure will this strategy work. And then there are those over used lines – "open ended" questions such as, "What keeps you up at night?" Every time I hear them I cring. Remember, executives sit through hundreds of vendor meetings. They've heard all of these lines, and you better believe they are sick of them. Can't someone be original? Executives need input from people who bring experience, understanding, and can communicate effectively.

So, addressing the robot comment, I would argue that great speakers never sound like robots or they would not be able to command such exorbitant fees. Actors who we recognize as "stars" take on the personality of their character so effectively that we forget who they really are for the duration of the picture. And sales people who speak with confidence, and who effectively illustrate their points with compelling stories, will deliver truth that is sure to defeat the objections and critical eye of the average prospect. On the other hand, sales people who have simply memorized sound bites from their data sheets are bound to lose long before the end of their first meeting.

It's Not About the Slides

The look of the slide is important. But it's the message that really counts. The slide is like a frame. It must support the picture by adding to it, complementing the colors and drawing your eye to its center, which is the main message. Marketing departments tend to be the creators of most sales slideware, while sales people are out delivering the message. My experience tells me, sales people are relying on the slides to be the message.

During a recent event I spoke at, the security practice director preceded my talk with an overview of his company. The first ten minutes of his presentation seemed to drag on for hours, and attendees around the room quietly drew their iPhones and Blackberries from their holsters. Bullet by bullet, he stuttered through each point, laboriously trying to keep track of where he was, straining from the stage to read the words. It was obvious he didn't know what they said. For seven slides he forced us to sit there, waiting for something of remote interest. At one point he even half-heartedly apologized, claiming that his marketing group would stone him if the slides were withdrawn from his talk. Finally, the company overview section ended and he went on to his own material. Suddenly he seemed to come alive, and become animated, and confident, as he expounded on newsworthy issues. The audience was reborn and rejuvenated. Blackberries were re-holstered and the audience began to tune in…he was lucky.

The security practice director did have good material to give us. But, it was his slides that enslaved him, and until he was freed of this bondage, he was boring us to death. When the slides are complex, too wordy, distracting, or simply don't match the message being given, they tend to take the prospect's eyes off of the speaker, placing them on the slideware.

Given these truths, the place to start is with your message. Does it speak value? Look back at some of the chapters we've already covered and make sure you are speaking value. Once you have it, it's time to choose which frame most effectively fits your message. Enter the white board, slide show, or table top dialogue.

White Boarding vs. PowerPoint

Do you use PowerPoint or go with the white board? Or do you just sit around the table and talk? There is a time for all three, but knowing what to use and when to use it is important; almost as important as the message itself.

Some Thoughts on Power Point

As far as sales calls go, I am not a PowerPoint fan. While PowerPoint is an effective tool, when used incorrectly it can put an audience to sleep, kill a discussion, and alienate everyone. On the positive side, it gives a sales person the ability to display diagrams and process, as well as photographs of products with bright, colorful images and flare. That said, once the lights dim, the propensity to slip off into dreamland grows with each slide. Slide shows also have a tendency to distance the audience and come off as canned – one size fits all. Many times I have pleaded with sales people to put away their slides in hopes of using our meeting time to address particular questions. But for some reason, they just couldn't hold a meeting without them.

Where does PowerPoint shine? I use it when speaking to large audiences, educational marketing events, or going through the details of a project plan for a larger group. In the first case, slides can be used as long as you don't lean on them. They provide a backdrop to you as a speaker. This is especially effective in educational marketing efforts because people do like something in the way of an outline to follow. The problem comes when speakers start reading slides or putting more text on the slide than one might see in a memo.

Try this. Use slides to show pictures – with just one or two words. Use the background formatting features. For instance, change the background from white to a picture – something memorable to support the message. As an example, in a recent educational marketing event about cybercrime, I used a slide of my two-year old son in front of a computer. The slide was black and only his face was visible, with the light from the screen illuminating his face and keyboard. This dark, sinister-looking, computer picture, with a child at the helm, underscored how easy this type of corruption had become. Four descriptive words to the left of the image served to drive home my message: Bots, Phishing, Social Engineering.

Using this kind of slide is both memorable and fun to watch. The speaker doesn't read the slide because the meaning is obvious. The audience is drawn into the speaker's story with the image reinforcing the message. This is a good use of PowerPoint.

Thoughts on White Boarding

I love the white board. Unlike PowerPoint, white boards allow for collaborative thinking. I remember one of my sales managers coming back from an appointment with great excitement, recounting how he and a perspective client had been up at the white board together, adding to a diagram, interactively creating the solution to a problem they were having. They went from one-way broadcasting to two-way brainstorming. This can't happen with PowerPoint.

Earlier in my career, I came up with a powerful story you now know as, *The House & the Cloud* (the title of my first book). Every time I was called upon to share my team's progress with partners or management, I used the *House & the Cloud* to illustrate my points. It became a brand over time. That is what you want; a personal brand or a signature story. It won't happen overnight, but as you begin thinking about it, using illustrations during your sales calls, and reviewing the results, your story will evolve. As it grows, don't be surprised if people want to meet with you to hear about your "House story." I have another keynote story I use as well — "my Chem Lawn Grass Story." People have heard it all over the world and it's even on my website. But when I speak, those who have heard me in the past will tell their neighbor, "Wait until you hear this guy's grass story." They want to hear it again, and they are disappointed if I don't tell it.

You can't close the million dollar deal with dried out markers...bring your own.

Start here. Learn the presentation you used to give in PowerPoint, strip out the boring statistics, and recreate the message employing a more informal, white-boarding style. Look for ways to make your sales story interesting, compelling and interactive. There is something powerful about watching someone draw. If you have ever seen a speaker use chalk drawings to illustrate their message, you know what I mean.

By creating knowledge gaps, interrupting one's thinking (which I'll describe in more detail later), and filling in the blanks in an interactive drawing session, you can magnify the energy in the room, drawing people into your story as you unfold it. This takes preparation, creativity, and practice.

Anyone can do it. It just takes some upfront planning and rehearsal. Start thinking through your presentation. How can you make it great? Your goal should be to create a story that can be told through pictures and colors, in fifteen minutes, using a white board diagram.

Bring Your Own Markers:

Let's continue on with the topic of white boarding – something someone should probably write a book about. It's one of the most frequently utilized tools in the sales process, but often misused by ill-equipped sales people. A few practical pointers:

- [ ] Always carry your own markers. I started doing this about twelve years ago. Many of my prospects thought it was funny, yet they appreciated my preparedness and the quality of the colors that brought my pictures to life. I always say, "You can't close the million-dollar deal with a dead marker."

- [ ] There is no reason to recreate the wheel on every new sales call. You use the same brochureware, why not use the same illustrations? I can think of several speakers that use chalk drawings as part of their gig. It's highly effective and the pictures look great every time. Why? Simply because they have practiced. Get your storyboard together, learn to draw your diagrams, and use them often. You can adlib as needed.

- [ ] Learn to draw while you talk. There is nothing worse than watching someone draw with their back to you. Practice drawing without thinking about it so you can put your attention on the client.

- [ ] Learn to write neatly. It always amazes me when, in an interview, I ask someone to whiteboard something and, while writing in a falling arch format, they turn to me to explain that they aren't very good at white-boarding. My response to them is, "You must be an expert if you want this job."

- [ ] Use the entire board – I don't mean the entire wall of the war-room…but I do mean, don't make your pictures so small that no one can see them. Spread things out so that the room can view what you're talking about.

- [ ] Don't call your white-boarding process a presentation. One big advantage of white-boarding is that it gets you away from the canned presentation. So even if it is well rehearsed, you can do it in a casual, yet specific way. This invites collaboration and interaction.

☐ Always erase the board when finished. It's the courteous thing to do. But more importantly, you don't want to give away valuable information. I have learned a lot from those who did not bother to erase their figures. Once I walked into a sales meeting with one figure in mind, saw my competition's notes on the board, and raised my price 60%! I won the business while making a much larger commission.

The Mighty Flip-Chart:

I was recently speaking in Cancun, and just before my session started, one of the hotel staff members ushered in a flip chart that I had not requested. Then I saw a familiar face, someone who knew I really like flip charts, and obviously had remembered to request one. Sure enough, I did use it!

While white boarding is great for sales meetings, the mighty flip chart stands out as one of the best tools for facilitation. It's absent from most training centers and boardrooms these days, and when I do request one, it seems to create a sudden emergency; like placing a special order at McDonalds (also something I am known to do).

When the chart and stand arrive, I am not surprised if the tripod cross bar is missing – the one that holds the flipchart in place. Most easels come with them, but they are quickly misplaced, leaving only the tripod, which is now only useful for supporting marketing posters. Invariably the chart is presented with white board markers, not flip chart markers. Most don't know the difference. Another possible attempt to help results in permanent markers, which are not a great substitute for the mighty flip-chart marker! Like the white board, it is best to carry your own markers and Post-it Super Sticky flip chart pad, which is great for hanging various sheets on the conference room walls or the white board when the easel doesn't work.

Why do I like these so much? Here are several reasons:

☐ Strategy and training both require interaction. The flip chart allows me to move the working space closer to the audience or meeting attendees, and to angle it in such a way as to allow the audience to view my illustrations and bullet points more easily.

☐ Posting notes around the room. White board space is usually limited and cannot be reorganized. I especially like the Post-it charts for this type of work. Whether training or facilitating strategy, I find that posting key ideas in different colors, and then reorganizing information, is extremely helpful. This really matters when spending an entire day, or several days, together. No white board can keep track of that much information.

☐ Others may contribute. When using a white board, things get messy when multiple people contribute. The organizational abilities of flip chart paper make this much more manageable.

☐ Flip chart markers! I carry my own, so I always have good ones. White board markers quickly become hard to read, smudged, etc. Flip chart markers are bold, don't smear, and look crisp even after a day of moving papers around the room.

☐ Permanency. At the end of the day someone has to keep this information. When it's on a white board, you have no choice but to erase or leave it for the next group. Flip chart paper can be collected, organized and handed to someone to save. I know there are white boards that print, but most are very small, generating one small sheet of paper for each print; this is useless to a group of 8 or 10 people.

Presentations Create Business

Regardless of how you do it, presentations have the power to create business, proposals don't. Leads are great, but what do you say when you make the call, and if you get the meeting, do you have anything of value to present?

Company overviews and product data sheets are, in my opinion, a waste of time. No one needs them until they clearly see a necessity and make the connection. Take a look at your presentation materials. Look at what you present by phone, and then, what you bring to that first meeting. Does it educate prospects about something they really need, but don't really understand? Does it interrupt their thinking, causing them to be alarmed by what they missed? Does it create an urgency that reprioritizes their week? This is the making of a great sales call.

The Problem with Most Presentations

The purpose of a presentation is to sell. It is important to convince the prospect that you have a solution for a problem that they, in fact, have, and that you are the best problem solver around. The fee in turn, must be commensurate with the value delivered.

But here's the problem: First, 95% of the possible prospects in your territory don't necessarily agree that they have a problem, or at least have a problem that you specialize in solving. Second, most presentations are informational, offering no compelling value. They are not centered on solving a known problem. The other 5% of the people out there admit they have a problem, but have no reason to believe your solution is any better than the next guy. In this case you lack differentiation.

Since most presentations look pretty much the same, the client's propensity is to continue doing business with the known quantity, unless an incumbent's price is severely undercut. Don't overestimate your brand or uniqueness based on things everyone has, or at least say they have. Start treating your presentation as a commercial, or perhaps an infomercial. Put more time into making a great presentation and you'll waste less time on unqualified meetings.

10 Things That Will Kill a Presentation...

1. Opening with an agenda slide – your first task is to grab the audience's attention; the agenda slide is a sure way to lose everyone.
2. Using the standard bullet point format in PowerPoint – this makes for boring slides with too many words.
3. Showing slide after slide of meaningless numbers, statistics, and financials, with values that are too big to comprehend. The human brain needs a comparison when dealing with large numbers – a point of reference.
4. Talking about "Me." Especially true when presenting to new prospects – no one cares about your company before there is a reason to do business.
5. Bad colors and no graphics. Most people are visual. They want to see pictures. That is why people watch movies more often than listen to stories on the radio. If you want your information to be memorable, use attention grabbing graphics!
6. Reading your slides – no! Look at the audience. This requires that you know your material.
7. Too many words on the slide. If your audience can't read the whole slide at a glance (5 or 6 words) you've lost them. They will either listen to you or read the slide…most will read the slide and ignore you.
8. No climax. A presentation must build. If it's flat, people will lose interest quickly.

9. Obvious content. Most sales presentations look exactly the same. They discuss company background, offerings, features, a few client names, etc. This is predictable, boring, and obvious.
10. The presenter is not a speaker. This is the final presentation killer. If you're going to stand up in front of a crowd, you had better be good. Remember, this is not a genetic trait. It's simply a matter of learning the skill and practicing until you're great at it.

Stage Presence

Stage Presence starts with great markers (if you are using the white board or flip chart)...but there's far more to it than that.

Part of consulting and consultative selling involves communicating with executives and understanding or clarifying their needs. Learning to write on the board is a great place to start – this is a key part of facilitation:

☐ Bring your own markers

☐ If you sell networks, learn to draw clouds. Amoebas won't cut it.

☐ Don't let the IT guy draw his network. He'll ruin the show, while the execs check email.

☐ Practice using the same picture all the time. Keep it fast, simple, and generic.

☐ Learn to speak while you write – don't turn your back on your audience.

☐ There are many facilitation methodologies – learn one if you don't already have some in your toolbox. I personally prefer a practice called *lateral thinking*, which relies on *six thinking hats developed by Edward De Bono*. With this in my skill set, I feel very comfortable walking into situations without a lot of background knowledge. I can quickly assess where things are, where they want to go, and what stands in the way. This is the beginning of any good consulting process, and is the quickest way to establish a long term relationship; bound by ongoing sales.

> Don't let the IT guy draw his network. He'll steal the show while the execs check email.

Stories Bring Your Presentation to Life

You probably don't remember how to balance chemical equations, but chances are you do remember some great story a teacher or classmate shared in school. Mr. Gustafuson, one of my high school teachers, used to begin every class with a short excerpt from a book he was reading. I remember some of the details from those stories, but to be honest, I don't recall what class he taught! I do, however, recollect looking forward to hearing the next chapter in our reading; which encouraged me to show up on time. I even remember the title and author of the book! Stories are memorable, facts and figures are not.

Presentations which might otherwise be dry, come alive with great stories. When talking about a wrong approach or illustrating an idea, use a story rather than defining your position. A wise mentor once told me, you can't argue with someone's personal testimony. So use a real story, and if possible, use one you have personally been involved in. If you don't use a personal story, research the details and make sure it's true, before bringing it to the client.

One more important point; great stories are rehearsed and revised. My high school English teacher always said, "Great writing is rewriting." Coming up with a new story at the moment of truth is not the best approach. Develop your example stories before you get on stage. Practice them, record them, and share them with others. Tell them often and they will improve over time. The better you become at storytelling, the more life you'll bring to your presentation. Try it this week and let me know how it goes....

Using Controversy

Earlier I mentioned Rush Limbaugh. Love him or hate him – you are forced to make a choice. Even the bad press increases this celebrity's fame and reputation. He wins from both sides. Remember what Seth Godin says, "Obscurity is your biggest enemy."

When you present the obvious, lack any differentiating opinions, and look to please everyone, you end up standing in a crowd among millions. You are not a leader, you stand for nothing, and you bring no value. All you can do is represent another choice, but not one that stands out. Perhaps you'll win on price, if you are a large reseller with big discounts, but your sales life is limited. Eventually a discount etailor will pass you with an online sale. In their world, the high-involvement salesperson is not needed.

So look again at your presentation! Is it interesting? If not, change it...this is the hardest part of selling. Once you have honed your message, begin working it, making it perfect, and finally, learn how to deliver it with confidence. This has made Rush one of the most well known figures in American radio.

Note: Rush can do it because it is his business, but I strongly encourage sales people to leave politics, race, and religion out of their presentations.

Using Knowledge Gaps

"I have an idea!" "There are seven things IT is doing to enable hackers..." "You know how?" Bold, unexpected statements cause the brain to ask, "How?" or "Why?" The stronger the need to know, the better. A great presentation creates these *knowledge gaps* to draw the audience in. One speaker I listen to calls this *salting the oats*. In his weeklong seminar, he often says things like, "There are four purposes for money...which I will share with you tomorrow." Another favorite line, "While in school I went from D's to A's. I found the secret to success...which I will be sharing with you on Friday." This keeps people's interest for days! (By the way, I did attend, followed his recommendation, and actually went from a .9 to almost straight 4's in one semester! I'll share the secret with you another time.)

Your presentation should be no longer than 30 minutes and much of your time should be spent in discussion. But take a look at your opening presentation. Is it boring or does it create knowledge gaps? Another speaker I respect says, "We need an interruption every ten minutes to keep the audience tuned in." I don't know where his research comes from, but I can say I've sat through many predictable and painful presentations. Like another episode of Scooby-Doo...the outcome is known long before the presentation is over. It is obvious. There is no curiosity, no *ah-ha moments* and nothing to keep me from reverting back to my Blackberry – the ultimate time filler. Spend some today reviewing what you present and see if you have knowledge gaps or can find places where some might be injected into your delivery.

Using Interruptions

Interruptions are needed! People go to sleep when you present the obvious. Take a look at the presentations you are using for executive meetings/company introductions...are you stating the obvious? I see marketing departments putting out fancy slides that say things like:

- The Internet is becoming more important to business
- More people are using wireless computing
- Mobility is growing and people are using smart phones
- Duh!

Your presentation needs something new – a new point of view. Something that makes the executive say, "What are we doing about this…how did we miss this?" Only then can you expect them to tune in, want more, and promote you to the adviser status you've been looking for. Don't expect this to just happen – it takes you pouring over your content and looking for a new angle. Wait on your marketing department to think of this and you'll be waiting for a long time. That is, unless your marketing department is way ahead of the pack, and some are!

Sound Bites

"250,000 end-nodes are infected with malware everyday according to The Wall Street Journal!" Sounds bites are power-packed statements that grab people's attention. Using sound bites from trustworthy sources, such as The Wall Street Journal, will impact high-level executives. They make a statement! Here are several important observations about using sound bites:

- ☐ If you are quoting from credible sources, no one can argue with you. If you are presenting issues to executives about trends, threats to their business, or considerations for new technology, a business source such as the Wall Street Journal is like having the Gartner Analyst report in your hands. People believe it must be true if it is published in a high-profile document.

- ☐ Technology people don't generally read these news sources. You won't get much push-back from a systems engineer when quoting the Wall Street Journal, and if you do, the executive is likely to favor his favorite news source over the IT person's opinion or equivalent quotations from PC Week.

Sound bites tend to be analytical…once I have established credibility, I move back to emotional stories

- ☐ Sound bites allow you to connect at a peer level, demonstrating that you are reading business oriented news that impacts your client today. It's up to you to have current sound bites that are relevant to the industry you call on.

How do I find these sound bites? Every day I spend about fifteen minutes combing through the paper. I look at two sources, *USA Today* and *the Wall Street Journal.* I use these two simply because they are in just about every hotel.

That means that my audience, who probably travels almost as much as I do, is also reading one or both of these. I don't read everything. I just look for articles that matter to my business. I might read one or two other key items related to our nation's political situation as well, just to make sure I know what is going on. And if it's Super Bowl weekend, I check to see who won just in case it comes up in a meeting.

Tearing these articles from the paper (or clipping online with Evernote), I place them in a folder labeled *Sound Bites*. Wherever I go, I carry my folder and simply try to use the new sound bites a few times until they are part of my long-term memory. After just a few months, I have dozens of great sound bites that help brand myself as an expert in the areas where I am focusing.

In a recent demand generation event, as I was going through some of the trends, one of the more technical attendees insisted on interrupting me in a confrontational way. He threatened to derail my presentation with some technical jargon and barbed questions, opposing my point. I don't know if he was right or not, but I do know *The Wall Street Journal* disagreed with him. By simply restating my point and quoting a sound bite from a *Wall Street Journal* reference, the audience was right back with me. They believed me because I had strong evidence from a source they trusted. I could tell from their looks that they did not appreciate the interruption. My adversary sat down with the sudden realization that people were there to learn, not engage in technical debates. Because I had a credible source, my audience believed me and was satisfied.

Note: Sound bites are usually statistics or short news items. They tend to be analytical, which drives against the emotional response you need buyers to have. I use them upfront to build credibility, or as a response to a technical objection. Once this has been accomplished I move back to the emotional – back to the storyline of my presentation. Marketing studies have shown that when you feed people lots of data, it leads to judgmental thinking, not a buying decision. I need the credibility up front, so I use sound bites. But once established, it's time to go back to stories and insights.

How Did We Call on 100 Prospects at One Time?

With the right presentation you can sell to hundreds of people at one time. In a recent reseller marketing event, I met with nearly a hundred CIOs and executives in Charlotte, North Carolina. Most traditional sales calls target one company, and most *lunch & learns* can hardly be considered sales calls. But in this case we are combining the two to create a more efficient sales effort. How does it work? Well, I do cover demand generation events in a later chapter, but here, I'll give you some brief insights.

First, traditional *lunch* & *learns* are generally attended by existing IT-level clients, not executives. This is a great way to express appreciation to your clients while providing technology updates with the hopes of discovering new projects within the group. This is, however, expensive and the jury is out on actual ROI. In my experience, most of these efforts do not produce measurable success and rarely lead to anything you wouldn't have found just by staying in contact with your customer base; still, not a bad thing to do for your best customers, especially if you have a way to fund it.

Educating your market is different. This approach targets a group of buyers using educational, presentation material that is relevant to the executive audience; people who can approve a purchase. It's like casting a wide net to capture a large group of potential consumers. We promote the event much like you would a wedding, including professional looking invitations with an RSVP. It's an "invite only" in order to limit lower level attendees, and generally done over a meal to encourage networking opportunities. Creating a place for executives to network within their circle, guarantees this type of event will work.

The keynote I gave at this event was designed using the marketing concepts I teach and continue to talk and blog about; mainly, knowledge gaps, commitments, interruptions in thinking, and stories that create an *aha moment*. I want my audience to ask themselves, "Are we addressing these issues?" If the issues I bring up are urgent and credible, I can move my audience to the point of believing it would be foolish not to at least check! Educational content that leads to urgency, followed by an investigation, is the key to success. This process is used as the discovery aspect of the sales process, which then creates opportunity for remediation or other project efforts. In the case of liability issues, these sales lead to recurring revenue or annuity. In many cases we will motivate seventy-five percent of our audience to move to an assessment. Many of my clients find that up to ninety percent of these assessments lead to projects and managed services, provided they understand the follow up process.

This is the power of presentation. Every sales person should be capable of delivering this type of program, or perhaps putting this type of event together with an outside speaker, and then following up. The results far out perform traditional selling efforts.

Selling Remotely

Presenting by Phone

Sometimes you just can't be there in person, so what do you do? I am not a fan of cold calling when it comes to high-involvement selling. However, learning to use the phone is key when it comes to saving time, especially when you are in charge of a large geographic area. I cover the world with just one rep – me. The phone is not something I use to cold call. Rather, it is a tool I used to communicate with qualified buyers.

A call set up through email or a referral is no longer cold. The problem is, people lose their focus on the phone, so you can't really present anything. Keep your descriptions short, use a story to draw them in, and predict objections to staying on the phone. But, you will need more.

Here's a simple strategy that I've found to be effective. Since most of the people I schedule a call with are sitting in front of their computer or laptop, taking them to a website that has been set up correctly (meaning it has good content and graphics) is a great way to engage emotionally. There I have descriptions of what I am doing, along with customer testimonies on the side bar, and landing pages that spell out the value they will receive. Without having to set up WebEx and do a slide show or demo, I am able to take them to a page that outlines, or pictures, what I am talking about. This allows me to systematically walk through my value proposition, filling in the gaps with a story or two, to demonstrate success. While I am talking, I know they are looking at quotes and testimonies that sit between paragraphs, encouraging the sale.

Become great at phone selling and you'll save an incredible amount of time. An on-site meeting may take two or three hours considering travel, waiting, meeting, leaving, and driving back to the office; and that's a best case scenario. The phone might take thirty minutes to sixty minutes, tops. And that's only if they are really interested. I follow up with an email, linking them to the very same pages we viewed together.

Using WebEx

Some sales calls lend themselves to WebEx or some other form of web collaboration software. For the same reason I don't really like PowerPoint for an initial sales call, when WebEx is used to show PowerPoint, once again I find it takes away from the interactive experience. On the other hand, if you are at the point of demonstrating a software product, it may do the trick.

The secret to success is in knowing when and how to use WebEx. If you have a product you intend to demo, using WebEx can be highly productive and cost effective. Once again, shooting from the hip is bound to result in lost sales. On the other hand, if your call is qualified, you have the right people on the call, and your product is attention grabbing in a demo; you have the foundation for success. But, you still need a well thought-out sales strategy. Remember, like radio, dead air time is never good. You can't afford dead air while you navigate through countless software menus looking for something to show them. In fact, in my opinion, sales teams that rely on these remote communication tools require more training and practice than those who sell in person. Without the personal touch, your presentation must be executed flawlessly with a strong follow up plan. Don't underestimate your team's need for training on this.

Content and Finesse

I have seen presentations given by unappealing people with very strong content, and those given with less content but by people with very strong presentation skills. Content is king! But a poor presenter can destroy great content. On the other hand, a great presenter with an empty message comes across as shallow and selling hype. As we used to say, "Big hat, no cattle."

If you lack content, get some. Educational content delivers value while product knowledge is free online. Remember, Google knows far more than you'll ever know about your product. Personal viewpoints and stories give listeners new perspective and move them to action. Again, sound bites by themselves, while establishing credibility, rarely lead to change. Leave selling to commercials and become an educator. Spend time understanding the needs out there, discover lasting answers, and then find ways to communicate truth despite the mental roadblocks of your listeners. Become a catalyst; an agent of change. Develop a concern for those you call on and then spend time finding ways to improve your client's position.

Next, as you reach out to different prospects, focus on becoming an excellent communicator. Even with an urgent message in hand, you may discover people are still loath to take action. It's your job to find out how to move people to action when the need is real.

Summary

- ☐ Movie stars memorize scripts and practice for months; yet they never sound like robots – they're professionals that become great at communicating their lines.

- ☐ Speakers are made, not born. They learn their stories, practice their openings, and rehearse their close. Sales people are often called on to be speakers, and must learn to do the same.

- ☐ Slides are the frame around your message – not the message itself. Don't lean on slideware.

☐ Learn to use white boards and flip charts where appropriate and always carry your own markers. Don't leave sensitive data for your competition to see.

☐ Learn to use a facilitation tool such as the *six thinking hats*. This makes consulting with buyers much easier, opening up all kinds of new opportunities.

☐ Learn to use success stories – they are emotional and impossible to argue with. They defuse objections and lead your potential client to the discovery of concrete solutions that point to your product. Stories sell.

☐ Great presentations showcase your opinion, stand out, create knowledge gaps that demand to be filled, and lead people to embrace you or reject you. Either one is better than neutral.

☐ Sound bites are good for creating credibility and defeating technical objections. Learn where and how to apply them to the presentation and people will see you as the authority.

☐ Mastering the phone sale will multiply your time. Learn to communicate effectively with your voice and some online tools.

☐ Make sure you content is great.

6. MOVING UP – STRATEGIES FOR ACCESSING BUYERS

Thousands of incompetent sales people have preceded you, calling on executives and wasting their time with company overviews, product data sheets, and silly questions about what is keeping them up at night. No wonder managers have stopped taking sales calls. Yet, all sales books seem to say, "Call high." I don't disagree, but what these books tend to leave out is, when to go and what to say when you get there.

Getting a meeting with an executive may not be that hard. In fact, if you've been in sales very long, I'm sure you have had several. It's the second meeting that is more difficult. The executive may need time to forget how the first meeting went before granting a follow-up. Or, you may find more qualifying questions like, "What do we need to talk about?" or "Can you send me an agenda?" Interpretation: "Let me qualify this before scheduling," and in the back of their mind they are thinking, "This probably isn't necessary or important." If this is happening, it is likely a result of not having the right message first the time around.

While calling high is important, calling on executive management in itself is not all that useful. It's what gets accomplished in the executive meeting that matters, and if nothing significant is accomplished, it may do more harm than good. All of this comes back to our theme of going *from vendor to adviser*. Offer unique value, and this meeting becomes relational and important.

To restate value, the four things buyers buy - ROI, operational efficiency, competitive advantage, and risk mitigation must be at the core of your message. Trying to attack all four will lead to confusion, while focusing on just one can be powerful. As Jim Collins puts it in his book, *Good to Great*, you must be passionate about the one you choose, and become great at delivering value in that area. When we say *trusted adviser*, we mean, the rep. is able to actually advise in his chosen area, and when required, advise in a particular vertical market.

Then, when delivering in the context of say, operational efficiency, what is the impact and likelihood? There is a measurable impact to the business, but, what is the likelihood of achieving it? If the buyer does not believe there is a high likelihood, the probability of them buying goes way down, and in the end, budgets will not be approved.

Understanding System Thinking

When coaching sales people, one of the first things I want to know is, are they acquiring new accounts or just farming existing named accounts. Most are doing the latter. The next question is, are they supposed to be looking for new accounts? If so, are these existing accounts being maintained at an influencer level or have they managed to move up to an advisory role with an executive? How are they going to, or how will they, maintain that position long term? These are all important questions to ask in order to achieve success.

At this point in the book, we will focus on moving up. Then later, I will discuss maintaining that higher-level relationship. I like to break down the sales process into four distinct milestones, which I call meetings; Meeting One, Two, Three and Four. By doing this, I am creating a system that is repeatable and can be refined. If a sales person can develop a repeatable process that works, the job becomes much more definitive. The seller can now spend time reworking the system and perfecting it, making their job less stressful. In the end, they will enjoy predictable growth. I call this process *system thinking*.

The Four Meetings

Meeting One: Influencer Meeting

Generally meeting with IT or IT management, there are no decision makers and the meeting predictably centers around products, technology, and approved budgets. I refer to this group as custodians – data custodians, or people who oversee the systems you sell and implement. Perhaps this person is looking for technology or services and you are a possible provider. Or there may not be budgets approved, in which case you are maintaining a relationship and hoping budgets will be approved for your project.

The Four Meetings...

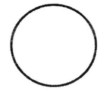

Mtg. 3 - Interview

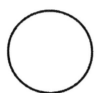

Mtg. 2 - Value Proposition

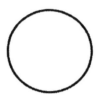

Mtg. 4 - Proposal

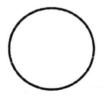

Mtg. 1 - Influencer

The Four Meetings

Meeting Two: Value Proposition Meeting

This is where the business is sold. If you make it to this meeting, you will have decision makers, but more importantly, a group I call asset owners. Asset owners and asset creators are those who work in, or run, profit center organizations within the company. They may also be the decision maker in a smaller company. This is the meeting where you will present business value in one of the four areas I described earlier (ROI, operational efficiency, competitive advantage, or risk mitigation).

Meeting Three: Interview Meeting

This is a short meeting, generally conducted by phone with someone who can make a decision. This should be a person who attended Meeting Two. The goal is to clarify the final project deliverables and therefore, proposal, and to determine their budgets and propensity to buy.

Meeting Four: Close Meeting

This is where you get the contract signed. Usually held with the decision maker, and anyone they deem important to the final closing meeting.

In most selling situations, I find that sellers are at the Meeting One stage and are writing proposals on unbudgeted business. Or, there may be a budget, but competition is there along with that budget, and everyone is bidding to win a product deal. There may, or may not, be services associated with it, and of course with every bid the margin is quickly shrinking.

As I previously cited, in my unscientific analysis, having polled hundreds of sales groups around the world in my sales training workshops, I have found that 10-20% of the proposals being submitted are closing. Most have been written directly to an IT contact or custodian. Far too often, there has been no discussion with an asset owner, and therefore no commitment was made. The seller is simply hoping their proposal will look good and they will somehow be selected. I love the book title, *Hope is Not a Strategy*, written by Rick Page. The message he delivers is absolutely true. Hoping to close your business simply means you have lost control of the deal.

And so I find sales people putting a fifty percent likelihood on most of the deals in their forecast, then moving them from month to month with some remote hope of being the chosen provider. Take a look at your forecast and honestly ask yourself these questions: How did you determine the likelihood of closing, and how many times have you moved the deals on your forecast to a later month, with a 50% probability of closing? If you are like most, this is a common activity you engage in every time you update your forecast for a sales review meeting. Again, It simply means, you are hoping it will close, and you have no control over the decision process.

When a sale is made following this scenario, it usually happens because you have many custodial level relationships going, and as you maintain those relationships, money does eventually come down the chain. The custodian, having built a relationship with you, offers the business. You then tell others, "I won the deal." But did you really *win*? This explains why only a small percentage of any sales team is successful, while the majority are just making it, or wallowing in failure. It also explains why sales managers treat this as a numbers game. By holding onto enough relationships, they believe the money will eventually come down

By building a system that takes us through all four meetings, with a well formulated strategy, and messaging built for each meeting, I believe we can have greater control, assign more accurate percentages to deals, and have more influence on what companies purchase, and when. This same system can also help us determine when it is time to abandon a deal, or at least, know when to stop putting all of our focus on it. There are times to pull back and market more to a company before proceeding to the next meeting level. And there are times to just move on. I'll address both in this chapter.

As a side note, earlier in the book I referred to the five percent rule. There are a small percentage of companies out there, let's say five percent, who are looking for something you have right now. These are the companies who have already approved a budget, already identified possible buyers, perhaps put an RFP on the street, and are determined to buy from the lowest bidder or a bidder that was chosen prior to writing an RFP (Which I will cover in more detail in the proposals section of this book). If you are the preferred seller, and you know it, go ahead and take down the deal. But if not, there are better ways to proceed than writing a response and submitting it along with twenty *other look-a-like* responses. If you know they need what you have, and can prove it, you have a better chance of winning it. This goes back to educational marketing strategies and is the best approach for finding new business.

Custodians Don't Make Decisions

When a custodial level person (i.e. IT person) calls for a quote, you need a sign on the wall reminding you that *custodians do not make decisions*. When the quote is requested, it is hard to say no. After all, there is a chance you could get the deal. At this point, your ability to identify who your decision makers are, who those asset owners are, and who will actually depend on the system in question to conduct business, can save hours or even days of work.

I remember the day one of my clients called with an opportunity. A healthcare organization in Florida had reached out to him for a security penetration test. We had been working on the information security side of his offerings, so this call was welcomed and generated a lot of enthusiasm in my client's office. Penetration tests are somewhat complex and often carry a healthy price tag, so this was a great opportunity to receive and it even had the potential to create some great follow-on business. However, the requester was not a decision maker nor was he an asset owner of any kind.

The prospect (IT person from the healthcare company) was making the request, but I wanted to know why. I asked my client to go back to him and explore this. There are many ways to assess risk, so why was he asking about the penetration test in particular? Why not just ask us to evaluate their security? After some initial probing, it turned out that the company wanted something to take to their healthcare patients that would show their facility was secure; a sort of competitive advantage. I encouraged my client to probe further. I was confident we would find holes in the healthcare facility's security strategy; making this a bad way to convince future patients their facility offered excellent protection. But the IT contact kept insisting on the penetration test. Why would someone, with custodial responsibility, be the primary requestor of this type of initiative?

Custodians have no liability, they simply maintain systems within the guidelines they are given. Their interests usually lie in things that will make their jobs more interesting or increase their worth to the organization. In this case, I believe our prospect was interested in learning more about security and penetration testing as a way to increase his knowledge level, and value to his organization. I did not believe his management was actually interested in a penetration test or even knew what one was. After several calls, we were unable to get a meeting with his manager, but he assured us that money was not a problem. With this in mind, I encouraged my client to put a high-priced general offering in front of him, with little detail. I didn't expect approval, in fact, it was my opinion that there was no deal to be had. We would never actually win this, so going through the discovery phases to put together a real price was a waste of time. Instead, we opted for the something safe, without actually refusing to bid.

The healthcare company never came back to us, and as far as we can tell, never contracted with anyone to perform the penetration test. I think they were hoping we would have something affordable that would somehow get approved. I don't know if they went to competitors, but if they did, the prices for penetration testing were probably out of reach for this non-decision maker.

If the deal had been real, someone with liability would have been the real requestor, and our prospect would have eventually allowed us access to them. Instead, it is likely his management didn't even know he was out shopping.

Discernment is an important part of saving time. If a deal is bona fide, you want to see how you can win it. When the deal is simply for educational exploration, you want to know before investing time. That being said, sometimes this type of opportunity can be turned into a real deal. When custodians are involved, you don't want to cut them out of the process, instead you should focus on their needs. Understanding where they fit and how to deal with them, is important to the sales cycle and can save a lot of time. After all, they do influence. Let's take a look at some of the options and how to engage with various people in the organization as we investigate the opportunity.

Meeting One: The Importance of Custodians

Custodians are important. Just about everything we have must be maintained, and without proper maintenance and oversight, the system will eventually fail.

In the CISSP (Computer Information System Security Professional) study guide, security administrators are referred to as data custodians and are charged with the critical tasks of making sure confidentiality, integrity, and availability of data and applications is maintained. But their authority and liability is limited to the scope of their custodial care, and the budget they have been given. In other words, as long as they do their job, as is outlined in their employment agreement, they have no liability.

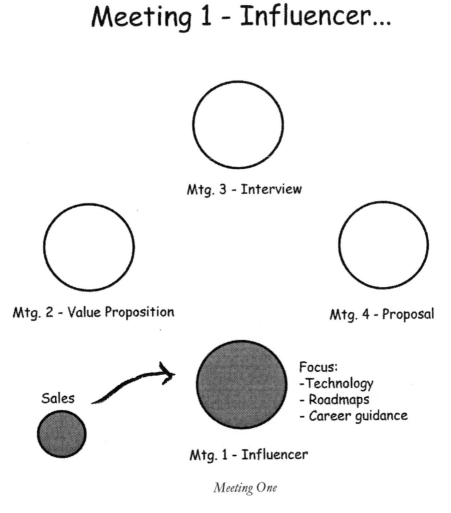

Meeting One

Let's not confuse these important custodial responsibilities with strategic decision-making and liability. While it may be easy and even informative to meet with custodians, it does not lead to big business deals if you stop there. Don't position yourself as a peer to custodians, but rather start thinking of yourself as an adviser to those leading the business – those who create and use assets, and those who own assets. If you don't have what it takes to advise at this level, get on a program to change. As you should know by now, advisers are made, not born…you can be one of them.

For many different reasons, most reps are calling on those that maintain - custodians. Therefore, they are primarily dealing with implementer and system maintenance; trying to sell technology. Even if the 20% close prediction is off significantly, the numbers are still bad and time is being wasted on proposals and follow up that go nowhere. The key here is not giving in to influencer requests, but rather having a plan of attack that includes those higher up in the organization. As I mentioned earlier, beginning with the end in mind.

Assume custodians will masquerade as asset owners and will request proposals, act like they care about cost, and talk down to you as though they are actually in charge of budget creation. Don't give in – don't believe it. Instead, start focusing on their real needs and how you can help. I find that, more often than not, they need your support and greater influence with those in asset owner positions.

Use Meeting One to begin mapping out the organization. Find out who, outside of the IT organization, is responsible for driving company revenue. Forget about your products for a moment and identify those who own assets, and those who are creating and using data that ultimately drives company profitability. From there, you can begin developing some sort of scorecard that will allow you to measure gains in operational efficiency or risk reduction, and then associate them with internal business processes.

Meeting Two: The Deal is Sold to Asset Owners

While there are four meetings in my model, the actual sale takes place in Meeting Two. Remember the adoption life cycle I presented in chapter two. Value and differentiation are demonstrated early in the sales cycle through one of the four things buyers buy. The product is then sold in the middle, and recurring revenue opportunities fall into place at the end. Meeting Two is where your value is presented to those who own assets.

The initial research is done in meeting one at the custodial level, allowing you, the seller, to identify asset owners and to gather all you need to advise in Meeting Two. Meeting Two is where asset owners are present, and where your presentation of business value makes sense. Assume custodians will be there as well, but the message prepared for this meeting is directed toward asset owners, not custodians. The custodians may not understand what you are talking about, or may not see value in what you are saying, but that doesn't really matter as long as you don't undermine them in the meeting. Remember, this is not an attempt to go around anyone, but rather an effort to understand the business needs in the context of the four things buyers buy. Your message around the four things buyers buy does not necessarily help custodians in their day-to-day tasks, but it does bring business value in areas of efficiency and risk mitigation which is where your asset owners should be focused. And it is this value that will ultimately justify spending.

Meeting 2 - Value Proposition...

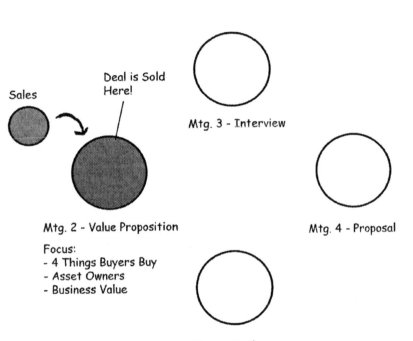

Meeting Two – Where the Deal is Sold!

Think of Meeting Two as a time to establish a vision. You are giving asset owners a vision for what could be. A vision, perhaps, for greater efficiencies that allow their traveling employees to produce more on the road, collaborate across time zones, meet face to face without having to get on a plane, or work from home without the risk of their children bringing malicious web threats into company computers. You may offer your clients a way to access sensitive data from coffee shops or work with smart phones and iPads, because now they have a way to do it safely.

Meeting 2 - Moving Up...

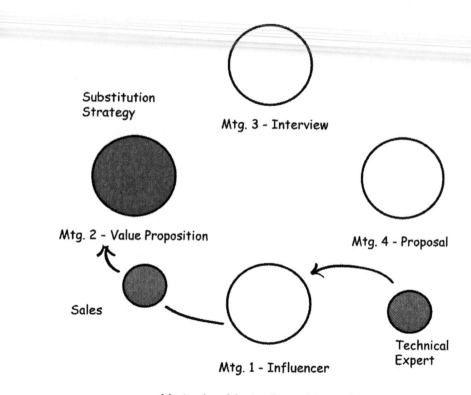

Moving from Meeting One to Meeting Two

By visualizing these advantages in the context of the buyer's business day, using their applications, locations, and processes (things you learned while in Meeting One), you are now able to speak their language and communicate complex ideas in a way that they can now understand (Note: this is no place for technology jargon – learn the language of the vertical you are calling on). Once the vision has been established, they should be asking how, and how much? When that question is asked, you know you have the vision planted securely in their mind. They see something, and now they want to know if it can be done. They see the vision and it makes sense - but don't move from Meeting Two until this has absolutely happened. Moving through these steps will establish that trusted adviser status.

Gaining Permission

Each step, from custodian to asset owner, to proposal submission, is a matter of value proposition. Access is gained by giving people what they need in a unique and differentiating way. In Meeting One, we discovered the custodian's needs and identified probable business issues and key asset owners. What do these people really want?

In most cases, what they really care about is respect for what they do, compensation commensurate with the value they bring, and a chance to actually make a contribution that people upstairs will recognize. Everyone has a desire to accomplish something meaningful, or to have a significant purpose in the business. Back in the days of the industrial revolution, leaders like Andrew Carnegie and political figures such as Woodrow Wilson, saw that our country's profits depended on building large companies with a few key leaders. This would require that the majority of the population be trained to work in lower level, worker-bee jobs. This "working-class" group would be large, have little input, and be stripped of their creative and entrepreneurial spirit. The school systems were actually designed to do just that. Even today's private schools, and many learning opportunities, turn out these drones. So as people enter the workforce, many are willing to just do their job, and nothing more, while others become frustrated. Help this discouraged group get somewhere and you'll be their hero.

Once in front of asset owners, another step is needed. Thousands of sales people just like you, are calling on these decision makers, simply following the methods proposed in every sales book written in the past decade. With numerous companies just like yours, and a limited number of businesses in a given market, leaders are inundated with calls from incompetent sales people, looking to show their wares. To differentiate yourself, and to see success in your endeavor, a discovery process is needed with those who create and use data – those who work directly for asset owners and are responsible for growing company profits at the end of each day (We'll be covering this discovery process in great detail later in the book).

Moving forward requires demonstrating value. In a recent demand generation event we targeted Meeting Two asset owners from the start and arranged for it to be held at an upscale location. I was brought in as a speaker (speaking on the trends of data security and cybercrime), and a follow up discovery program was designed. Our goal was to show them, as reported recently in the Wall Street Journal, that security is no longer a custodian issue, and that companies must have someone at the executive level overseeing this and reporting right to the top! This was a perfect introduction to a Meeting Two conversation. No products, no tech talk, and no Power Point slides discussing the hosting company's profits, employees, or certifications. Instead, we created a reason for attendees to meet us.

After just sixty minutes of presentation, these attendees were willing to stay and talk. They received books, signed up for assessments and looked forward to our next visit; a visit that would take place in their office with a focus on their risks. They wanted to know how to ensure that global cyber thieves would not victimize their businesses. In fact, we gained access to see them three times! The first meeting was at the luncheon. From there they agreed to invite us to their office for an assessment, and finally, a third meeting to deliver our findings. If a sales person can't close business with three executive meetings and compelling justification from an assessment, it may be time to change jobs.

Key Selling Principles – Understanding the Importance of Assets

Working with asset owners isn't easy. There are two selling principles and two board room principles I keep in front of me at all times:

Selling Principle #1: Forget about products; focus on the assets

Selling Principle #2: Find the asset owner

These two principles were spelled out in some detail in my first book, *The House & the Cloud*, but their importance goes much farther than just selling security solutions (the focus of my first book). Assets are another name for data in today's businesses and organizations. There are all kinds of assets one can point to, but data has surpassed most in value. In just about any disaster recovery plan, data is almost always the first thought. Where and how do we back up our data, and how will we restore it at an offsite location? Intellectual capital, trade secrets, pending patents, customer data, finances, and even money itself, is now a digital asset.

Even criminals have recognized the growing value of data. Organized crime syndicates are now making more money on stolen data than they are on drug trafficking. The bottom line is, data is of great importance, and if lost, could put a company out of business.

Every company has data, and that data is central to what the business does and is planning to do. So your first step is to focus on their data. Learn about it. Learn about the applications they use to create it, manage it, store it, use it and you will be focusing on the most important aspects of the company. Apply the four things buyers buy, and you have the recipe for success.

Secondly, find the asset owners. This is plural because there is often more than one. The decision maker is an asset owner, but there are other key influencers that also own or create and use assets. These influencers carry tremendous power, power that often exceeds that of the traditional economic buyer (the one who writes the check). The power of influence is strong when the economic buyer cares about the asset owner. Take a parent-child relationship for example. The parent should be the decision maker, but how many parents cave in when their little girl or boy continue to ask for something? It's hard to say no.

While custodians may be hesitant to ask for budget, or perhaps powerless to do so, an asset owner is different. Anyone responsible for company profitability owns assets. But there are others. People who manage critical profit-producing departments, own assets. At another level, those working within a profit center department are expected to generate sales in their own company and probably rely on applications and data throughout the day. There may be a technology decision at hand and the technology managers (perhaps the CIO) will make a final decision. But, you can be sure the needs of the Investment Bank's Executive Vice President will be heavily considered in the decision making process. As I write this book, I am working on a major technology sales training initiative. The funding will come out of the training department, however, my focus is on the asset owners and those who rely on assets to do their job. They are the people who oversee the international sales team; those who will carry the quota and fight to get the training they need.

Key Board Room Principles – Establishing Value

Board Room Principle #1: Ask a custodian level question; expect to get demoted.

Board Room Principle #2: Present price before establishing value and expect the deal to stop.

Both principles are important when dealing with asset owners. The first is a sure sign that you are really a vendor or technical guy. The Asset Owner most likely does not understand technical jargon and has delegated this function *down* to someone in a technical role. The other day I was on the phone with my email hosting company about an issue concerning a lack of delivery. While I do have a technical degree, as soon as he started talking about MX records and email routing, I was ready to direct him to my web hosting company who handles my domain registration. Email administrators speak another language, and getting wrapped up in this discussion is a waste of my time. Asset owners are no different. They pay someone to handle the technical details so that they can remain focused on the business. At the end of the day, they will be asked questions like, "How much money did you save us in total cost of ownership?" or "What return did you give us from this investment you insisted on?"

In my workshops I encourage sales reps to leave behind all technical jargon, three-letter-acronyms, and sales buzz words (including: *partner with you, earn your business, and value-add*). Learn their language, and speak it. If you find managers sending you back down the ladder, or saying things like, "You should talk with our IT people," assume you have slipped into tech speak. You've been demoted.

The second rule is about value you deliver. Everyone wants to know the price, but to what are they comparing it? If you give someone a price on a project, but they don't really understand it's value to the organization. They can only compare the value to a budget they have. Picture yourself wanting something you have never bought before. For instance, you are going to buy a new mountain bike. As an avid mountain biker, I frequently get asked about mountain bikes. When shopping for this purchase, you will find several price ranges. The novice generally has no idea where to begin. All bikes seem to look the same, carry Shimano components and have rapid-fire shifters. So why are some $3500 and others only $350? The buyer has nothing to compare the bike to, so if I just say, I'll sell this to you for $3500, all he does is look in his wallet. If I start probing, I might find out that he only wants to ride on some dirt roads occasionally, to get some fresh air. Unless you just want to own the best and money is no object, I am going to recommend the low end of this spectrum. But usually I start by breaking down price categories and explaining the break points.

The point is, the buyer must understand what they are looking at in terms of value and functionality. They must compare it to their personal, or in this case business needs, and then make a decision. Unless they really don't have any money, asset owners will reallocate funds once they determine the real needs and options.

Central to this point is gaining access to those who work for asset owners. These are the people who evaluate the need and really understand the proposed solution. Find this group, discover their needs, and you can be sure they will influence the asset owner's direction. Mahan Kalsa's book, *Let's Get Real or Let's not Play*, does a great job of pushing sales people to speak frankly about prices and needs with asset owners. There is no reason to pass papers back and forth, avoiding the price discussion. Instead, once real value has been demonstrated, talk openly about investments and operational costs. On the other hand, don't bother talking about price until you have uncovered the needs, figured out how to help, and have presented some unique differentiating advice about how your client should proceed. With this in mind, we can now put a price on it along the lines of the value we have demonstrated (I will be speaking on fees and prices in a later section in much greater detail).

The Four Things Buyers Buy

Of course we have covered these already, but in the forefront of your mind should be, that value must be demonstrated through the four things buyers buy:

-   ROI – Return on investment
-   Operational efficiency
-   Competitive advantage
-   Risk mitigation

The Strategy

Years ago, while working in the IT department of a large national bank, I was called into a vetting process for PCs. We were rolling out standard desktop computers to over 50,000 end-users; a deal that any sales rep would be happy to take down, even in today's commoditized PC market.

The choices were Compaq EISA (before the HP acquisition) or IBM Micro Channel. IBM was the incumbent with their mainframe relationship. They had their big iron computers spread throughout our company, and were working hard to sell the Token Ring IBM system next, along with PCs on every desk.

Early on in the sales process, Compaq came to see me. They brought with them their senior engineers from Atlanta, and gave me some product to appraise during the vetting process. In addition, they made their engineers available to me throughout the sales evaluation process. During the months to come, I spent hours with these guys. They also introduced us to a reseller they brought in from Atlanta, who provided all kinds of great insights into the future of technology, PC architecture; and backed it up during visits to their lab. They educated me, picking up where college left off, and armed me with questions for the IBM sales people.

IBM never came to see me. Their relationship was strictly with the executives. Over the months, I learned more about PCs than I could have imagined. Both about IBM and Compaq, but none of this information came directly from IBM. In the final weeks of our search, IBM offered to host a meeting in Florida at their Boca Raton center. They flew several bank representatives down to their facilities for a two-day meeting. IBM had not invited me, probably because they misunderstood my importance to the whole process, but the bank saw value in my attending, and asked me to join them.

Over the next two days we went through competitive analysis discussions and slides, looking at the future of PCs from IBM's perspective. IBM's Microchannel technology sported a 50MHz bus, and from what IBM was telling us, no other bus would ever exceed 33 MHz! They also insisted that network speeds over 16 Mbits/sec would not happen outside of fiber optics and type one cable. As we went through these meetings I was asking questions; questions that came from my meetings with Compaq.

In the end, the decision came down to our group for consideration. The asset owners made a decision to buy, but the management was not about to make this decision without input from their technical people; those with custodial responsibility. Had IBM courted my team the way Compaq did, we might have chosen them, but they didn't. What lessons can we learn from this?

☐ Data custodians are important. We didn't make the buying decision, but once a buying decision was in process, we were consulted. Custodians influence, so the seller's job is to ensure that those charged with implementing and maintaining will vote YES. We didn't in this case, and our managers chose to believe us.

☐ Compaq did move up the ladder, however, they first substituted key technical people for the sales person's relationship with IT. Given the relationship with a top engineer, IT was not about to block the salesperson from visiting the management team. Technical people generally value a relationship with senior consulting engineers over a sales person who takes them to lunch occasionally.

☐ IBM called high, but neglected the technical team (they also neglected business-side asset owners). They only addressed this project at the executive level. IT wanted involvement, however, the only education we received came from Compaq. Therefore, when we were asked to choose which horse to ride, we choose the one we were comfortable with. A loyalty was established with one brand, but not the other.

☐ Technical people have needs. Education is always at the top, along with recognition, compensation and benefits. The technical team probably won't actually have to use the new equipment, at least not like those with asset responsibility, so what liability do they really have? Just their reputation for technical expertise. Compaq, in this case, gave us the education we needed, so that's all we knew. Not much different than doctors who recommend prescriptions based on the education they received from pharmaceutical companies.

Summarizing the Strategy

The Seller has Value

Sales people have little value to give when it comes to dealing with technical people. They don't know as much, don't have the same level of interest, and often don't speak the same language. Sales people are business people, working on commission, selling products and services. Technical people are people who work with their hands. They do things — they take care of the process. Technicians are task oriented, work for a paycheck and like things to be predictably stable. Sales people are more like entrepreneurs; high risk, high reward people, perhaps building a territory from scratch, living on commission and selling things that may not actually exist until sold and developed.

The seller's value to the technician is in connecting them with future opportunity and education by introducing them to senior technical people in the seller's organization; those who have higher earning power, have seen more things, fixed more problems and know the future roadmaps. They may even have advice about a better career path for the technician they are calling on. The sales person's value must be in the four things buyers buy. They must become a consultant of sorts. Not a technical consultant, but an adviser.

There is a Time to Move Up

Timing is everything. In my events, we are moving up on the first meeting, but we have an industry speaker, usually a thought-leader, who speaks with non-bias expertise to business audiences. In the typical sales call, IT is usually the starting place. But knowing that the IT person is really a custodian should provide motivation for moving up. When to move is the important question.

Move when a request is made, when an evaluation product is requested, an executive briefing is asked for, or when a demonstration is required. Say, "Yes, we can do that." But first, there are things to discover. You are liable for what you deliver in the form of recommendations and ideas, so insist on seeing asset owners as part of the discovery process. You are asked to do an evaluation or proof of concept. Great, do it. But first, you must gather some information to develop your success criteria (something I'll cover in more detail as we go along). Start with peers, then perhaps those who work for your primary contact. But in the end, you must see the people who are liable for data; you must see the asset owners. Only then can you really understand the business implications for what you are recommending, and only then can you discuss value and pricing. Don't give in, or you will enter the endless sales cycle of influencer meetings and lunches.

Don't Ask, Tell

Notice I said, insist on seeing asset owners. If you ask, they will likely say no. They may still say no, but don't give them the option. If you are liable, you just have to. But there is no reason to put forth this requirement if you don't resolve to walk away from the deal, when necessary. That doesn't mean you never sell to them again. It simply means you are going to continue marketing to them, but will not deliver the requested proof of concept or evaluation until they provide access to the right people. Continue selling them on the solutions they have asked for, but don't provide it until you have the right people involved. To do otherwise is generally a waste of time and in the end you will lose.

Liability is the Key.

When you say, "We are liable," what can they say? In fact you are. Perhaps not legally, but what if you recommend a direction without the proper facts, and they are attacked by cyber thieves the very next week? It doesn't matter what you recommended, the last person giving the advice will be in trouble, and that could be you.

Going Wide

Sometimes the answer is no. Before giving up, try going wide. Talk to their peers, and keep going wider until you see a way up. But don't provide anything in the form of proof of concept or evaluation until you meet people responsible for assets.

Substitution

The risk is always in going over the custodian's head. Every sales person fears doing this, but substitution is the key strategy here. When you, the sales person, hold onto a custodial relationship like it's your best friend, you are in trouble. Substitute the senior technical person for yourself. Let them be on point for technical things. I'll never forget going into a major US bank years ago as a technical presales consultant. The salesperson had been able to set up a meeting with a large group of middle managers along with some technical people. Instead of introducing me as someone important, my rep simply said, "this is our technical guy." No formal introduction, and no justification for them to get to know me. I ended up sitting on the sidelines for this one, and our heroic sales person never moved up. His problem, not mine. I wasn't looking for status or glamour, but rather to be positioned in such as way as to help his cause. In my opinion, he blew it.

The Two Year Marketing Plan

Finally, plan to continue your marketing efforts. Assume half the people you meet will not allow you to move up to the asset owner level. It's okay. Continue to market to them, showing them value at their level and providing the education they need and desire. Use the substitution strategy to keep things moving forward, and you will be surprised at how many accounts eventually turn your way. The ones that don't aren't worth chasing.

The Goal

Of course the goal is to close the business. But always keep in mind what executives and asset owners really need; to know the measure of impact and likelihood. The risk mitigation sale is predicated on understanding the impact to business if something goes wrong, but the motivation to buy requires a credible measure of likelihood. The operational efficiency sale is similar, but seeks a high likelihood of a positive outcome. If the client or prospect doesn't believe the likelihood of something going wrong or improving is very high, expect the deal to head south.

The Impact / Likelihood Chart

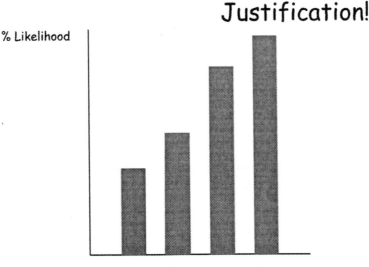

Impact / Likelihood Chart

In the case of the Florida healthcare deal I mentioned earlier, the client believed the penetration test would show his clients that their security was good. I disagreed. I can't think of many organizations who have withstood penetration tests, and if they did, my assumption is that the security team didn't understand how to get in. In other words, the security of the company wasn't necessarily good, and the team performed poorly.

Whether you are looking for an efficiency gain, or a reduction of risk, the impact must be identified by the asset owner, and the likelihood must be high. The company is either losing business due to its inefficiencies, or in jeopardy due to some high risk issue. In either case it must be urgent. Communicate the urgency of this issue to the asset owners by explaining what this really means in business terms, rather than glossing over it with techno-speak.

Once you have access to asset owners, your goal is simple; find something urgent. It can be a risk issue, or an operational efficiency/cost savings discovery. I recently heard about a young man, just out of school, who approached large corporations with a study he did on the amount of money being wasted through incorrect accounts payable procedures. He proposed a program to audit and fix these issues before payment was sent. His fee? He simply wanted 1% of the savings. His project resulted in millions of dollars in personal income. He was able to gain access to people who cared, convince them that the likelihood was high, and then show through proof of concept that he was right. It cost the hiring company nothing, because they were saving 99 cents for every 1 cent paid in consulting fees. I think I would have asked for 5 or 10 percent.

Given access to the right people, the discovery process begins. I cover this in another chapter in greater detail, but for now a simple outline of what it means to assess or discover is all we need.

Assessing and Discovering.

The discovery process is more than just asking some sales questions. Every sales person who wants to become an adviser must become a consultant. That doesn't mean you start charging a fee for input, but rather it means learning to ask questions that lead to solid justification.

In a recent sales opportunity we were charged with providing a competitive quote on unified communications (UC) products. The company already used UC, so the quote was simply to upgrade. The seller assembled the quote, listing all of the necessary hardware, software, and services to move their client to the latest version. The problem here was that the proposal had no differentiation! It listed product, installation services, and a price. You might say your uniqueness is in your people or your certifications, or perhaps "yourself" as the go-to provider for that brand of system. But in this case, you don't have a platform to demonstrate it. How do you demonstrate uniqueness?

Demonstrating Uniqueness in the Discovery Process

The answer is in the discovery process. Most of these projects are assigned to a presales technical person. The sales person has simply become a relationship manager, adding no value to the client relationship. The technical person is generally too technical to effectively interact with asset owners. So the sales person and asset owners wait on opposite sides of the deal. The sales person hoping for a "yes" decision, and IT managers looking at budget. Instead of sitting on the sidelines, you, the seller should be in there communicating with those who will benefit from the technology your company wants to provide.

Remember to focus on the urgent issues – things with high impact and high likelihood. Many of the things we deem critical, are not important to asset owners. We can either work to educate them as to why they really are important, or move on to the things they are concerned about.

Meeting 3 - The Interview...

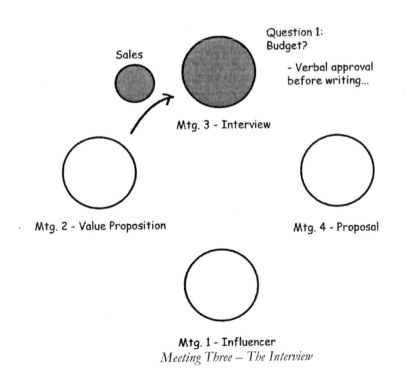

Sales

Question 1:
Budget?

- Verbal approval
before writing...

Mtg. 3 - Interview

Mtg. 2 - Value Proposition

Mtg. 4 - Proposal

Mtg. 1 - Influencer
Meeting Three – The Interview

Meeting Three: Clarify the Budget

For some reason, discussing money is the major hurdle. Yesterday I was on the phone with a potential buyer. We had discussed the need, talked about options, come to a conclusion on a promising next step, and even picked dates to begin. My prospect then said, "Send me a proposal with some options and pricing."

I was tempted to agree, but then that little alarm went off in my head – don't do it! Why would I write the proposal before agreeing on options and pricing? Paper doesn't sell, I do. We have verbal agreement on the vision, but no specifics. Why waste time and possibly ruin the opportunity by putting the wrong thing down on paper?

Instead I simply said, "Let's review some options right now and make sure we are in agreement on how to proceed." I verbally gave him my interpretation of what we were planning to do, offered a couple of options, restated the value, and then offered a fixed fee. I then said, "How does that sound to you?" He said, "That sounds great." Now I know that I have been selected, and can write the proposal, which is really an agreement, with confidence. I converted it to a PDF, attached it to my Evernote contract software, and wrote, "Here is exactly what we've agreed to." "Simply sign the attached and we'll get started."

The likelihood of closing this kind of agreement is much higher than the elusive agreements made in most sales meetings. Meetings end without any real commitment, and the request for proposal is often just a polite way of ending the meeting. There is no agreement, and there are no specifics from which to craft the proposal. In the end, this type of proposal goes nowhere, leaving the sales person's forecast at fifty percent.

The budget should be clarified in Meeting Three. In most cases, Meeting Two includes both asset owners and influencers. Your value proposition (using the four things buyers buy), is presented to the group, in business language, surrounding the business issues. However, the custodians are still there, whether they are actually listening or not. When Meeting Two comes to a point of vision – when the asset owners finally see it and signal their new revelation by asking the question, "How much will this cost?", you know you have sold it. However, the price and specifics have yet to be agreed upon. At this point, I recommend packing up and heading home, with a plan to put together the options and prices.

Some have said, "Why not give them the price right now?" There are a couple of reasons. First, it is always a good idea to get your team together and make sure you have the right understanding and solution. Write down all that you have heard the client say, discuss services with your technical people, and make sure your pricing strategy is commensurate with value. You don't want to give your product/services away, and at the same time, you don't want to overcharge or propose the wrong solution. Second, and just as important, custodians will often hear a price and compare the services to their own income level. If you propose $100,000 in services, and the custodian makes that or less in a year, they are going to compare your four week project to their annual income. It is not a good thing if they are asking themselves how your people can be worth that much?

A third issue comes to mind, and that is, the seller needs to be comfortable with the price. The first few times I quoted $100,000, I was unsure of myself. I would ask myself, "Are our people worth that much?" Only after having delivered this pricing model numerous times was I absolutely confident that the value was there. Assume there will be some push back unless the buyer perceives that you are confident this should be the price.

There are times, at the end of the meeting, when the buyer pushes hard for a price in Meeting Two. I always try to delay that discussion, offering to put together some options. But as I am considering options, I ask for permission to contact the decision maker mid-week if I have any questions. I always have one, and it is about budget and commitment to buy. I make the call after I have considered the options, come up with alternatives, considered the least possible solution and figured out the best recommendation. I then make the call directly to that decision maker. The call is brief and to the point. It contains the following:

- A restatement of value
- I remind them of our recent meeting and the vision they had for success
- I recall the reasons for buying and the ideas we came up with that seemed to work
- I describe the best recommendation on how to achieve the desired results
- I then offer the fee, followed by an explanation of how we came to that number
- I end with saying, "How does that sound to you?"

Notice my question is not about the price, but rather it covers the entire discussion on solution, logistics, and how we arrived at the pricing. I am looking for either a yes or a question. If the price is too high, I rearticulate the value, offer some alternatives, and work to gain commitment on what it is we are trying to accomplish. This is not just a sale, we are trying to solve a problem. A lesser solution may not solve the entire problem, and should be clarified. By getting the client to focus on the issues at hand, and not the price, I am getting them to visualize what success looks like; and the ineffectiveness of anything less.

On one recent call, a potential buyer was wavering back and forth. I could see that they really wanted me to include the options for the better solution, but use the pricing of the lesser solution. This is never possible. If the price is too high, we look for some creative ways to help the client overcome this. But, I don't just give them a lower price. That would be dishonest. Once the price has been verbally agreed to, I can move to the next step which is closing the business.

Meeting 4: Trading Proposals for Agreements

When Meeting Three is complete, I am ready to move to Meeting Four; the close. If Meeting Three ends without a commitment, it's time to go back to Meeting Two's value proposition. I can stay at Meeting Two forever if needed. If the client is not ready to buy, the value is not obvious. They don't see a clear path to one of the things buyers buy. If they did, and they really believed the likelihood was high, they would probably buy it. It's time to reconsider my value proposition and justification.

Meeting 4 - Proposal...

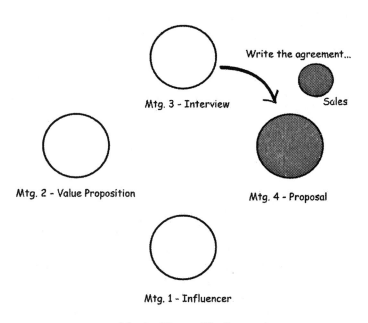

Meeting Four – The Proposal

If they do agree, it is time to write an agreement. I used to write proposals, but proposals are just that; a proposal. They offer to do something for a price, but with no prior commitment. I am proposing to do something and waiting for your approval. In this meeting, Meeting Four, I have approval. I gained it in Meeting Three and I am now ready to put exactly what we have agreed upon on paper. The document should be short and to the point. It should be concrete, spelling out the things we intend to accomplish. It does not need to detail your methodology, and it does not need to sell. The deal is sold.

My recommendations are clear and concrete. I don't want to use jargon, or high-level, meaningless business phrases that can't be pictured. It is important that this document clearly state what we are doing, so if there is a scope creep in question later on, we can go back and be clear about what is included and what is not. I am not talking about being too granular here, but rather being clear. We really do want our client to get what they need and be happy at the end, and by providing a fixed price based on value, we should have room to make sure this happens. After all, we do want future work and we do want references.

Summary:

- [ ] Understand the four meetings – there should be a process you take the client through, with definite milestones and a close plan.

- [ ] Identify the decision makers – Asset owners and economic buyers must be part of the plan. Identify them in Meeting One and make their acquaintance in Meeting Two, where you are prepared to present value and a go-forward plan.

- [ ] Sell the deal in Meeting Two – This is the meeting where deals are sold. Come prepared to sell one of the 4 things buyers buy: Operational Efficiency, Return On Investment, Risk Mitigation, or Competitive Advantage.

- [ ] Use the strategy here to move up – Move up using the triggers mentioned in this chapter. From Meeting One, you are looking for a request that requires some upfront research. This leads to Meeting Two – when they see it, they'll ask for prices. Move to Meeting Three, discuss budget and gain verbal agreement. With verbal agreement on something concrete, you can replace the proposal with an agreement – which will be presented in Meeting Four.

☐ Justify the deal through the discovery phase – Always involve higher level managers in the discovery process – this is where you reposition yourself as an adviser and create justification.

☐ Gain agreement on budget in Meeting Three – Ask. There is nothing wrong with presenting options and a price, and asking them for their overall feeling on your offering.

☐ Write the agreement for Meeting Four – Apply the proposal tips presented later in this book.

☐ Get a signature and begin selling the next project as you work to accomplish all that has been agreed upon.

7. THE MOST EFFECTIVE MARKETING PROGRAM EVER

How will you get to the right people? This is the question every sales person should be asking and is the focus of numerous sales training programs and methodologies. Several years ago, I had been working to get a meeting with a large healthcare organization in the southeast. Our team had successfully met with the IT people several times and had established a fairly good relationship; however, sales were slow in coming and budgets seemed to be our primary obstacle.

Our strategy was to land a meeting higher in the organization where perceived business value might move some budget our way. Finally, I was granted a meeting with the Vice President of Operations. This person had the authority to approve money and would certainly be central to a successful proof of concept or pilot type project, if we could convince him to move forward. Our meeting started with the Vice President showing up late, but we were ready with our list of promising questions and discovery skills.

After an initial greeting and introduction, I launched into my "solution selling discovery process." Giving me just enough rope to hang myself, our VP prospect answered the first question. But as soon as I began presenting my follow-up question, he looked over at our IT advocate and roared, "I thought you said these guys had something important to share with us. So far all I've heard are a bunch of open-ended sales questions. What is the purpose of this meeting?" How do you recover from that?

There are all kinds of tricks and strategies for getting that meeting at the top. However, in my experience, this is not the real challenge. The real challenge, which is not adequately addressed in most sales books, is that of building peer level relationships at the executive level. We have all gotten the

"Big" meeting at some point in our lives, but how many are consistently staying at this level after the first meeting?

At first glance it may appear that I did everything right on this call. Questions, after all, aren't a bad thing. But typical sales questions are predictable and stale. While the individual I was meeting with may have lacked some manners, and certainly he did, he provided a much needed wake-up call. Something more compelling is essential, when meeting with people at this level in the organization, as we are coming in behind thousands of incompetent sales people who have wasted their time.

Education Can Go a Long Way

My first exposure to a strong value proposition came on the heels of being fired from a great position. As Vice President of a technology solutions firm, I thought I had it made; until one day when a number of bad things came together in our business, all at one time, and the bomb was dropped right on my corner office desk! While cleaning out my office, I was plagued with this important question, "How do you find another one of these?" No one advertises for such a position.

After the initial shock of being in this unbelievable situation, it occurred to me that I had bestseller material sitting right in front of me. Our company had achieved some unbelievable success, so why not put together a short seminar on how to take a company from "Good to Great" (borrowing here from Jim Collins). Rather than sifting through job ads and contacting headhunters, I went right to the phones. I called every decision maker I could find in the southeast and started setting up thirty minute meetings with presidents and CEOs of technology firms, offering to share with them research on business performance, growth factors, inhibitors, etc. The demand was strong and I found myself landing five and six meetings a week!

Rather than going in with a resume, begging people to buy "me", I showed them undeniable value. The presentation would often end with an agreement to explore further how we might work on such a strategy to grow their company. Within a couple of weeks I was getting offers. It was so much fun I wanted to do this full time – but of course no one was paying me. Eventually I settled on a position similar to the one I had left. It was three years later that I discovered a way to take my material to market on my own.

I relate this to selling technology. The connection is easy, people need help with business growth and if someone appears to have answers, leaders will listen. As you're heading out this week, are you carrying with you lasting answers to your prospect's biggest problems?

Where to Market?

My son asked me the other day, "Dad, what happens when you run out of people to call?" What a great question for a 16 year old to be asking...this is the problem every sales person has at some point in his or her career. That's what marketing is for! But how many companies really have their act together when it comes to marketing? In most cases it is up to the sales person to generate new interest - it would be great if marketing and sales would get together on this...

There are three primary platforms for marketing consultative and high-tech solutions:

- Customer events
- One-on-one seminars
- Social media

But using any one of these platforms for something other than education builds distrust with the prospects you call on. In other words, effective marketing (in B to B sales) must be founded on education, not hype.

It's through this well-thought-out process that a continuous stream of new names will come through your office, giving you a growing source of new people to call. Let's take a deeper look.

Local Events

My favorite marketing platform is local events. My first major *lunch* & *learn* came on the heels of moving from an IT position to a presales support role in the wide area networking space. A major manufacturer sponsored our meeting, the marketing was taken care of by our in-house marketing person, sales people were charged with getting clients and prospects to the meeting, and I was offered an opportunity to be one of the speakers for our half-day event. I hadn't done much speaking at this point in my career, outside of a local Toastmasters club I had joined and some oral reports I did in school, so I labored over my presentation material determined to make it perfect. As a presales guy, I wasn't involved in the logistics of this event, just responsible for great content. I had no working knowledge or experience with marketing, demand generation, follow up, or anything, other than articulating what various technologies could do; all from a speeds and feeds mentality.

Finally the day came when I would present, and for the first time, I was given an attendance list. I had dreamt of presenting to 50 or 75 people; maybe even 100 would show up to hear my presentation! But, to my dismay, there were only 6 on the list. Six! I couldn't imagine presenting to an audience of six. Do you actually stand to do this, or just sit at a round table? We decided to go forward anyway because we had some pretty good names on our list. You've probably guessed already, but as I've come to learn, attrition is the biggest enemy of any event, and only two showed up. I thought six was bad, but two is horrible. I think I would have rather had a one-on-one meeting and made it a sales call. We had two companies with completely different businesses. It was a total flop. And I was in the middle, working hard to hold their attention.

That was over twenty years ago, and since then I have learned that events really are a great way to market. However, it doesn't just happen. It takes a strategy, commitment from sales and marketing, and contribution from every person on the team. When done right, it is an excellent investment, done wrong it can be a very costly mistake.

Funding these Events

How much does it cost to put together an effective *lunch* & *learn*, educational marketing event? This is a question I am frequently asked – "Will my partners sponsor this, do they speak too, should this be half a day or a whole day, etc.?"

If you manufactur products, this is probably not an issue. If you resell, you should try to acquire some sort of joint marketing funds (JMF). The perception is, if the event is not product focused, JMF won't pay for it. This is a misconception. Vendors who provide their resellers with JMF are looking for a return. Given the current US economy, return on investment is key and every dollar must count. Therefore, you must show compelling reasons for your agenda.

Smaller resellers continue to hear, "We don't have any money this quarter." This is also not true. The fact is, millions, if not over a billion dollars of JMF will go unspent annually. The truth is, they don't have JMF allocated for your company for some reason. That may be because your company does not produce enough business to justify an allocation. JMF may be marked for certain companies, certain types of events, or just not available from the vendors you have chosen to partner with. All of the above can be overcome. The following tips were derived from working with vendors on all kinds of events including customer appreciation, marketing, training, and demand generation:

☐ Getting JMF is a bit like acquiring angel investor money; you need a compelling business plan. The plan must have substance: strategy, target market, planned marketing, planned follow up, investment requirements, and expected outcomes. The plan should be concrete and in process, not theoretical. Let your potential investors see that you are doing this with or without them. Ask them if they would like to join you and reap the rewards! A letter explaining this, followed up by a call, is the right way to proceed. This means setting a date, having a speaker, a venue, a topic, and an invite list ready to go. You can always cancel, but you want potential sponsors to see that their competitors will be there if they say no, and you intend to close big business at this event.

☐ Some companies don't provide JMF at all. Managed services platforms tend to fall into this category. They either don't provide any JMF or their program is so weak, it's not worth it. Not true for all, but do your research and understand what kind of participation others are getting. I recommend partnering with companies that are willing to invest in you.

☐ Some companies only invest in their larger resellers, leaving SMB solution providers to fend for themselves. If you fall into the *larger* category, you're in great shape and probably don't have an issue here. If you fall into the *smaller* category, I recommend you consider switching brands, unless you are getting some other tremendous benefit by partnering with this company in question (for instance, numerous qualified leads).

☐ Learn what other companies are experiencing with the vendors you are targeting. Online forums are a great way to do this. Leverage this information when going to bat for funding.

☐ Provide results from past events, even if they are not yours. For instance, I frequently help my clients by sharing results from other events I have done with the same partner or competition. This increases the chances of winning in the mind of the sponsor. Remember, they must show a return to their manager for this to go well.

☐ Track results and share it with your sponsors as you go along. This increases the likelihood of future investment.

The Basis of All Marketing Events

A couple of key points to remember when planning a successful marketing campaign:

☐ Marketing, while considered to be very artsy, is very scientific. Learn what motivates people, what turns them off, what causes them to be judgmental, and what creates open-mindedness.

☐ The goal is to gain access to continue the sales process through the four meetings I've discussed. Marketing cannot be interruption driven, using mailings and billboard type selling – people are tired of this approach. Events like we described here are just one step in gaining access to the right people; to consult and advise with decision makers.

☐ Persuasion is an important concept. I like the definition from The Character Training Institute, "Guiding truth around other's mental road blocks." Truth implies honest delivery of a client's situation and your ability to improve it. Roadblocks exist simply because the 95% you call on don't really understand the issues like you do. Demonstrate a need for risk mitigation or operational efficiency and you're on your way to helping them.

☐ Finally, remember that executives need your input. Don't shy away from communicating value. Thousands of incompetent sales people have addressed this group in past meetings and phone calls, so don't be surprised if there is some convincing to do up front. If you have prepared properly, you are doing them a favor by contacting them.

Seven Principles of Educational Marketing:

1. It Must be Educational

When I say educational marketing, I mean that the presentations, collateral, blog posts, etc., shed new light on subjects your prospects are interested in. One of the first educational events I personally attended (as a prospect), was just after having received great news, "Your wife is going to have a baby!" It was our first of seven, and what an exciting time it was. In the process of signing up for things, buying at baby stores, and perhaps visiting the doctor, we ended up on the marketing call list for Baby Tenda-care, a company that manufactured and sold a multi-purpose contraption for babies. It served as a high chair, porta-crib, and several other things. As you can imagine, anything that looks like a porta-crib, can't easily turn into a height chair, but they claimed it did. Our first introduction to this amazing device was through an invitation to attend a free dinner at a low-end buffet steak house; a place where you pay about seven dollars for steak, sides, and desert. The setting should have been a sign that this wasn't going to be good.

While the speaker did spend time on educating us, most of the talk was high-pressured sales. It was distasteful and aggravating. I told my wife about ten minutes into it that we were absolutely not buying anything. We didn't buy that night, but it was uncomfortable not to. Many did, and the guy signing up new customers did his best to make the husbands feel like they were cheating their wives out of a great, time saving tool that was almost guaranteed to take the work out of parenting. As far as I can tell, this product is no longer on the market, and I know why. This cannot be your approach to educational marketing if you plan to succeed.

The difference between old school marketing and educational marketing is in the message content, format, timing, and location. Old school marketing interrupts someone's day. It shows up in the middle of a great movie, places pages between the start and finish of an exciting article, or stands in the middle of a car dealer's lot in the form of a giant inflatable gorilla. Who likes this stuff? Getting an unexpected call in the middle of dinner from a credit card company, or having a lawn care company representative call your cell phone on Sunday afternoon, while you are spending time with your family, is not the way to attract new clients.

However, being invited to speak at a technology conference, and showing up with educational material vs. a product pitch, will be greatly received. I remember well the day I was asked to speak at an educator's conference in Greensboro, NC. Attendees from the state's major universities included technical support, IT managers, and CIOs. My topic was security, but rather than showing up with a firewall pitch, I put together a talk on industry trends and how universities might be at risk. With applications for receiving charitable funds and other school administrative functions, sitting on networks shared by students and teachers who download and share all kinds of pirated music and video files, or host student projects while at the same time accessing grading systems, this was a recipe for disaster. At the time, people hadn't really thought through segmentation, and VLANs (virtual local area networks) hadn't yet been invented. By taking my audience through traditional network designs, evolving risks, and recommendations on how to reduce risk, my audience now had concrete information about how to approach IT and security.

The results spoke for themselves. Several organizations arranged follow up meetings with our company and we landed a number of very large assessment deals. Not only did these go on to the remediation stage, but the referrals fueled new opportunities in state universities all over North Carolina. Since these schools really weren't competing (at least at the IT level), the network of IT managers gave us entrance into numerous new opportunities without having to go through the cold-calling process. This is network selling.

Three Aspects of Educational Marketing

The inflatable gorilla doesn't work for me, but neither does obvious education. I want your opinion, not just facts. I want perspective, not just the vanilla, left brain statistics. If you want people to listen, you're going to have to step out and say something. Three key elements of educational marketing sum it up:

Credible. Educational means believable. It has to make sense to the target audience. That means people understand what you are showing them, in a language they can grasp, not jargon that is outside of their ability to comprehend. Too many marketers have given us meaningless sound bites using phrases like *integrated, adaptive, scalable,* etc. They've put together phrases that sound good, but have no practical explanation and leave the prospect confused. Educational marketing seeks to show a prospect something they have not considered, convince them there is something they need to be doing, and show them a high likelihood of achieving a desirable outcome if they will simply follow your program.

Unexpected. It can't be obvious. The prospect has to be hit with something they have not considered, in a way that is almost shocking, whether good or bad. It interrupts your day, not like the inflatable gorilla, but by moving you to action suddenly. If I show you malware on your own computer and then begin to describe the potential its owner has to steal your data, you should be moved to action. When the vacuum company shows you how disgusting your mattress is, you are suddenly shocked into wanting their vacuum, although in a couple of weeks you will likely be back to your old habits and realize this is just part of life; no different than having dust mites crawling all over you right now. Of course, you have already made the purchase, so the marketing department has achieved their goal.

Opinionated. This is where sales people and marketing fall apart. It's your opinion as a thought leader that matters. Too many sales people rely on vanilla slides that speak through statistics. Statistics are left brain sound bites that hold some credibility, but move the listener into a state of judgmental thinking. They question what you are saying rather than being drawn into your story. Good marketing is emotional and opinionated. When you hear Howard Stern or Rush Limbaugh, you think emotionally. They are thought leaders that represent a certain way of thinking. Sure, there is a group that hates them, but then there is another group that loves them. And the more the haters hate, the more the lovers love. They are men who are willing to stand up for their brand regardless of what the opponents are saying, and it builds their brand. People who want to be liked by everyone end up standing for nothing, and therefore have no followers. Look at the ratings and you'll have to agree with me on this.

2. You Must Have the Right Speaker

Who should speak at your next marketing event? John Chambers or John Maxwell would both be great choices, but chances are they won't be able to fit you into their schedule this year. You can go the other extreme and hire your own sales manager or perhaps convince a local channel manager, or worse, presales SE (Systems Engineer) to take the stage. Both mindsets are wrong. So who should speak?

Decision makers don't want to leave the office for techno speak, and a product pitch is sure to put them to sleep. But industry news, with business relevance, can be worth taking time out of a busy day. Depending on the size of the companies you target, you will have variance here on the caliber of speaker you need. But no matter who speaks, the person must understand the goal; "Educating business leaders in the community." The speaker must be able to connect with the audience at the business level. That means speaking in terms business people understand. They must also understand how the marketing aspects of this event work. If you are too analytical, expect your audience to get bogged down in analysis paralysis or worse, fall asleep or leave. Remember, sales are emotional, so we are looking for stories and events that solicit an emotional response.

At some level, this speaker should also be entertaining. Not a humorist, but certainly able to tell their story in a way that draws in the listener and provides a fun experience. They must also speak with authority – again, with respect to the market they speak to. Most free speakers are free for a reason; they don't add any value to this event. Some of the speakers I have used successfully have included FBI Cybercrime Investigators, Gartner Group Analysts, technical superstars that may have started a company or invented something, and industry speakers who have authorship or have earned a name through some association such as SANS. A customer case study can work, however, make sure your customer really can speak to a group. I've seen some disasters that were hard to recover from.

Once you have a speaker, what will they speak on? There are four topics that matter and you've heard them from me countless times: ROI, operational efficiency, competitive advantage, and risk mitigation. Executives need all four, but your speaker must be an expert on at least one. If the speaker can convince the group that they need one of these, and that the educational message being given offers enough concrete information to deliver it, you will have achieved success.

In the Baby Tenda-care example, the speaker was offering us operational efficiency in the form of purchasing just one gadget that did many things. However, it became obvious to me that it was actually going to be more cumbersome to own this thing than to have discrete devices. They also offered a risk message by showing how some baby products were dangerous, but theirs was not. I was not convinced by this either. Finally, they were going to save me money by putting it all into one purchase, that was more expensive than one separate item, but much less than two or three higher end products. Had they focused on one area more intently, the message may have been more effective.

3. You Must Have the Right Audience

A few years ago, I was scheduled to speak in Chicago at an executive breakfast. I flew all night from southern California to make this event, almost got stuck in Philadelphia where I was re-routed due to storms (which could have caused me to miss the event), and finally made it in at 3 AM that morning. When on the ground, I learned that they had lost my luggage. Undaunted, I finally made it to my hotel by 4 AM, checked in, took a three-hour nap, and arrived at the breakfast. The room was full, however since I had not been able to get the attention of the sales manager in weeks, I had no idea who I was speaking to. Remember, the speaker must be able to connect with the audience, which requires some understanding of who the audience is.

Through some questions, and a raising of hands I learned that I did not have an executive audience at all. These were IT managers. They seemed to appreciate my insights, but my client and I had planned to sign people up for risk assessments, which target the decision makers. Generally I get about 75% of the group to sign up, but in this case, almost no one did. This is typical for a technical audience; they have no liability, therefore they have no urgency. When technical people do agree to an assessment, it is usually because they want to learn – they are looking for security experience to add to their resume. Follow up calls were made, but in the end the results were poor. Why? Wrong audience.

There are four types of people you want at your next marketing event:

Decision Makers. This is obvious; you want people who can spend money. Depending on the market you call on, this could be anyone from the president of an SMB company to a vice president of a company in a Fortune 1000 list. CIOs are also great candidates in most mid to upper accounts, but in the SMB space you just need the president or owner.

Asset Owners. Presidents are asset owners, but not the only ones. Asset Owner simply means someone who has ownership and responsibility over key business assets – in this case, data. These people oversee and make money with assets. And while most decision makers are asset owners, there are many more who fall into this category. Anyone who oversees a profit center would fall into this group, in most cases, especially if their division or group is a profitable one. A great example would be the manager over Investment Banking or Card Services at a bank. If these people see a need and push for it, they often get it.

Customers. I always start my invite process with customers in good standing. Having a bunch of prospects sitting with the CEO or President of a company that really likes you, never hurts. It also helps to use their name when inviting new people. Of course these clients must also be asset owners in order to make this work.

Prospects. This may be obvious but I am amazed at how many demand generation events are customer only! This is the perfect time to reach out to new people, especially those at a higher level. Every sales person knows how difficult it is to land a meeting with a new executive level prospect, but how much easier to invite them to a well organized event with a speaker that promises to be good.

What about technical people? Most executives don't want to attend something that is technical, however, expect a few to sneak in, and if you have some customers that are big buyers, and your primary contacts are technical, it doesn't hurt to invite them. I would not invite technical prospects to this event. They will only try to derail the meeting with technical questions, and will not benefit from anything presented on the business level. It's a wasted seat in my opinion.

The great ending to my Chicago event was that after the meeting, I headed back to the Airport (without my still-lost-luggage), only to find that all flights were cancelled due to weather. I made a trip down to luggage and there was my suitcase. No one had called me; it was just sitting there in the corner. I grabbed it and headed back to the Marriott, finally having fresh clothes.

4. You Must Have an Effective Marketing Campaign to Fill Your Seats

The hardest part of any educational marketing program is filling the seats. You can say, "We are focusing on decision makers," but getting them there is a challenge no matter how you look at it. In my examples I have talked about technical people being in the seats and not responding to the message. That's normal because technicians have no liability. It's not that the hosting companies didn't try; it's more likely they didn't know how. They assumed an email blast would do it.

In a recent event with a large integrator, I started off my relationship with marketing, letting them know I could indeed help them get their marketing event set up, as well as be the keynote speaker. Whenever a company contracts me to speak at an event, I offer to provide some upfront coaching to help market the event to decision makers. The event isn't successful unless we have the right people. My marketing contact was certainly open to the idea, however, the sales team, and more importantly, the sales manager didn't give it much attention. Instead they chose to contract out the cold calling process to a firm they'd used in the past. This is not unique – many larger firms do this. Having worked with these firms before, I offered to provide some coaching to the contracted firm. They agreed to a call, however, once on the phone, the call center manager assured me that he was a professional, and that his team was highly capable and would fill the seats with decision makers.

With just two weeks to go, the marketing manager contacted me to let me know that only two people had signed up so far. They were having trouble getting to decision makers, simply because most of their customer contacts were at the IT level. There wasn't time to change course, and so we re-engineered out program for influencers, and as predicated, the response was good in terms of interest, but low in terms of assessments and follow on business. What happened? Here's my analysis:

- ☐ Sales teams rarely have higher level contacts. For this type of event, it is essential that the sales manager get involved, see the vision, and push the team to reach out to people they normally would not call.

- ☐ Outsourcing this type of activity never works. It takes passion, zeal, endurance, and understanding of the value this company is offering to their prospects. No script will make up for the sweat equity built by a sales team.

- ☐ The sales manager's failure to engage sets the priority of this event low. The message to the team is, "This is just another effort to drive sales. Show up if you're interested."

- ☐ No follow up plan. If the manager doesn't engage up front, there is no momentum or accountability in the follow up process. As a speaker, I have no authority to push for strong follow up, I can only recommend a direction. From there, the team must engage and execute. This requires management level leadership.

Understanding the Invite Process

Why would an executive attend one of these events? Only if the education is directed toward them, and they believe the messenger will be life changing, and worth the effort of leaving the office. An equal motivator is the networking opportunity. Many high-level managers don't have frequent interaction with peers from other companies, so creating this type of gathering has merit. Consider the events you attend, I'm sure you've attended company meetings, distributor conferences, or perhaps Gartner. The same things that draw you to these events must be true of your marketing events.

With this in mind, start your invite process with a letter directed to business leaders in your community. Keep it short and to the point, but make it clear that there are issues to consider together as community business leaders. This can be Fortune 1000 or small businesses, but include yourself in this group of people who should be concerned about the topic. I recently used trends in cybercrime to create such a letter, noting that we are all under attack and we all need to do something about it. With this in mind I was bringing in a certain industry expert to give everyone direction on this. I explained that my follow up value proposition would show that I had been formulating a team of experts within my company to address this growing emergency; which created some urgency around the problem.

Assume that your prospects will not see the letter if you mail it first class and make it look like an advertisement. Hand written letters are more likely to be read, and there is actually a service now that will digitize your handwriting and print it so that it looks handwritten. You can learn more about this at www.sendoutcards.com.

Talk up your speaker, promote your venue, and name drop people who have already committed. Invite your key clients first so that you have some names to drop. Finally, work out a call script and make the calls. The letter simply gives you something to refer to. Be prepared to sell the administrative assistant. Most decision makers have one, and if it's a prospect, chances are you will have to work through this person. It's okay, they have been trained to take important messages to their manager, so make it important, and build a relationship with this person. If your event sounds meaningful, the message will get through. Assume you'll be making more than one call.

I like to think of this process as if it were a wedding reception. The wedding invitations look nice, they demand an RSVP, and they promise a good meal alongside friends and family. As a follow up, ask your attendees to pick a meal. Preordering requires them to commit one more step. By selecting *steak* or *fish*, they realize you are spending money on their seat, creating another level of obligation. I find this to be a higher level of commitment than signing up online for a massive event where no one is really counting.

5. Networking Starts Now

I am amazed when I attend these *lunch* & *learn* events, and find the sales team standing over by the food, huddled together commiserating over lost deals, comp plan discrepancies, management issues, or a recent loss by their favorite sports team. What a waste! Not only does this look bad, it squanders your time.

When people show up to the event it's time to network. You're the host and therefore responsible for making sure your prospects have a great time. If they are clients, you should be introducing them around to your team, building a stronger brand in their mind. But don't stop there, reach out to people you don't know. I have personally sat in these events as a prospect and remember being bored and alone. I might shuffle through a trade rag or check in on email, but would much rather be engaged by the hosting company.

This is where it starts, but how do you transition from chatter to business? It's a matter of value. What do you have that will help the visitor? Networking is not just exchanging cards – especially with executives. Give an executive your card and it will be in the trash hours from now. You'll have their card, but when you call, they won't really remember you or have a need. They might say something charming like, "Thanks for the invitation, it was informative...have you met with our IT people?" But this too is a waste of time.

Before your event ever begins you should be collecting great articles, putting together a study of some type, or writing a white paper. I often use my first book, *The House* & *the Cloud*. It's unique, written to sales people (who I call on), and from what I hear, provides real value. When I meet someone at a trade show, such as the RSA show I attended this year, I offer new contacts a free PDF copy of it. You might say I am losing a $16.95 sales opportunity, but I'd much rather give someone something that has real value in hopes of engaging further in the near future. Remember "My enemy is obscurity." A hand full of people will buy my book, but thousands will take it for free. And if it really does offer value, the door is open for further conversation. I've landed many workshops and keynotes as a result, and you could use this same technique to land assessments and projects; simply by offering some intellectual capital of your own, or something great written by someone else, but discovered by you. Stop exchanging cards with a promise of a sales call, and start collecting cards to follow up with something worthwhile. This is the start of a great follow-up program.

6. The Follow up Begins Before the Event Ends.

One of my first successful events was in Las Vegas. I was scheduled as a break-out session speaker; a small part of a very large conference. I was a no-name, but people did show up to my session. I launched into my program. No introduction was given, no one knew me, and no one really knew what to expect. I had just forty-five minutes with this group, and no pipeline to speak of on the horizon. Somehow I had to make this event count if I was to make my business a go.

The content was well received. The people in the room seemed to connect with the points I was making as I demonstrated the difference between strong resellers and those struggling to get by. I shared stories of how we had built a company from nothing, forged our brand in a city that already had strong competition, and made our way into some serious accounts. Over the years, we had taken our company from selling small software programs at the SMB level to large Fortune 500 businesses, selling mid-range systems, storage, building out data centers, securing perimeters, and staffing some very high-end expertise. This audience was hungry for more. They wanted to see their businesses, some which were twenty and thirty years old, grow with this kind of success.

Many of these businesses had once been extremely valuable, but the owners, having grand visions of early retirement, did not sell; instead they pictured their fortunes multiplying into the next decade by holding on to their technology companies for just a few more years. Then the dot.com bust ended their visions of grandeur, leaving entrepreneurs with nothing but debt, inventory, unpaid bills, and longer hours in the office. The models I described seemed to transcend the economy and offer hope, so these people wanted more.

As my talk came to a close, I felt the need to provide more. I had a day and a half left in Las Vegas, planning to attend some of the other sessions, meet people, and perhaps have a look around, but for some reason, I felt the urge to help these people. As I closed I offered to spend the rest of my day setting up thirty minute coaching sessions. Within three or four minutes, every slot was filled, spilling into the next day's schedule. Others handed me their cards asking for some phone time, and a few people asked about executive coaching services, which at the time I had not really considered as an offering. My final count; 50 cards – all decision makers, and about 16 onsite coaching sessions!

> Every door is available; all kinds of business awaits the entrepreneurial thinker.

I immediately found a corner to conduct these meetings and began my coaching programs. We spent our thirty minutes looking at my new prospect's business and applying the concepts from the meeting. People were grateful. This was not a sales pitch, but real educational help. I was as interested in selling as I was helping these people and seeing practical applications of the material I had presented. In my mind, this was win-win. They were getting value for their business and I was learning how to really apply this stuff to all types of situations. Refining my material for small, mid-size, and larger markets.

Upon returning to my office I had more calls doing the same, and within weeks I had several paid coaching agreements in place. Some of those resulted in contracts I still hold today, six to seven years later; still coaching, still helping, and still learning. It's a win-win even today.

But the most important lesson I learned that day was about networking. Presenting great material is satisfying, but meeting people's needs right there on the spot, and having something to follow-up on that is not just a warm lead, but actual value, is like the master key to a mansion. On the other hand, there were events where I didn't follow up with coaching, didn't find a way to collect cards, didn't sign people up for anything. I left with many handshakes, people smiling, people even saying, they'd like to follow up, but in the end, no business resulted. Why?

Sales are emotional. Value is short lived. Once people return to their office, unless some commitment is made, few will take proactive steps a week or two later. In fact, the rate at which your value diminishes is not a linear curve, but rather it is exponentially downward like a decay curve (if you remember anything from Algebra II). If I ask people to sign up for my blog or a newsletter while I am speaking, by putting a sheet in the back of the room (meaning they won't actually sign up until I finish), I can guarantee a twenty-five percent sign-up rate. If I wait until the people go home, and follow up with a phone call, I'll get two percent. But if I pass around a sheet while I am speaking and have them sign up right there in their seat, I will get at least ninety percent, maybe one hundred! While people are sitting there, their emotions are high, and the learning part of their brain is in motion. They will sign up for more. As time goes on, the emotions fade, and their busy day kicks in. Before long, I've lost them.

The follow up starts now! It starts when people are getting seated through networking, it continues as the presenter is giving them an educational message, and as the speaker winds down, there should be a call to action. Many times it is not practical to send around a signup sheet while the presenter is talking in this type of marketing event, although it works well for me as a speaker. But here are some steps you can take to put this into motion in your next event:

1. Make sure there is some type of assessment or discovery process in place as a follow up. Let's say the talk is geared to security. A risk assessment is a natural follow up. In a unified communications meeting, there might be an analysis to show companies what they would save or gain by moving to voice over IP. I talked to a business owner recently who did an event on social media marketing and online reputation. He followed up with an analysis of their marketing effectiveness. There are many ways to build your program but you need something. Even a webinar can be more effective if you present ways to connect through LinkedIn or offer sign up for something online during the presentation. I have often done this and had people "Link" right in the middle of my program. Is it okay that they left my presentation to do this? Yes! I want them to. I want that long term connection.

2. Assign seats. This seems foreign to many of the companies I work with, but seating is important. Put your best sales people (even if it's the company owner) with your best prospects. If you have presidents or CIOs coming, you want people who can talk to them and help close them, sitting with them. Put clients and prospects next to each other, and place clients right across from the sales representative. When it's time to sign up, that client will give your seller credibility and encourage the table to follow, simply by putting their name down (of course, this would be a client who has not had an assessment recently).

3. I like to informally pick up the signup sheet and announce that I am certainly going to sign up. As the speaker, people laugh realizing that I am not really a qualified buyer, but it eases any tension that may come from the offer. A rep can do the same, saying he at least wants his company to visit his home after hearing what was said. If the speaker is from outside, this works, because the seller is new to the message just like the rest of the table. This makes the transition to selling easy. When one person signs up, people tend to follow suit.

4. Have your reps practice asking others to join. When people are asked, they often say yes. Once they commit verbally, they may later cancel, but it's not likely. Reps should practice a friendly way of making sure everyone has had an opportunity to participate.

5. Remember, an urgent message is more likely to get a response than something that is just "nice to have."

6. Serve dessert. I like to ask the waiters to bring out the meal while I am speaking, and then serve dessert right when I close, as I am bringing back the

host – in my case this would often be a sponsoring executive from the technology company. As dessert comes out, the host is reminding people of my message, pointing out the complementary assessment, and encouraging people to stay for a few minutes to ask the speaker some questions, and network. Dessert tends to keep most people from heading out early. Dessert has been one of my biggest lessons over the past few years. Breakfast meetings are not nearly as effective for this reason.

Failure to begin the follow up process in the meeting is a big mistake, and will cut your return on investment by ninety percent.

Follow Up Continued

The follow up continues. Getting people signed up is great, but those companies who wait three weeks to actually follow up on their signed up attendees are in trouble. The message has worn off, and people are on to something new. When my clients ask me how many people I think they can get to an event like this, they are usually hoping for a huge number. Some have suggested numbers up to 100 people.

My reply is, "How many people can you follow up within the first three weeks?" Each study or assessment might take half a day to conduct. Some might be shorter, some unqualified, but others might be well qualified and worth taking extra time on. It must be done right away, and I would recommend prioritizing your list to get those significant companies in first. Here are some thoughts on the process.

☐ The study or assessment process must already be in place. Don't wait to see if people sign up before building this. Not only should your questions be ready, but the deliverable should be in place. Remember, this is a marketing document, so treat it like one. Make sure it looks great, appeals to executive management, and will communicate solid justification to move forward.

☐ Executive questions are critical. Start with executives – this should be done by sales people to establish that consultative trusted adviser relationship. Sales people always use that term, *trusted adviser*, and then when an assessment comes up, they delegate it to engineers! Why? This is your chance to be a trusted adviser. Once you have on your consultant-adviser hat, you can talk to anyone. And since they didn't pay anything, you control the process. You don't have to continue if the client won't give you access to the right people.

☐ Technical discovery comes as a follow up to validate or prove out what happened in those executive meetings. This may involve some questioning, as well as data collection, but there is no need to spend months in there. All you need is justification. If that takes thirty minutes, then spend the thirty minutes. If it takes two days, and the account is worth a two day investment, do it.

☐ Analyze the results. The questioning process is a place to demonstrate value and credibility, but the deliverable must reinforce the value you bring. But remember that paper does not sell the deal, you do. Make sure you present it in person, and again, if the prospect won't give you access to the right people on delivery, you don't have to deliver. They didn't pay, so you don't owe. Demand they attend, and present it in a compelling way.

☐ Make sure your written document is great. It must be well formatted, easy to read, business level, and prioritized with just enough detail. Don't rewrite *War and Peace*. Consulting documents used to be priced by the pound but in today's day of texting and IM, keep it short. No one reads through those documents anymore. Future proposals might even be sent in a YouTube clip or Tweet.

Multiply Your Follow Up.

In a recent event I did in Philadelphia we marketed to four thousand people. This solution provider was significant in size, so getting an audience of fifty to a hundred seemed manageable. About ninety people signed up, mostly decision maker level, and about sixty five attended. We had three speakers, one from a sponsoring manufacturer, which I don't generally recommend, followed by an executive level client who reinforced the value of the reseller, and finally I presented a message on risk and the need to investigate possible data theft.

Of the sixty five attending, about fifty people signed up for our assessment! We were very happy with this outcome, however there's more. The sales team for this group was large, and with inside sales support available to us, it made sense to keep going. We had conducted two days of sales training prior to the event where I took each sales person through security technology sales techniques, and showed them how to present portions of my message. There were 25 people who had signed up for our event, but for some reason or another, had not attended. Once the follow up for the fifty assessments was underway, I worked with the inside sales team to contact those who had not come. We expressed our disappointment that they were not able to attend, and urged them to let one of the reps come by to show them what the speaker had said. "This urgent message must be heard, so if you'll give us just twenty minutes, we can give you the highlights." A large percentage agreed, giving us an opportunity to present value in an educational format that was not seen as another product focused sales call.

But it doesn't stop there either. We had another 3900 people waiting to be contacted. Some of this was done by phone, and some by mail or email, and of course the hit rate on this group will be lower, but still, these prospects are much more likely, than a pure cold call, to introduce your company. They already know about your event, a good number may have actually considered going, but for some reason decided not to. Call them, explain how great the event was, drop some names of those who attended, and offer to bring them the message. I encourage people to follow up my events with my book, *Data@Risk*; not to leave the book with them, but to show it to them. Show them some of the diagrams, review the message by white boarding it (as we did in the training class), and move them to a possible complementary assessment. Since this group did not attend, the emotional high is not there, so your follow up time can stretch into the next two months. Once you run out of steam on the follow up, it may be time to hold your next event. Remember, the success of your event is determined by the effort you put into it.

The goal of each appointment is to begin the four meeting process. Access to asset owners, with an objective of looking at their systems and networks, and to discover what their problems, is what you are looking for. As you go through the process, you are looking forward to presenting urgent findings to asset owners and decision makers.

Remember, where there is urgent impact and high-likelihood, there is budget. Budget is a non-issue when someone is having a heart attack, and the same is true when someone is losing thousands or millions of dollars in overpriced technology services, or losing millions of dollars of data through unsecured systems.

7. This Program is Ongoing.

One company I worked with has completely stopped cold calling. Hiring expensive reps to sit at their desk all day, making phone calls to people about company introductions and product specials, is a waste of money. In their first event they landed 25 assessments, and closed about half of them. Twenty-five represented about 75% of that audience, so the sign-up was strong. However, the close on assessments leading to more business was somewhat average. Some purchases were big, others small, but overall this company was very happy with the results.

But that gave them an idea. Why not do it again, and this time work on the assessment process to improve it? Refining the document was one step, but then really working with the sales people to bring up their presentation skills.

This is such an overlooked area, yet one of the most important factors in closing business with executives and business owners.

The next quarter they had similar sign-up results, but a much higher ratio of closed business and recurring revenue. They continued doing this quarterly, each time practicing the delivery process and perfecting the assessment. They introduced new technology into the assessment process, and trimmed down the written deliverable as they observed the interest from executives. Quarter after quarter they continued this process, making it the primary means of adding to their pipeline. Last year that business owner reported closing up to 90% of the assessments, turning them into project work and recurring revenue. This success allows them to operate with a small sales staff and few cold calls. Now, most of their marketing effort is directed toward building attendance for the next event.

They also do similar programs each time. They are not trying to get the same audience in for new material, but rather casting a net for new prospects; bringing them into the funnel, moving through assessment and discovery, and into a customer relationship. This is a well oiled machine that leads to strong business growth. The topics must appeal to executives, so they stick to things like cybercrime and cloud computing trends, not storage, telephones, and other techie topics that won't draw a decision maker crowd. Once in, they can move the sales effort around to drive adjacent offerings and widen their presence in an account.

Demand generation events that are educational, and are conducted by well spoken presenters, with the right audience, and which use an effective invite process, with immediate follow up, make selling much easier regardless of the economy.

Summary

☐ Don't assume old techniques or outsourced call centers will bring in the right audience. It requires a new approach, backed by management, and committed to by the sales team.

☐ Three platforms for educational marketing make sense in today's market: Customer events, one-on-one seminars, and social media (which I cover in a later chapter).

☐ Funding events with JMF is not hard – but it requires a plan. Sell your partners on supporting you through this by showing them a well thought-out execution plan that promises a strong ROI.

- ☐ Educational events must be focused on awareness and education, not high pressured sales. Make sure your speaker understands the goal and is able to communicate effectively to the audience you are targeting.

- ☐ The audience must consist of asset owners. Custodians have no liability, no budget, and no ability to sign up for anything.

- ☐ The invite process is the hardest part of event marketing. It must be invitation only, conducted like a wedding reception, and committed to by managers and sales people.

- ☐ The follow up process begins at the event. It must be well planned, executed immediately, and followed through within three weeks.

- ☐ A second sales opportunity follows, calling on those who signed up but did not attend, and then those who did not sign up, but may have considered coming. This group is large, and promises additional sales opportunities if the sales people can learn to present a summary of the speaker's message.

8. HARNESSING THE POWER OF DISCOVERY

One of the most overlooked tools in your bag is the discovery process. I have been through countless sales meetings where the discovery process was conducted in that first or second sales call, a product was quoted, perhaps a sale was made, and then maybe a ten percent margin was realized. Next came the commission check that was too small to write home about.

Last week I was working with a rep from New York. He has been selling for years, but the market is changing and competition is fierce. Margins have gone down, and commodity technology is just about all he has to offer. He promotes the same products every company like his sells; storage, unified communications technology, network components, etc. My client had just come across a new opportunity to upgrade his prospect's unified communications platform. The initial step in his sales process, is to assess what is in place and recommend a strategy for migrating to a new platform. In our call, he explained that he is charging twenty-five thousand dollars for the assessment, but is not very confident this company will actually buy the upgrade project from him. This is new business for my client, so somehow he must convince the prospect that he is someone to partner with on future projects, and should be selected as the adviser.

As we spoke it became clear that the discovery process was already underway. I asked him, already anticipating his answer, "Who is leading the charge?" He recited a name I had heard many times before, a technical consultant who also lived in New York. "Are you engaged in the process?" I asked. "No," he replied, "The consultant will be getting back to me once he completes his analysis, and from there I will draft a proposal and submit it to my contact." I asked him if he was in communication with the asset owners and found that he was. I was confident that would be true as we had been working hard on gaining access to the right people before committing to assessments and discovery work. So why was he not involved in discovery? Simply put, it is not part of his company's protocol to include sales people in the discovery process. This is a sad commentary on where technology companies have gone with their process.

However, it was not too late. The assessment had just started. I encouraged my client to get back in there to parallel his consultant. "Let's formulate some asset owner questions," I said. He agreed, and the brainstorming began. "What business are they in?" I asked. The company in question served as an investment company. They have offices all over the world, investing in new companies; mostly in the high-tech areas. Their needs included collaboration, finding new investment opportunities, rolling out financial performance reports and analyzing their portfolio in a million different ways. Unified communications and new advancements in social media integration, video, and mobility with smart phones, could drastically change the way they do business. Sadly, the technical consultant looking at their current system would probably never discover these things. He is too wrapped up in how many phones they have, operating system releases, and patch levels. He probably cares more about their current server environment than he does about their next major investment decision! How can this technical person possibly understand the next generation of this company? He can't. So who will figure it out?

My client's tone began to change as we talked about the outlook for technology and how it might affect the future of this business. We explored ways of collaborating. In most cases, my client did not seem to know how business was conducted in China or India (both major growth areas for technology), or how his client's headquarters, now located in the states, monitored their investments in those parts of the world. But he did see the vision. It was up to him to get into the bowels of this company and figure it out. It didn't really matter how many phones they had, rather it mattered how collaborative technologies could be used to put this company out in the lead.

It was in this call, that my client began to realize how much power he had with this twenty-five thousand dollar contract in place. It was now that engaging asset owners really mattered. By changing his approach, and becoming more of a consultant, my client could gain access to just about every senior manager in the company. By moving from vendor to adviser, my client has now earned the right to ask whatever questions seem relevant. In this chapter we will explore how to make the most of these opportunities, not only to be sure we sell the project at hand, but to reposition ourselves as the future adviser for all kinds of projects.

The Impact / Likelihood Chart

Justification!

% Likelihood

3. How comfortable are you with your ability to detect and respond?

2. What are the relevant threats?

Business Impact

1. What are you trying to Protect?

What Every Executive Needs

Just as a review, every sales person must have in the forefront of their mind the impact/likelihood graph. This is the final outcome of every discovery process. What is the impact, and what is the likelihood of achieving gains or guarding against high-impact loss? Your competition focuses solely on impact, however, it is likelihood that really differentiates. If you can show this in a compelling way, the chances of success go way up.

What Every Solution Provider Needs

Whether you consult, sell for a manufacturer, or resell products along with value-add services, every provider needs a strong value proposition that will precede the commodity product sale. Once the product is in view, the value is gone. Everything you know about the product is on Google, so demonstrate your value long before you get there. This is done through the discovery process where value is shown in an advisory fashion. The one who successfully demonstrates impact and likelihood wins. Every executive needs an adviser. In fact, they need many advisers.

The discovery process is exactly the place to reposition you and your organization as advisers. We've talked about various kinds of assessments; penetration tests, vulnerability studies, optimization studies, risk analysis, proof of concept, etc. It doesn't matter what you call it, the point is, you have access, so use it. In the end, it's marketing that wins the deal, not technology. And, though the highly technical mind tries to make this into a scientific analysis, you the sales person, know that if you fail to persuade the client to act, you have done him a disservice.

I have heard many complaints in sales training classes I have conducted; "That takes too much time," or "We never conduct assessments for free." Here are few things to consider when going through the discovery process:

The ROI of Complementary Assessments;

☐ You determine the involvement. When the client insists on delegating the process to IT, you can say no. If the client pays, they control the process. At some point it's worth having them pay, but when dealing with less expensive assessments, control is more important.

☐ This is your opportunity to meet every asset owner influential to the project. I would rather assess than continue making sales calls. You control the questioning process and have the opportunity to ask anything without people holding back. The assessment is powerful, so offer it over continuing to sell.

☐ This type of assessment does not demand a long deliverable, so don't compare it to paid assessments. Instead, think about the value of assessing over sitting through more meetings.

☐ The delivery audience is up to you. You don't have to show them your findings until the right people are available. So wait for them. You can't do this in a typical sales meeting, nor can you hold back on a fee based assessment.

Eight Steps to Successful Discovery

The discovery process should be fun. I remember some of those early sales calls where we would argue and run out of things to say. It was painful. Once I learned the art of asking business level questions and engaging decision makers in their business, I found a whole new aspect of selling. All of the sudden it was fun. In the remaining pages of this chapter, my goal is to have you discover this world and give you some simple tools that will take the stress out of meeting with asset owners.

Step1: Wear the Right Hat

The first step is trading hats. I started out as a technical guy, and of course my value was seen in my ability to be technical. Not surprising, most of my meetings were with technical people, looking for technical things. They were interested in road maps, features, and learning about future technology trends. While interesting and easy to get a meeting with, my prospects were not buyers. When I would follow the sales books out there, telling me to call on higher-level people, I would come face to face with people who did not understand why we were meeting. I felt pressure to engage them, and often sat across from busy people, who were not interested in my offerings.

The hat I am talking about here is the technical hat; the propeller head. Get rid of your techie hat, and replace it with a consultant's hat. Consultants are often hired by senior managers and invited to speak at board meetings. Companies spend millions on consulting firms, while paying technicians by the hour. Now, granted, the big consulting firms often have accounting relationships with the companies they call on. They can open doors I cannot open. However, coming in with the right attitude and positioning can really turn things around.

Another term thrown around out there carelessly, and one I've already mentioned is, *trusted adviser*. The trusted adviser is trust-worthy, meaning they possess strong integrity and character and can be trusted to steer the company in the right direction. But they are also able to advise at the asset owner level. In order for this to happen, the sales person must become a student of the business, taking an interest in the daily functions of the company and the language spoken by the asset owners. Start by learning who the decision makers are, who owns critical data, and who creates and uses that data – and how. Also uncover who the technical go-to people are. All three groups matter, but two of them will demand most of your time; those creating and using data assets, and those asset owners overseeing them.

In the discovery process, your goal is to find out what they do, how they do it, and what kinds of improvements would change and grow their business. In order to do this, you have to see yourself as a peer and a counselor to these people. If you view yourself as less; as a mere vendor, you will likely be shot down. Self image may be the biggest obstacle in this business. You may be thinking that this prospect is a manager or executive, and I am only a sales person. This is wrong thinking and must be corrected at the outset. You are an adviser, an ambassador for your company, and one who brings value to the client. If you don't change any negative attitude quickly and get back in the game, you can't possibly win. Put on the right hat and start acting the part.

The Discovery Process You Go Through Will Be:

- Asset focused
- Business driven – starting with asset owners
- Verified through technical observations
- Backed up by technical data and appendices
- Documented in business language
- Presented to business people (who are asset owners)
- And done with remediation and new projects in mind

2. Consider Business Level Issues and People Related to Your Project

Remember our two key principles:

1. *Forget products; focus on the assets.*

2. *Find the asset owners.*

And the board room principles I proposed earlier:

1. *If you ask technical questions or speak in technical jargon, you can expect to be demoted to IT.*

2. *If you present prices before establishing value, expect the deal to be shopped or put on hold. The deal has no value and therefore cannot be justified.*

> The more value you provide in the discovery process, the more valuable you are, and the more likely you are to remain at a peer level with asset owners.

In the previous chapter I discussed marketing and points of entry. Keep in mind, the discovery process takes place in the Meeting Two phase of the sales process. You can get there through educational marketing or through the strategies I have presented on moving up. Either way works, but don't begin the consulting process until you are there, and don't give away intellectual capital until you have asset owners present. This is where the deal is sold, so don't try selling it before you get there.

As a consultant, picture yourself climbing the ladder, gaining access to each level, and gaining more ground within each level. The more value you provide in the discovery process, the more valuable you are, and the more likely you are to remain at a peer level with asset owners. This is how consultants stay in accounts for so long. At each level, learn the business. Following is a list of things to be looking for during the discovery process:

1. Company Vision. Most technology projects never consider the company's vision, but you should. Chances are this company has spent more time and money on their vision statement than they will spend with you. Learn it, and understand where it came from. I recently met a business owner from China. He's an American, but has made major inroads overseas. How did he do it? He spent time learning about the history of China, the culture, the language, and the significance of their letter characters, operas, and many other things important to the local population; including the business leaders. As a result, his company is growing exponentially. The Chinese people care about their heritage, and so by understanding these things, he has gained their respect, and their ear. They call him *the egg* – white on the outside, but yellow on the inside. This is a personal brand, and it has immeasurable power. Do the same with the managers you meet.

2. Understand the Company's Growth Strategy. Every company is working hard to grow. Learn how they are approaching this, and understand the challenges. Most managers will take time to talk to someone who understands their vision, especially when that person has ideas and valuable input.

3. Management Philosophy. The culture of a company is important and how their managers operate is central to this. Learn about their decision-making process, their metrics, their systems, and other processes. Study the company, looking for ways to improve it. I had one client in my coaching program that embraced Michael Gerber's book, *E-Myth Revisited*. In this volume, Gerber reveals some of the most common misconceptions of the small business owner and what causes small businesses to fail. My client studied this, not to grow his own business, but rather to have greater relevance when talking to his clients. He was selling technology, but instead of focusing on products, he sought to serve his customers by learning the ins and outs of small business. When he would quote from Gerber, people listened. They were amazed at his wisdom and not only embraced his products and solutions, but him as well. Consequently, he received a number of job offers from his clients. People wanted the knowledge he had gained. Become valuable to the managers you call on.

4. Customers. Know your client's customers. Know how they deal with customer service, how they attract customers, what value they bring, where they might be losing customers, what customers represent the greatest profit, and where the company might be bleeding. Your client's customer base is likely their most important concern, so get to know more about it.

5. High Performers. Know who the high performers are. It is likely that these people will not have much time for you, but if you can somehow get a few minutes with them, discover their secrets, and help them grow; and as a result, you will bring value. I have a colleague in the speaking business who has built his entire business on this concept. He has gone into large insurance companies, interviewed their top performers, systematized their processes, and put together training programs for the other lower performing agents. His clients love him and they pay him handsomely for his work.

6. Use of Technology. This seems to be the first concern for most sales people, but it's nearly last on my list. It is important, but far more useful when put into context of the larger aim of the company.

7. Competition. Know their competition, and how they are going to market to compete. How can your solutions help them stay in the game? Can you secure them from data leakage or loss of intellectual capital, or perhaps help them cut operational costs or implement unique systems that would put them ahead of the competition? You can't deliver this type of value until you fully understand where they are headed and what they are up against.

Step3: Ask the Right Questions

How should sales people spend their time? One of the best and most valuable uses of your time is in asking questions – but they have to be great questions. Most sales meetings are monopolized by long presentations and talk about the seller's company. Stop and listen. This all starts with the right questions asked of the right people.

I often joke about the four things that keep executives up at night; financial problems, health issues that stem from financial problems, marriage problems that come from working too hard – to fix the financial problems, and rebellious children, a product of not being with the family due to too much work. Of course none of these issues are funny, but now that I've shared this with you, there is no reason to ask the age old question, *What keeps you up at night?*

My friend from China shared with me the business philosophy that produces the greatest success. It starts with understanding problems, then building solutions. Jim Collins, in his book, *Good to Great*, actually suggests that people build a team, figure out a problem, and then go to market with a solution. Mack Hanan, author of *Consultative Selling*, says something similar. He recommends selling, and then building rather than the opposite road taken by so many vendors. Value is in solving problems, and questions are the catalyst to understanding the surface issues and root problems. Too many of our solutions are simply band-aids placed over surface issues.

Asset Owner Questions

Asset owner questions focus on impact to the business; good or bad. They are business relevant, application focused, and measureable. Asset owners are focusing on profits and building shareholder value, not creating a more complex computing environment. If they automate something, it's not because it looks cool, but rather, it adds something to the business. They focus on applications because that is what their team uses to build the business. You don't hear knowledge workers talking about networks and routers. They speak about the applications they depend on to access data, analyze issues, and solve problems. They track their clients, their own progress, develop offerings, and manage profits in custom software; and when something is down, it's the application. So learn their key application names and understand how these applications are used by the business. In the coaching session I mentioned at the start of this chapter, my client and I formulated some questions – here is a short list from our brainstorming session;

- How does the company attract new clients?
- What is the profile of a great investment?
- How does this company measure the performance of their remote offices and investments?
- What tools do field offices rely on to do their job?
- How do remote workers collaborate between offices and clients?
- How will technology be used in the future to further automate the systems currently in place?
- What key systems exist – what strategic initiatives are planned?

At this point, order is not important. The idea is to brainstorm, without considering the current technology you sell, about where the client is going and how they plan to get there. Then we can consider how the technology fits into the overall picture, and finally where you, the salesperson, fit in.

The Three Question Framework

Specifically for security or risk related sales, I have developed a three-question framework that has served me well for over a decade. I offer this as an example of how to approach the questioning process:

1. What are you trying to protect?
2. What are the relevant threats?
3. How comfortable are you with your ability to detect and respond?

In question one, *"What are you trying to protect?"* I am looking for assets. I may ask the question just like this, or I might reword it. In both cases my focus is to drill down into the specific data, systems, and applications that make this business work. With information such as, the company's most important application, secret formulas, or differentiating intellectual capital, I almost become an insider just by asking this question. This knowledge will guide future discovery as I meet with high performance employees and sales people, executives, and profit center managers.

The second question, *"What are the relevant threats?"* is a loaded question when used correctly. The simple version of this question might be answered by IT, but it is not a technical question. The threats to this business change with business climate and strategy. If a company is in the midst of a lawsuit, IT may not know it, and certain data may help the opposition with their case if they can gain access to it. If this is the case, the threats are suddenly greater, and focused. The opposing company may even hire someone to break in and steal the data in question. If the company is on the verge of releasing some new discovery, and competitors have heard about it through the rumor mill, it is likely that someone will attempt to access this information before it is released to the public. Of course these things are illegal, yet they happen every day. Question two requires some help from the seller, and will aide in creating awareness with the prospect; especially at the business level.

The final question is a measurement. *How comfortable are you with your company's ability to detect and respond before it's too late?* The temptation is to answer for the client, but don't. Allow the client to answer honestly, as this provides you, the seller, with some very important information.

Now, look at the results. As I explain in my book, *The House & the Cloud*, these three simple questions give you a picture of the Impact vs. Likelihood graph, from the client's perspective. Question one provides insight into the X-axis data set. In Algebra, this would be the domain or input

The second question now gives you data for the Y-axis; the range or output. The things that have likelihood, with some idea of how likely they are. Each data set or application should have some threat level that can be measured. But how likely is this to happen?

The Impact / Likelihood Chart

Justification!

% Likelihood

3. How comfortable are you with your ability to detect and respond?

2. What are the relevant threats?

Business Impact

1. What are you trying to Protect?

The final question is overarching. It gives us a feel for how the prospect views this Y-axis. Do they really think something will happen, or are they under the impression it won't happen to them? This is where most deals fail. The client sees the impact, they understand there are threats, and they understand where the threats might come from. But when it comes to likelihood, they don't really believe they will experience a threat. It is like trying to sell an alarm system to someone way out in the country. They see loss and theft on television and they can see how someone might break into their own home, but they don't buy simply because there are no reports in their area of burglary, and it just doesn't seem realistic to think someone will actually make their way out to this small town, and target them. Go to North Philadelphia or Los Angeles and the story will be different.

Watch Your Language

I have said this many times, but bad language get's a demotion. By bad language, I mean talking products and features. Start talking about technology or use jargon, and you're finished. Expect the executive to introduce you down the ladder. Questions like:

- How are you connected?
- How do you encrypt data?
- What types of operating systems are you running?
- How does your back up process work?
- Are you up to date on something technical?

All of these questions are out of bounds and should be saved for IT custodians. On the other hand, the IT person will likely attend some of the manager meetings, so expect them to continually insert technical view points. Think of them as landmines or bait on a million hooks just waiting to catch you. Don't go there.

Your Goal

It's simple – find something urgent! Don't leave without it. A second goal should be stated – reposition yourself as a peer to those in charge.

Step 4 – Apply the Right Sequence

Armed with the right questions, wearing your consulting hat, you are ready to go; ready to take on the world. Patience is important at this point as this is not a simple product sale, and you are no longer a coin operated vending machine, dispensing firewalls, disk, and servers when requested. It is the larger architectural deals you are after, the ones that land you larger accounts for the long haul. Rushing this process will mark you as a vendor in disguise, so approach it with the right sequence of events in mind. As stated earlier "Keep the end in mind before you begin."

Case Study – Moving From Product to Project

In workshops, I often recount my experiences on a sales call in South Carolina, working with a regional bank there. They were a new prospect, and we had hopes of selling a simple firewall upgrade. One of the sales reps on my team received this lead from a vendor competing for the upgrade business. I was asked to join the call simply because the rep didn't know much about the firewall they had in place. I didn't really know much about it either, but I agreed to go on the call with one condition; we needed an asset owner there.

It took some time, but using some of the tips I gave in an earlier chapter, we were able to obtain a meeting with the executive vice president of operations. He didn't understand why he needed to join us, but he did agree after some insisting. The key here is in positioning your team. The rep wisely positioned me as a peer to that executive, rather than a technical resource. And rightly so, as I was a director, and came with executive level discussion in mind.

Our meeting started with their technical person trying to lead, however the meeting was quickly refocused on business as I launched into my three question framework. The technical person tried to answer my questions, however I continued to look to the EVP for his asset owner level input on mission critical applications and bank systems. Over the course of an hour I used the white board to explain some of the trends and areas of risk in an effort to pull him into his responsible role as asset owner. The more we talked about it, the more I piqued his interest, and by the time we had finished, the IT person had been repositioned to a listener, waiting for instructions from his commanding officer.

The firewall no longer mattered. We had established the bank's primary business, we had identified the primary banking systems, third-party processing partners, and future direction of the bank. We had agreed on relative threats, and looked at the company's likelihood of detecting something destructive in time to stop it. With this information on the table, the only question in the room was, "What do we do now?" Our illustrative executive could see that his armor was weak, and wanted some direction about how to shore things up. We had succeeded in getting him to see a high likelihood and he was ready to take action.

The meeting ended with a verbal agreement to conduct a larger, fee based assessment. It covered the key systems including mid-range computing platforms, third party connections, remote locations, messaging and a host of things in the network, server, and application computing environments. This was a great deal, all because we didn't run in with a firewall sale. From there we created justification for intrusion detection systems, event correlation, virtual private networking and even managed services; a recurring revenue contract that would continue to pay for years as long as we managed it correctly. How did this all happen? Were we just lucky?

Understanding the Sequence

In an earlier chapter, I reviewed the four meetings that lead to the sale. The sequence I am referring to takes place within the discovery process, which is part of Meeting Two. It looks something like this:

- Start with asset owner questions
- Meet with those on the asset owner's team
- Use technical questions to validate the hunches you get from numbers 1 and 2

- Collect data to prove what you believe to be true
- Don't quit until you have something urgent

Asset Owner Questions are Your Number One Asset

While most assessments go right to the technology, your number one goal in the assessment is to find urgency, while being repositioned as an adviser and solution provider at the business level. Without input from the asset owners and their team members, you can't do this. Think about the relationship first. How do they view you? If your local family doctor suspected you had cancer, you would probably go right to an oncologist. The family doctor's value is no longer very high in this kind of situation. You might be grateful that they discovered it, if they discovered it early, but the reality is, nothing would be conclusive until you visited with the specialist.

In the discovery process you must first be seen as the specialist, before anything is discovered. Then, when you do discover something, you have the credibility to continue with analysis and recommendations. Those on the asset owner's team, having interacted with you at this level, will then become endorsers of your value to the asset owners, and ultimately the decision maker.

Technical Questions Flow Out of the Asset Owner Discussions

Armed with input from the asset owners, you will likely have hunches as to where things are probably out of order. These might consist of overly complex processes, unsecure practices, or archaic applications. If someone refers to a dBase III application, and you're old enough to know what that is, you can be confident that there is work to be done. In one assessment I was involved in, loan officers were emailing information out for loan approval. I asked them to show me how they did that. It seems like a simple process, so they didn't really understand why I was asking, but it revealed a lack of security and compliance. The next step for me was to interview the technical people, asking questions about data leakage and encryption methods. They actually had encryption software, but it was not being used. IT had no idea that the loan officers were doing this.

When working with the technical team, your technical experts should be leading the charge. Drawing from your asset owner interviews, recall the red flags – times where you suspected problems or inefficiencies, or if you are aware of application features now available, but probably not being used in this account. Walk through the IT environment with your client's key business processes in mind. You already know what applications are being used, where people use them from, and where third-party companies access internal data or provide some sort of third-party processing. You know about mobile workers, home workers and perhaps unstructured data applications such as SharePoint that may be set up in an unsecure fashion. You are ready to prove what you already suspect.

Data Collection Validates Your Findings and Provides the Much Needed Justification

Scanners and network diagrams are often the first thing out of the bag. Technology professionals usually start here, but this is not wise. Only after you understand how their business works, have positioned yourself as an adviser, and have established rapport with the technical team, does it make sense to collect this data.

Find Something Urgent

Your mission is to find something urgent. This is why I like selling things that relate to security and risk in some fashion. You may discover a process that could be done more efficiently, thus saving the company money. However, finding something risky creates urgency, similar to the pressure of having a heart attack. It must be dealt with now. There is no waiting and the budgets don't really matter. Spend an amount of time commensurate with the value of the account.

Step 5 – Have the Right Data Interpretation

What does it all mean? One of my favorite workshop activities is reviewing deliverables written to create next steps. It may be a proposal or an assessment report. The question I always ask is, "So what?"

This is the question that needs to be asked before you write anything. When you return from the discovery or assessment process, pull together results for a POC (proof of concept), or conduct a penetration test or application walk-through. Don't forget, for every finding, ask the question, "So what?"

Sometimes it sounds rude, when the consultant begins going through their findings and I stop them with the question, "So what?" I don't mean to be rude, but I do mean to interrupt. I want them to think! I want them to get out of the technical closet and think about the business, the initial business questions we asked when we spoke to the business people. What do these findings have to do with the business? How will they impact profits or productivity? Will your clients be impacted by your findings?

Another question to ask is, "Will the asset owners care?" Will they care if your discovery report shows "There is an open port," or "That config file should be changed."? In most cases the answer is no. Only the business impact matters, not the actual technology issue.

So how do we make this data relevant? It goes back to something I mentioned earlier in the book – the scorecard. Early interviews with those working on asset owner teams give you the information you need to develop some sort of scorecard that will be used throughout the project or proof of concept to measure improvements. The ultimate position to reach as an adviser, comes when the company managers are sending their own employees to you to hear how a certain quality area is improving or some growth area is taking place.

Data interpretation is more than understanding facts. It is helping them see what they have and what must change; either to realize amazing improvements or avoid impending disaster.

Step 6 – Have the Right Focus

The right focus is urgency! In a recent coaching session I was reviewing a salesperson's findings. The first issue on their report was that the company must hire a security officer. I asked my client how long he thought it would take this company to hire someone at that level, and he rightly assumed a six month process. I asked my client, "Is this going to cause your client an immediate problem?", and he rightly guessed it would not. This is not an urgent issue. It may be important, but it is not immediate. In fact, it cannot happen quickly.

For every finding you should ask the question, "Is this urgent?" Not that everything has to be urgent, but leading with the non-urgent is a mistake. Getting your foot in the door on urgent matters is much easier. From there you can branch out to explore all kinds of adjacent opportunities.

Step 7 – Have the Right Deliverable

Every day I receive mail, email, magazines, newspapers, and a host of papers from my children. Between work and family, I have a million things to read. Some of them I request, others are spam or junk mail. The papers from my kids are just a necessary part of home schooling, a decision I'll never regret, but one that doubles my reading. There is no way to keep up with it all and still read great books and stay on top of trends and news. So what gets left out? Anything I don't absolutely have to read. Then there are things I want to read, but hold less weight; they get stacked and usually go unread. Then one day I finally toss them too.

The same is true for every business person. They have too many items to read, too many emails and too many things grabbing for their attention which don't actually require their involvement. Executives put gatekeepers in place to try and stop anything that could be delegated. Their employees just ignore anything that doesn't contribute to productivity and profitability. It's a matter of survival.

Prioritize

Your document should be asset focused. If the reader recognizes their key applications on the first page, they may continue reading, especially if they note some issue or graphic representation calling for their attention. I like to start with the *impact vs. likelihood* graph on the front cover, with my client's data on the X-axis.

From there, I would go right to the issues list. This list should be ordered, showing the most critical issues right on top. "Customer Information – "A" is accessible by anyone on the Internet – including your competition." This is urgent.

An outline I recommend might go something like this :

1. Graph – Impact vs. Likelihood
2. Key Data Applications – ordered according to the asset owners
3. Urgent issues discovered followed by other issues
4. What we found as a result
5. Recommendations – broken out by things we should do, and smaller things that might be done by the internal team if they have one
6. Technical appendix

In projects that represent efficiency gains, such as data center consolidation or collaboration projects, I might start with major areas of gain, pointing out what the company is losing by not having something in place. This might be a large sum of money spent every month unnecessarily, showing the client instant savings if they act now.

Step 8 – Deliver the Right Presentation

This book is full of ideas on presentation, but the point here is, most sales efforts stop short of a great presentation. Sales people don't like to make this final presentation since it may lead to rejection. Well thought out, rehearsed presentations that allow listeners to visualize the future in a way that saves money or greatly enhances their business, will create the emotion you need to move to the buying stage of the sales call – Meeting Three. Make this the focus of training, meetings, and internal strategy sessions. One client I worked with thought about creating a video proposal rather than lengthy written proposals. This is out of the box thinking. Will it work? I don't know. But this kind of creativity is what's needed to take your business to the next level.

Summary:

☐ Executives care about impact and likelihood. The latter is the missing ingredient needed for a buying decision. While your competition focuses on impact, start measuring likelihood and close the deal.

☐ Providers should learn to assess as part of the discovery process. Control that sale by putting on your consulting hat, and start talking to business people with business needs.

☐ Complementary assessments allow you to maintain control of the sales process. You control how much time to spend, who should be involved, and how the deliverable should be written.

☐ Successful discovery means: wearing the right hat, asking impact questions, applying the right sequence, interpreting data correctly, having an asset focus, creating an effective deliverable, and learning to present effectively.

9. PROPOSALS THAT WIN

I hate writing proposals. It seems like half the meetings I have attended as the seller, end with, "Why don't you send us a proposal?" I write it, send it over, and it seems to disappear into a black hole, forgotten, and never to be seen again. What happened? Why did they seem interested enough to ask? Was I dreaming? In the end, it would seem I have just wasted my time. How often do your proposals actually close? How many end up in the black hole?

There is an answer to this conundrum. Moving from vendor to adviser means aligning your actions with the clients. It means becoming an insider, and working with the client to solve a problem. It completely changes what you write, and when you write it. I am convinced that most sales calls end with a request for proposal simply as a polite way of ending the meeting. Once the proposal is written and sent back to the prospect, control of the deal is lost to the prospect.

So when and what to write? That is always the question, even among some of the most experienced sales people. A wise mentor of mine told me long ago, "When they are ready to buy." Of course, it is rare that you'll actually know when they are ready to buy unless you have somehow moved to the inside and become a trusted adviser.

Two things stand out in my mind as important factors:

1. You must have identified the people who actually make the decision and somehow become a peer to them. If you don't know the people you are writing to, you can't possibly know what to write.

2. You must have established the value of the deal with the buyer before presenting your price. Without a solid understanding of value, there can be no evaluation of price.

Your proposal should never be asked to build your relationship for you, or to sell the deal without you – it can't. The sales person gets paid to sell the deal, then the document formalizes the agreement. If the buyer is asking for a proposal (usually it's actually a custodian asking), and if you have not completed both of the tasks above, you are just not ready to write. Submitting the proposal too early means you are destined for failure.

Instead, find ways to continue the sales process through discovery or a demonstration that will allow you to further establish a value based relationship and then discuss the prices and budgets before writing. If the prospect is unwilling to work with you, not allowing you to take them through the proper steps, then consider yourself one of their possible vendors. What can you do to move up? It may not be on this deal, but I would pull out and continue to market your value for the next one. The last thing you need is another vendor-client relationship. Assume they'll be looking for the best price from now on, stripping you of all value and margin.

In Summary: Don't even think about writing until the deal is won

By Definition

Before you write, you should be clear about the need and the opportunity. Marketing groups and managers have done a disservice to their sales team by creating mammoth proposals with unreadable terms and conditions, and a format that looks more like a legal will than a friendly agreement to buy.

What is a Good Proposal?

☐ Think marketing! This is the final marketing piece. You might have delivered data sheets, presentation material or perhaps a findings document, and hopefully you had marketing in mind. Your documents should have been professional looking, easy to read, and pleasing to the eye. What about the proposal?

☐ A summary of everything you have agreed to. The deal is done, now we are agreeing in writing, so this should clearly reflect all we have discussed and agreed to.

☐ Boundaries of scope. The proposal outlines what we did agree to, but also clarifies boundaries to stay within.

☐ A contract. This is your written agreement, so it should clearly state what you will deliver and how. There should be no questions.

The Proposal is Not:

☐ Another selling tool. The deal is sold at this point – but the agreement is only verbal until this is signed.

☐ Ideas, guidelines, or negotiation. You should have already agreed to a scope at the point of writing, and the fee should already be established. If there are fee changes, there will be scope changes.

☐ A dissertation.

An Effective Proposal

It takes me about five minutes to write most of my proposals. Whether my fee is $200 or $100,000 dollars for the project in question, the proposal looks the same and communicates the same information. The difference in fee has to do with the value I am proposing, not the format of my proposal.

Much has been written about systematizing business. If your company is to be positioned as the best; as the elite solution in your space, then your processes must reflect top-shelf value. The systems you put in place should be million dollar systems that position you as the million-dollar solution. The proposal is one piece of that system. It is the final agreement that cements the arrangement to provide a service or product for a predetermined fee. Most proposals that fail, fail because the process is not well defined and the proposal is written without the proper ground work taking place.

To solve this problem, the proposal process must be defined, refined, and systematized (I use an online tool called EchoSign to automate the signature process) till it becomes a simple document that is quickly assembled, once the sale is verbally agreed upon. Write the following steps down and educate the entire team on this process. Some of the steps involved might include:

1. *Waiting Until Meeting Three is Complete.* We've talked about the four meetings. You, the seller, must have completed Meeting One where the asset owners are identified. This is your target audience, and the value restated in this document will address specific insights you have gained while

interviewing them in Meeting Two. Then in Meeting Three, the price will be agreed upon.

2. *The Desired Results are Well Defined.* What is the outcome of this project? Too often, proposals go into great detail about methodology, when it is the results that matter the most to your asset owners. While technical people are more interested in process, because that is their value, the user of the system wants to accomplish something you have justified through analysis or study, and shown will return value to the organization.

3. *Know the Milestones and Final Success Criteria.* The proposal agrees that you will accomplish something major. But along the way, there may be other milestones that will get met, and they should be stated with some sort of timeline.

4. *Agreed Upon Fee.* There is much debate about when to share the price. My opinion is, you will waste a lot of time writing if you don't discuss price in Meeting Three. Agree on the price, and also spell out some options that enhance the project. I have found that gaining general agreement in Meeting Three is possible, but then by offering a couple of upside options in the proposal, the buyer has time to consider some additional value while signing. Like buying additional coverage on a car purchase or extended warranty; the final deal can only be increased.

Note: I have read in many sales books, that a *choice of yeses* psychologically moves the buyer from seeing their option as a simple yes or no, to believing it is a yes or yes or yes, or no. Somehow this holds more persuasive power. In my experience, this has been true. I also believe, that it is helpful to the client if your additional offerings really do represent value to the client. Never do anything that might be construed as a manipulation tactic.

Creating the Proposal

1. The Opening

I like to think of my proposal as a letter addressed to someone rather than a sterile document opening with a third-person narrative of the company I am selling to. I address them personally.

Example:

John Smith,

RE: Fall Seminar Series

I understand you are working to build your sales over the next twelve months through a series of customer facing events that will target executives in midsize companies.

I *like this better than:*

Network Integration Company "A" is developing a series of seminars to be conducted in multiple cities in their northeastern territories.

My opening consists of one or two short paragraphs that sum up the overall aim of my client's initiative, reiterating our conversations and agreement concerning exactly what we are working on, and what we hope to achieve over the coming weeks or months. This approach also recalls the relationship I have been building with the buyer as I am looking for some sort of emotional resonance.

2. Overview and Objectives

The next paragraph introduces a series of bullet points that define specific objectives upon which we have agreed. My goal here is to use language, taken word for word, from discussions I have had with my client. If they used phrases such as *sales ready messaging,* or *technology solutions conference,* then my document will use these same phrases. This makes the connection with everyone who reads this list, that I am talking about their company and not some boilerplate program I am running with every reseller and distributor I work with. An example might look like this:

- Evaluate current messaging (to end-users through partners) and marketing plans – what's working? Assess effectiveness.

- Create effective messaging specifically for *new products* to be used by *current managed partners*

- Identify top performing *managed partners* who represent the strongest opportunity for the *new product launch* over the next 12-18 months, and how best to motivate and equip them with this messaging.

- Finalize plans to equip channel managers for taking messaging and training into the *managed partner community*.

* The italicized words indicate key phrases or labels this company uses when dealing with their partners or new product code names (which I have made generic here).

3. Value to Your Organization

In this section I reiterate concrete statements of value that have been affirmed as justification for doing this project.

- Measurement of your current messaging and marketing strategy.
- Clear value statements to provide to your key resellers, allowing them to better promote our new product.
- A target list of partners to focus on with new products.
- Plan to mobilize your current channel organization, allowing them to move products to market more quickly.

4. Methodology and Options

In this section I am writing out exactly what was agreed to in Meeting Three. There should be no question as to whether they want this, and you should already have a verbal agreement on price. In addition, I will have alluded to some options for enhancing the project in Meeting Three. But rather than gaining agreement, I let my buyer know they will be listed in the proposal as options. This makes Meeting Three less confusing, and gives my client time to consider additions. This section might read like the following:

Pre-Meeting Preparation: Before meeting, my goal is to understand as much as possible about your situation. I will be sending an email once the agreement is in place, outlining information we will want to gather for my preparation prior to the meeting. Here is a quick summary:

- Current performance (financial), along with goals by quarter.

- Successful regions/partners/channel managers, etc. to better understand where the strengths are currently.

- I would like to conduct a few interviews if possible, with the above (2-3 people).

- Messaging currently being used to educate partners concerning the onboarding process or through regular product and sales updates.

- Plans that have been discussed for the future – future product roadmap, etc. Planned announcements that may affect future business (positive or negative).

Notice I have not gone into detail about my personal methodology for conducting these meetings. My methodology is not aimed at what they are buying, rather it is focused on how I get to the deliverable they are expecting. Next I present phase two of my methodology, followed by some options:

Strategy Meeting: This is the one and a half day strategy session we spoke about by phone today. As described above, I will provide some pre-work to help collect information before the session, research and review any materials that will help me understand your company, and then, through a collaborative session, work with your management team to discover the best way to grow sales for your newly announced product set over the next twelve to eighteen months. Most of this process will involve flip charts and brainstorming, so I recommend that you invite an administrative person to document our progress, and distribute notes in an orderly fashion for review and follow up.

Option 1: Executive Coaching/Collaboration: As a follow-on, I recommend using a 90 day follow up program for working together to refine this process. This provides us with unlimited access by phone and email over the next month (start dates are flexible depending on your travel schedule). The goal is to complete the process by allowing us to deliver final plans and messaging to your team in the shortest time possible.

Option 2: Channel Management Strategy: During our call, I mentioned putting together a one day channel management strategy workshop. This is a program I use to help channel managers understand how resellers make most of their money, where the problems exist, and how to help them grow profitability (gross profit) through your product set. By doing this, we can help them move from product channel managers to strategic advisers – gaining the mindshare of your key managed partners and building greater loyalty.

These options build on each other, making the project more valuable to my client. None of these options are new; we have already discussed doing some of these things. Generally I want two to three options that grow in value and increase in price. The first item on this list is a given, the rest are options. As long as the first one is worth doing, I don't really care if the others close now. Some may close now and some may come later, as they make more sense to my client. Also, notice I have not listed my prices here. The value of the option stands alone; the price will come later.

5. Schedule and Logistics

In this section I list timeframes or exact dates, not hours, to complete the work. In fact, it really doesn't matter how long I spend on the work. The question is, do I deliver the value I promised? Fees should have nothing to do with time, just make sure it results in a profit. Use timeframes like:

Phase 1: 2 Weeks

Phase 2: 4 Weeks

Etc.

In my business I do a lot of speaking, so this is where I list the date of the speaking engagement, the time, and length of my keynote. I also list equipment I may need such as a projector or cordless microphone. From here, I provide some terms and conditions to ensure the project is handled correctly; followed by my fees.

6. Terms and Conditions

This is where most proposals lock up the customer for weeks. Assume the number of conditions you list lengthens the time, exponentially, that it takes to approve the proposal. People do read them, and often send them to legal. I like to keep this short. If you are in a business that holds a great deal of liability, you might not be able to keep it short. However, most of us misuse this section so try to make is simple.

7. Fees

I have an entire chapter dedicated to this subject. For the sake of building the proposal, I do something like this:

_____Workshop fee; $10,000

_____ Follow up Program; $6500

_____ Channel Strategy; $10,000

Here I list any required travel if I am charging that separate from the fee. Then add the following:

** Fees are invoiced upon contract agreement to hold the dates, due upon receipt. All fees are non-refundable, however, we may be able to change dates depending on availability.

8. Agreement to Proceed

Finally I have a place for both of us to sign, and a statement indicating that payment, PO, or signature all signify agreement with the contract.

Long Proposals Make Great Landfill

That's right – Long Proposals Make Great Landfill…

The Wall Street Journal reported recently, we are in the "texting" generation, and those writing proposals might take note here; people want it short and to the point. The days of writing lengthy documents to close a deal are long gone, and long documents are destined to be delegated downward to the lowest common denominator. But don't expect that group to read it either. Some tips on keeping it short:

☐ Cut out all company overview commentary. By the time they buy from you they will know who you are. Plus, it's all online.

☐ Don't bother writing about your client either. Why an executive would need to read about their own company in your proposal is beyond me. If they don't know what they do, you're selling at the wrong level.

☐ The more technical specifications you include, the more likely the reader will require IT personnel for interpretation. Instead, focus on bullets that outline the proposed benefits and leave it at that.

☐ Your longest section should be your options. Make them easy to understand and build them one upon another. Stop at three or four options; all stated at a high level.

☐ List fees by milestone and avoid lengthy explanations about how your prices are computed or how many hours will be spent. When asked, be ready with a concise answer. I usually just say, "We'll spend as long as it takes to complete the project successfully."

☐ And to really make this simple, avoid proposing until there is a verbal agreement. At that point your document becomes an agreement.

☐ Make the signing page big and easy to read, but cut down on terms and conditions which make text lengthy. If you don't plan on suing your client, you don't need every detail covered. Limit your liability and cover your ability to fix those things not acceptable to the client.

Agreements; a Necessary Evil

Boundary stones have been used since the beginning of time as a way to identify property. Made of stone and often marked by owners, they stand as a reminder of past purchases, conquered land, and other formal agreements. The old adage, "Remove not the ancient landmark" stands as a warning to those who would change the boundaries set up by constituents.

While most of us are not going to spend the money on lawsuits when dealing with smaller projects, formal agreements, like these boundary stones, must be put in place regardless of company and deal size. They should be placed in obvious locations, easily readable and agreed to by all parties involved. More clients are lost over poor communication on agreements than I will ever be able to count; usually with regard to scope or price. When deals are done without an agreement, two excuses are often raised:

1. The sales team fears putting it into writing. They may think it will slow down the sale or draw attention to elements of the agreement that may not sit well with management (on either side).
2. The client refuses to sign anything binding, usually because they don't have the authority to do so, or don't want to be locked into anything long term.

There may be other reasons, but these two pop up often, and as you can see, both spell trouble down the road. It is definitely faster and easier to agree with a handshake and get started, rather than drawing up a formal agreement and getting a signature. But what happens after the project or service begins?

- The client thought they were also getting _____
- The client expected the price to be _____

And notice, it is always in the client's favor! I can't remember too many clients coming back and saying, "Oh, I think we owe you another $10,000. We'll send it over right away."

So, while proposals may make great landfill, agreements are necessary boundary stones. Without them, there is no proof of what you've agreed to and the client is always right. Push the issue, and you are likely to be out of a client.

Pricing Your Proposal

I will cover fees in greater detail in a later chapter. For now, we'll just address fees in regard to the proposal writing phase.

☐ Most resellers are pricing things too low. The thinking is that SMB clients can't afford more. The problem is, you can't afford less. Pricing is related to value...not your client's perceived bank account.

☐ T&M (Time and Materials Pricing) pricing is amateur.

☐ T&M with a cap is foolish – you take all the risk, your client has no skin in the game.

☐ Deals that schedule a given resource on Tuesdays and Thursdays (as an example), mean you must now fill their down time (every other day) with project work or their utilization will be too low to net a profit for the company.

☐ Too much detail. You don't have to break out every detail of a project's pricing. Start quoting in milestones, and price based on value. Break it down into days and weeks, not hours and minutes.

☐ Present options…*a choice of yeses* Give them the best option, an upside option, and a phased option to allow for tight budgets.

☐ Don't present pricing before value has been established. Remember, business value can only be understood by a business person.

After You Write The Proposal

Sometimes the proposal, or what I've now rebranded as an agreement, is just red-tape. The deal is done and the check may even be in the mail or credit card issued over the phone, or a PO number shows up in your inbox. Now you are headed for the final step in the sales process. Whatever you do, don't put this in your forecast at 100% yet; it's not signed so anything can happen. I change it to 90% once I have verbal confirmation, and then pray that it comes to completion shortly.

☐ Once I am done writing, I like to create a PDF of the final proposal which I can then send over to my contact (using Echosign as mentioned earlier). The proposal should go to your primary point of contact, but at this point in the sale, I would like to think I have established enough rapport with the actual buyer to send it directly to them, rather than going through my initial point of contact. Sometimes that means I send it to two people. By using Echosign, I am notified that they have it, have looked at it, and if it's been forwarded to someone else, I'll know that too.

☐ In the above proposal recommendation, I used the word "send." I don't generally hand this over in person simply because the number of proposals I have closed on the spot can be counted on one hand. Almost always, a meeting at this point is a waste of time. My buyer is going to want time to look the proposal over. There are many times when I will arrange a call just prior to sending it, ask a few questions to clarify, like in Meeting Three, and then send it over for review. That gives me a chance to explain the options and hopefully reignite the fire.

☐ Before ending the call, I look for a time to reconnect or possibly get a decision. I always ask for a tentative date to start or have a meeting, whatever begins the project. I am holding that date for my client which sort of commits them, at least at some level, and allows me to choose a date that works best for them. I don't want this to cancel simply because we could not find an agreeable date to begin.

☐ I like to submit my proposal early in the week and plan a follow up at the end. If there is no decision, I may check in again in a few days, but at some point I am pestering. I find that it helps to have some other items of value, news, or an update to send the following week, as a way of checking in with something more than, "Have you decided yet?"

☐ I often ask for all, or at least a large part, of the fee upfront simply to avoid cancellation. Many projects have been signed off on, only to then have the money reallocated, halting the project. Getting paid upfront ensures this won't happen to you. Of course, not all deals warrant this type of upfront payment, but do what you can to solidify the agreement. This will often benefit the client as well – since there may be someone above them able to pull the money, which leaves them without funding they thought they had secured.

☐ Whether the deal is signed or not, I want to know why. If they sign it, it really helps to know why they chose me. If they don't sign, it's important to find out why. Was your price too high? That means your value statement failed. If someone else took the business by positioning themselves as the expert, you want to know that, too. If they chose you as the lowest price provider, you really want to know that as well.

☐ If they are looking to discount, don't negotiate through email (I address negotiation in detail in the next chapter). You lose all control. Negotiations should take place by phone or in person. When someone emails, asking you to cut the price down to an even number or something lower than you've quoted, it often appears as though they will simply sign it and send it over on the spot. Don't believe it. I've had many deals dry up, not really knowing why, just after responding to one of these emails. I have made a commitment to never do it again.

In many ways you lose control of the deal once you present your proposal. This is why I am so focused on Meeting Three and gaining verbal agreement before writing. There is no silver bullet or magic formula, and while many sales books make selling sound simple if you will just follow their method or use a certain CRM program, it just isn't true. The only thing you really can do is set things up in such as way as to demonstrate value, and build enough rapport so you have an open relationship. Better to have someone tell you up front, "We just aren't going to do this now," than to say, "Just send us a proposal," in an attempt to avoid having to tell you, "No."

Submitting the proposal at the right time, with the right information, to the right person, will certainly get you closer to controlling the deal as long as possible – the best thing you can do under any selling situation.

Request for Proposal

Proposal writing wouldn't be adequately addressed without some specific words on the infamous, request for proposal (RFP). In just about every sales coaching relationship, the RFP comes up; usually in the form of a very large opportunity that will make the quarter if it comes through. The question is, "Do we fill it out or move on?"

The confusion comes when you, the seller, try to relate this to the sales strategies I've described in this book. The four things buyers buy – is this operational efficiency, risk mitigation, return on investment or competitive advantage? Moving to the front of the adoption curve I described in chapter two means selling to the 95% who don't know they have a need, but this person seems to know all about their needs. Am I coming up with one of the four things or is the client? How about the four meetings? Which meeting are we in and where are we entering the sales cycle? All of the rules suddenly don't fit. How about the fee setting rules? Is there a way to value price this request?

The request is almost always initiated by the custodians – those without liability. So where is the urgency? In my sales model, it isn't until Meeting Three that you would be discussing budget, and that would take place only once value has been demonstrated and quantified in Meeting Two, which is an asset owner level meeting. Meeting Three is usually a phone conversation to review the needs and pin point exactly what we are going to deliver, and finally, bringing out the price for a verbal agreement. Without a verbal, there is no written proposal in this process. So now, in this new situation, you can see we have violated almost every rule. We are taking a request for a meeting with one person, bypassing the value proposition phase in Meeting Two, which means there is no discovery or assessment taking place, and now we are sort of in Meeting Three with an unqualified Meeting Three participant, looking for price to be delivered ahead of value. It doesn't make sense because it isn't a good way to buy or sell. In most cases, you will lose this sale to the person who was chosen before the RPF was ever written!

That's right, the person who will win this contract may have already been chosen. It happens all the time. I was meeting with a person recently who is responsible for large contract RFPs (He writes and submits them). Our families were attending a conference together, so talking outside his normal work function, he shared with me that most of the time they know long before the RFP is written, who will be selected. In my own experience, working for a large bank, I can remember going out with an RFP several times for large project work. In our case, the RFP process was used to put pressure on our pre-chosen candidate, simply to bring down the price. Usually it worked. In other cases, we had technology companies actually help put the RFP together, knowing they would also win it. In those cases it was simply a request from our management team, who required that we get three competitive quotes. Most people realize this is happening behind the scenes, but for some reason, we continue to play the game. So what do we do?

CASE STUDY:

Working to get into a large newspaper company, we were handed an RPF to redesign the network infrastructure. It was a great project, but the RFP was distributed to over twenty qualified companies – all of which claimed they had great experience and should really be considered for this project. Twenty companies? What are the chances? I knew from previous experience that we would be spending about forty hours on this request – forty hours that could be used to sell or bill. And, in this case, we would be hopping over hurdles to obtain a deal we had little chance of winning.

Instead of responding, I requested a meeting with the issuer. I was able to convince him to have the meeting and to invite his manager. Often this request is denied, but in this case, the prospect finally agreed. Lesson one; don't assume you can't do it until you have tried. Had they refused, I would have walked away from the opportunity.

We prepared a number of exploratory questions, brought compelling success stories and used a few disaster anecdotes to demonstrate the need for more discovery. Most RFPs are written to strip out any differentiating value you might have. What is the point of selling to someone without your value proposition?

In the meeting, we showed the need to bring some of that value back. We explained that this type of project is rarely successful without some in-depth analysis, and that any company who simply responds to their offer, without taking a closer look, will likely fail. Near the end, they didn't seem convinced, so I resorted to the last and final question. "Have you ever sent out an RFP this complex, received a response within your budget requirements and then had the winner deliver on time, on budget, and produce exactly what you needed?" They looked at me across the table with puzzled expressions and finally the manager admitted, "No, we probably haven't." At that point he agreed to let us do some discovery.

Using many of the tools I've written about here, we began working through the process, meeting with the right people, demonstrating value and coming up with a completely different approach than our competitors offered. No one else was given this chance, and as a result, the other companies submitted ideas that only addressed the limited scope of the RFP. In the end, we won the deal, but the deal had become something much better than what was presented in the RFP.

Lessons Learned:

- [ ] RFPs are often won by those chosen before the RFP is sent out. Only an upset can win this, and that calls for a strategy that disrupts the normal process.

- [ ] Don't sell the deal on their terms. Instead, change the rules by demonstrating the need for discovery based on your prior experience with the same type of projects.

- [ ] Don't deliver a price when you can't first deliver value. Walk away from the deal if they refuse to meet with you.

- [ ] Understand that RFPs are written to put pressure on the competitors to drive down their price, or to deliver competitive quotes before being allowed to go with the company's preferred provider. Don't bother getting involved if filling out an RFP is all you are allowed to do.

- [ ] You can't negotiate if you are not willing to walk. If they won't work on your terms, be willing to leave. But always depart on good terms, explaining that you will be happy to come back if things don't work out.

When the RFP process doesn't go your way, it's time to walk, but not from the client, just the opportunity. Sometimes it helps to offer something high-level and out of bounds, just to say you did submit something. I gave an example of this earlier with the medical penetration test. But most of the time, companies will stay the course and require a response on their terms. Here is what I did on my last RFP opportunity:

The request came for an ongoing, exclusive training program. Now, you see the irony here. I teach not to directly respond to RFPs, yet I was handed one for training. I couldn't possibly respond – it would label me as a hypocrite! The RFP was detailed, required hours of work, and in my opinion, focused on the wrong things. Having worked in the high-tech reseller market for years, I felt that my programs were built to specifically address the challenges of selling technology, both direct and through the channel – but the two are different. I don't offer any generic training programs.

First, I was grateful to be considered. So I emailed my contact, explained that I was happy to receive their request, but I felt there was something missing from their proposal, that would be critical to the selection process. My primary concern here was that the RFP process contradicted what the people being trained really needed if they were to be successful in this market. I offered to meet with those responsible for selection and provide input for what they actually needed.

As you can imagine, my request was rejected. I received a simple thank you, with a note stating I was still invited to respond, but that the company felt it best to continue down the current path.

From there, I continued marketing to my prospect. I was already doing business with them in other divisions, but not this branch. My marketing consisted of content, success stories from other things I was providing in other divisions, and occasional idea letters.

Almost a year later, I was asked to speak at a meeting for this same division. During the discovery process, I was introduced to the person responsible for training. So I contacted him about the current speaking opportunity, which I had already been selected for, with an offer to review my training program with them.

After a brief call, I learned that the company who had won the contract a year ago, was not providing what they had hoped! The future was unknown, but they were looking to provide something better. At this point, I was able to have input directly into the process for the coming year. The lesson here is simple, don't give up, don't burn the bridge. Just understand, if they proceeded incorrectly the first time, it's bound to fail. Make sure you are there to help restore things to order once they realize it.

Summary

- [ ] When do you write? Write when the deal is ready to be won. Make sure you know who you are writing to (those who really make the decision), understand exactly what is needed, and agree on price before writing.

- [ ] Proposals are marketing documents. Make sure they are easy to read, and sell value, not methodology.

- [ ] Systematize your proposal writing process. Make it simple, quick, and easy to read and sign.

- [ ] Complete Meeting Three before writing the agreement. That means you have completed the discovery, sold them on value, agreed to price, and gained verbal commitment to proceed. This saves time and keeps you at the helm.

- [ ] The written format is important. Treat it like an agreement that assumes you are doing the project. Write your prospect and agree to deliver what is needed, restate the deliverables they are looking for, and provide pre-authorized pricing in a simple milestone format.

- [ ] Use options to create a *choice of yeses*.

- [ ] Apply value pricing principles (detailed later in the book).

- [ ] For RFPs, change the rules by gaining access to Meeting Two asset owners. If this doesn't work, continue marketing efforts.

10. STRATEGIES FOR GROWING YOUR BUSINESS

Living in a small town south of Charlotte, North Carolina, I have often heard my family members say, "I wish people would stop moving this way." We've watched farms turn into shopping complexes, wooded areas plowed and paved for neighborhoods and traffic that demands new stop lights and additional lanes for our once desolate country road. Suddenly our town is actually on the map.

While we covet the sanctuary we once lived in, I tell the children, if the town isn't growing, it's shrinking. Nothing stays the same. And if the children of this small town begin to move elsewhere as they grow up, and no one comes our way, soon the store fronts will be empty, homes will be abandoned, and our quaint village in the south will become a ghost town. The town must grow because without growth, not only will our town shrink and lose its livelihood, but our personal land could become worthless. Growth is necessary. The same is true in business.

Three Things to Be Doing: Adding clients, growing current clients, adding annuity revenue…

Branding

Some have tried to brand themselves by offering lower prices, others by offering outstanding customer satisfaction and still others by building great relationships with their clients. I see companies touting their specializations and certifications, or their status as a reseller of some product. "We are gold partners," or "Platinum and security certified!" But these things really don't work as distinctive branding contributors. Your business, and you yourself, must offer something unique. Exceptionality comes with specialization; a unique process, or intellectual capital that others don't possess. You need a product or approach no other company has. I have already covered a number of topics in this book on marketing and positioning, so let me summarize; you need a brand that stands out if you are going to grow your business.

Something memorable, something unique; a solution to problems others are not adequately addressing will help with this process. I was on the phone with a client the other day, and at the start of our call to discuss our first contract, she said. "I remember you. I have heard you speak before." She remembered me as the guy with seven kids and one wife. The guy who homeschools his children and has them involved in all kinds of entrepreneurial business ventures. In this case, it was my personal story that caught her attention. She couldn't remember my name, but my story was memorable. The fact that I have children is not impressive. Having seven children is somewhat memorable. However, the businesses run by thirteen and fifteen year olds, combined with seven kids who are homeschooled, was highly memorable. I find people often recall these things and it works for my branding.

5 Tips on Branding

Here are some points to consider as you build your personal brand and go from selling products to advising clients; as you move from vendor to adviser:

1. Constantly Writing

There are many ways to create memory recall and writing is one of them. Content makes you an expert, if you can write some knowledgeable, opinionated subject matter. Short books can be written involving very little cost. You can write articles for free, and of course, social networking is free as well. It will only cost you time. Some have said that you need a publisher, but I disagree. Everyone should be writing a book. In fact, I had my children begin writing books in their teen years. My daughters are working on developing seminars for young ladies right now, and the first step in accomplishing that is to write a book. By doing this, they will have documented, published and copyright protected their content. It will be easy for their prospects to understand the foundation of their seminars, where they are coming from, and what they hope to accomplish, simply by picking up one of their books.

In a conversation I had today with a client, he asked, "Okay, you are connecting with people you don't really know through LinkedIn. Since you don't really know them, what can you do to market to them? You can't just start sending them spam email!" He was right, that type of marketing outreach would frustrate and infuriate anyone willing to connect through social networking. Instead, if he had something written, when he gets a request to *link* or *friend*, he could offer them his book or article. Try using a landing page with an opt in, allowing you to take the next step in marketing to them. When you provide content with sound advice, you will reposition yourself to adviser status.

One of the purposes in writing is to establish yourself as a thought leader in your industry. If you don't consider yourself a thought leader, and many sales people don't, you need to rethink who you really are and become one. Remember, this is not a technical function. If you read *The Wall Street Journal*, you already know that the reporters are not experts in technology, yet they write for one of the most popular business journals in the world where people pay to read their ideas and commentary. What stands between you and them? Probably writing experience, but not actual experience. Writing experience comes from writing and rewriting. Start working on this now and before long, you'll find writing is fun, helpful in developing creativity, therapeutic, and a great contributor to your personal brand. Try writing just a few minutes each day, and perhaps look to someone for critique and input. You'll be an expert in no time.

2. Putting on Educational Events

We've covered this in detail, but here I want to reinforce the strategy. You start by writing thought leader type material and then present it. There are cases where it makes sense to bring in outside speakers, but the follow up should always be conducted by you – the seller/consultant, at the asset owner level. Learn to build content (or take it from your written content), and start presenting it. You might also try to speak at meetings held by your Chamber of Commerce, or other local groups. Speaking is one of the best ways to brand yourself and establish a name.

3. Social Media

This topic deserves some attention, so I address it in detail in the last chapter of this book. However, I mention it here to underscore the need to include it in your growth strategy. Make sure you plan this out using the information covered in the Social Media chapter.

4. Networking

When I ask sales people where their business mostly comes from, the first answer is usually referral business. This is the best type of lead, but to keep it happening, you must ask for referrals and reach out to meet new people -

networking. The key to networking is having something of value to say when you meet new people along with a list of satisfied customers supporting your efforts. I will address customer service in a later chapter, but for now, let's focus on meeting new people.

Ditch Your Elevator Pitch

That's right, get rid of it. No one wants to hear your elevator pitch. Everyone has one, and no one wants to hear yours. The elevator pitch is all about you – it's self-focused and makes you sound like a slick sales person looking to close another deal. If you sell something people need, you won't need this type of sales pitch.

Advisory Positioning Statement

Here are some examples: "You know how companies keep getting hacked into and are losing data daily?" "You know how annoying it is when you call customer service and have to work through a thousand menus, only to be cut off?" "Have you ever known someone who lost their laptop or had it crash while on the road? Do you know how hard it is to recover from something like that?" These are positioning questions that demand a response. I call them *advisory position questions*. If they are good questions, my prospect will answer with a, "Yeah, we've had that problem." Or "I hope that never happens to me."

My response is simply, "That is what I specialize in." I was on a plane a few weeks ago and introduced myself to the guy sitting next to me. I asked him what he did. He responded that he managed a division of a company that works with large concrete projects. In turn, he asked me what I did. Rather than saying, "I train sales people," which would have landed me a training group referral or nothing at all, I decided to test what I teach and said, "You know how these large companies like…keep getting hacked into? I just read in *The Wall Street Journal* that…was broken into last week." He replied, "Yeah, that was something." I then said, "I specialize in helping companies ensure that won't happen, and if it does, finding out why it happened, and making sure it doesn't happen again." It worked flawlessly! We started talking about information security, and for the next thirty minutes I had him engaged in a discussion around assets and asset protection at a business level. He was happy to give me his card after that conversation, and if I were actually a sales rep working in the network security space, I would have been able to follow up, get an introduction to someone in his company, and gain an appointment. Try this, it works!

Give them Something of Value

Next, always have something on hand to give them. I use my books, but you could have a white paper, article or study you keep on hand to send people. When I meet potential prospects out in the field, I mention I have a book to send them, then I take their card and write on the back a reminder to send a copy in the mail. This provides an immediate next step. At a recent dental appointment, my new dentist asked about my work. He was interested in the sales topics I speak about, so I took his card and sent him one of my keynotes on CD. He liked it so much, he sent it to his brother who manages a sales team. This is networking.

5. CRM: Organizing Groups and Mailings

My first CRM (Customer Relationship Management) database was a software application called ACT! While the application itself isn't my favorite, the *groups* aspect of it really makes sense. In fact, as soon as I converted to Salesforce.com, my first task was customizing the application to support groups. Groups are a way of organizing clients and prospects, to provide a better way of tracking and communicating.

If you look at old school marketing plans, they call for mass mailings of postcards, or some other archaic outreach media, to millions of people in hopes of hitting 2%. This is insane and expensive, and in today's computerized world, completely unnecessary.

Here's the problem. How can you keep up with everyone, and reaching out to a very specific group of new prospects, without incurring outrageous costs to do it? With social networking, new clients, lots of prospects, and years in the business, you have probably met thousands of people who are either qualified prospects, influencers, or partners. Your prospects alone break down into many different categories of people such as executives, technical, primary contacts, clients, business owners, departmental managers, etc. The list goes on. You can't really mass mail these people, nor can you contact them every few years with the expectation they will remember who you are. So what do you do?

We'll be talking more about social media towards the end of the book, but let's look at some simple ways to make CRM applications do the work for you.

☐ *Leads and Contacts*: First, there are leads and there are contacts. Some applications separate the two – I think of leads as people who might have some interest in what I do. It might be someone I met through LinkedIn or someone who attended an event, or just a name passed on to me by a colleague. Contacts are clients, real prospects, or another name I've collected from someone in a key account.

- *Everyone Must Belong to a Group.* Whether a lead or contact, they all fall into a category. When I look at leads, I have people who work for solution providers, others who work for software companies or hardware companies. These also break down into marketing people, meeting planners, solution provider business owners, sales people, etc. You would have groups that relate to the areas you sell in, such as: executive management, end-user, department manager, etc.

- *The Marketing Calendar.* In order to make sure I keep in contact with people, I keep a marketing calendar – a spreadsheet I use to list all of my groups down the first column, with dates across the top row. Every month I mail things to different groups, making sure that mailing has valuable content – content the receiving group will appreciate. Often I will send the same content out to several groups, but will change the language in the email body to reflect the audience I am addressing. When I email, I can sort my list by *last activity*, to avoid including people I have just contacted in the past week or so, or people with whom I am currently working.

- *Content is Key.* The key here is to be collecting content and only mailing it out when you have something worth mailing. Sending emails asking for more business is viewed as spam, so don't do it. Be sure to use an *opt in* process of some sort, to make certain the people you are mailing are okay with receiving the type of correspondence you put out. Also, follow email laws that require your address and an *opt out* instruction for those who wish to discontinue hearing from you.

- *Attitude is Important.* Your message should be important. If you are a trusted adviser your content reflects this, and your clients and prospects benefit from what you send. Expect people to *opt out* along the way, but don't take it personally. It used to bother me when people unsubscribed to my blog. It doesn't anymore. There will be others who will join, and a few will drop off along the way. If you find people are running from your emails, you might need to update your content. Whatever you do, don't send out advertisements or solicit money for fundraisers. Even those who have *opted in* will be annoyed at this misuse of communication.

Using Your Time Wisely

My father bought me my first Day-Timer when I was 12 years old. People laugh when they hear my story, exclaiming, "That explains a lot." But the truth is, my father saw the value of time and the need to teach me to use it wisely. If we just used our time better, we would accomplish much bigger things. But for some reason, it is easy to just fritter away time and waste the hour.

I mentioned Todd Duncan's book, *Time Traps,* earlier. What if you could just spend three hours each day in concentrated selling mode? Could you double your production and double your income? I don't know, but as I have studied time management books and learned to plan my time, I have seen the value of using this aid effectively. I have discovered, it is easy to spend a day with little productivity.

Duncan recommends segmenting your clients into *VIP, Premier,* and *Standard* Clients and then spending your time focusing on strengthening the *VIP* level with 60% of your customer time, and splitting the remaining 40% between the other two. I like to set up my week with certain days for project work, and others for prospecting and customer follow up. Duncan may be right about these time allocation amounts, but you can allow some flexibility, as long as it's reasonable. Set up days for selling, such as Wednesday through Thursday, other days for arranging meetings, and then allocate time for clients, prospecting, and administration. Be disciplined about doing this, and don't fill up your week with lunch appointments or wasting time with people who will not actually contribute to your bottom line. Social lunches are fine, but make sure you know when to plan them and don't convince yourself they are business meetings.

I also like Seth Godin's recent blog writings on the concept of *shipping.* He has written several posts, and even has a work book out now, about moving project work along to completion. Proposals, call lists, event planning, etc. often go undone simply because people are afraid of failing. So instead of getting down to business, they set it aside hoping to be inspired at some point. You can't wait. Get it done. *Ship* it. Don't worry about 100% perfect work – strive for 80% and get it done. Another friend of mine, in the speaking industry, tells me that it's easier to edit than to write. Therefore, just write the draft without worrying about quality, then come back and edit it. He's right. Give me something to edit and I feel a much greater level of confidence. Sitting in front of a blank Word Doc is intimidating and leads to writer's block.

Ideal Emails

So what do you send people? No one wants to be nagged until they finally buy, so at some point I began studying email, looking at what works and what doesn't. Here are some tips.

- ☐ Twitter or texting are the new email. No one has time for long, detailed emails anymore. It might be okay to write pages to your grandmother, but don't do it here. Keep mail short and to the point. Edit it, then make it shorter.

- ☐ I have actually started using texting with some clients instead of mail. It's short and real time. For others who have an account, I use Twitter; so I can direct message them.

- ☐ Have an idea, here's a sample email: "Jack, I have a great idea I'd like to share with you about how to change…, or fix…, or improve *something*." I don't explain in the email as I am just looking to set up a call. I find I will get a 10% response to this approach if I mass mail it to a group. Mail it to several groups containing one hundred people and you may find yourself with ten or twenty meetings lined up. But make sure you have some ideas. I call this the *idea meeting*.

More Examples:

"Jim, I just got back from a meeting with a Security Analyst, and have some important ideas to share with you from our time there…"

"Sue, On my way back from Palo Alto I came across an article that I think will help you as you are reorganizing your team. Do you have a few minutes for a short call tomorrow?"

The idea is to propose some new content, spurred on by a credible source such as a conference you just attended, book you've been reading, or article. Your ideas must be relevant to the client's situation, so using the *groups* allows me to target specific people in a specific situation. For instance, business owners that might be interested in ideas surrounding cloud computing and cost savings, or larger companies dealing with full-size data centers, may be looking at consolidation projects. Security is also a hot topic, when combined with groups that might deal with high-risk data such as healthcare, government or financial operations. The important thing to remember here is, you must have something worth sharing once they respond.

Partnering

When speaking about business growth, many turn to partnering. There are different types of partnerships, and much that could be said about them, but it would be outside the scope of this book. Here, I am talking about partnering with companies to provide additional services, or to create leads in exchange for leads from the partnering company. I am not addressing formal business partnerships where equity is involved.

As you, the sales person or sales manager, or perhaps a business owner who oversees a sales group, consider adding to your offerings by partnering with other companies, it is important to know how to determine which will be beneficial and which partnerships offer no value. This is what I have found in my own personal experience partnering with other companies:

☐ Rarely do peer-partnerships work. This is a partnership where we expect equal exchange of business. Most of the time, one party needs the other to perform a function necessary for a larger project, such as a network company partnering with a cable company. This makes for a good situation as the cable company adds to the value of the networking company's project. But don't expect the cable company to come up with an equal number of network project leads. In other words, don't look for an even exchange.

☐ Look for partners that you hand work down to – this may be a subcontract where you actually oversee the project, or a referral fee situation where you take a finder's fee for referring business. If there is no money exchange, the likelihood of continuing this partnership is low. In the case of the cable company mentioned above, they perform the work as a subcontractor, so the networking company is compensated for both their work and that which is provided by the sub.

☐ Also seek partnerships where you will be the subcontractor, or paying the referral fee. This is a great way to book lots of business with little cost to you or your company.

☐ Predefine how money will flow, and how the presales portion of this will be handled. Generally, if there is a finder's fee, it is not a problem. If there is subcontracting going on, there usually is not enough money for the subcontractor to invest much presales time.

Case Study 1:

I was working with a network integration company that had a need for some cabling. It did not make sense for us to build a cable division, given the different business models, so we decided to look at partnering.

The margin on this type of relationship was high because we did not need their input on the sales process. We only needed their quote. From there we would mark up the cable portion of the project, giving us a healthy profit for overseeing the project and bringing them the business. I don't remember them ever bringing us any business. But then, there are few cable companies that understand how to make a high-end systems integration sale. The cable company generally works with an entirely different group of people, so we couldn't expect quid pro quo. However, in the end, it was a great partnership for both of us.

Case Study 2:

In another arrangement, our company partnered with a software company. In this case, our engineers were trained to implement and troubleshoot problems with their software. From design to support, our company provided the expertise to implement high end storage systems while the software company made profits on their product sales.

Our company did resell their products, so we did bring in incremental business, however, our sales were not related to the department this partnership served. We functioned as an extension of their implementation team, fulfilling business in other parts of the country that our sales team did not serve.

This was highly profitable because their sales people were able to quote much higher install rates than our regional reseller business, and then sub the work to our people, paying us our normal rate. This was a win-win relationship and lasted several years.

Setting Fees with Partners:

A business coach I once worked with gave me a formula that has helped me establish a consistent means of compensating those I work with. It works something like this:

1/3 - To the sales process
1/3 – To the technology or intellectual capital
1/3 - Delivery

So I take the total gross profit in the deal, and then determine what percent of the sales process I am responsible for. The balance goes to my partner. If the deal is worth $9,000, the sales process is then worth $3000. If I am 100% responsible for closing the business, I get the $3000. If we partnered 50/50, we'll split $1500/$1500. We would then carry this same thinking through to all three areas.

The Technology area is made up of methodology. So, if we are using my process, we might be using my training material, and then I would take the entire one third for intellectual capital. This may not always apply, but where it does, it makes sense that we come to an agreement on how to split this part of the fee. In this case, I would get the $3000 for methodology.

Finally, delivery might be installation, content delivery, or a support call. Again, it is split up according to how much each party contributed. The key here is to agree up front, so that there is no contention on the back end of the deal. In the above training example, my partner is delivering the class, therefore they get the entire $3000. In the end, if we both sold, they delivered, but my material was used, I end up with $4500. If I sold the deal, I would pick up an extra $1500, giving me a total of $6000; my trainer then gets $3000. This may sound lopsided, but in reality, it works well. I've done many projects like this, and as long as we agree up front, there is no problem. I don't hide the amounts from my partner, we just agree right at the beginning on the percentages, and make sure there is enough in the deal for both of us.

Look for these types of partnerships. They expand your offerings, leverage your time, and create a tremendous flow of business when you are on the receiving end of the deal. Look for partnerships with product companies that create a lead in for your business, regardless of whether you are a services or product company. In other words, you are looking up the food chain for this partnership. Then look down the food chain to explore possible additions that would fill out your offerings and offer commissions on work your people don't actually perform. This is a profitable way to expand your business without giving away equity, or going into debt to build out an aspect of your company you can't afford. If there's enough business in that area, save your money and then build the addition to your company over time. Meanwhile, use a partner and consider if you really want that facet to be part of your company.

Building Your Team

Another strategy is to build your team. If you are a sales rep, start thinking big. If you sell ninety minutes a day, like Todd Duncan predicts, what if you had time to sell more simply because you had more time to sell? What if you had inside sales people dedicated to you, presales technical support people, and perhaps administrative help?

It may seem like a stretch. You may be saying, "My company would never do that for me." I've heard this before, but many of my clients (in my sales coaching program) have attained additional help from their company. It's a simple matter of return on investment (Remember ROI – one of the four things buyers buy?). If your manager felt sure that you could double, triple or quadruple your production, would it be worth it to add to your team? In most cases it would. The problem is, your current production does not support it. Impact and Likelihood – can you prove there really is an ROI to be had?

Your business plan, which you as a salesperson ought to have, should describe a road map that gets you to this level. What is holding you back? Is it your company? Perhaps the product you sell isn't big enough to build this kind of business? Then maybe you should be looking at something different to sell. Or possibly, you are just not used to that kind of success, and have told yourself you can't do it. This is a personal problem; one you need to overcome. Think big. Most sales people have unlimited potential. It may require a move to a different company, but it is out there. Too many people blame a lack of success on their company, when truthfully, they aren't really working at their own emotional roadblocks, or have stopped learning. Technology sales are growing and the opportunity to be involved with this type of business is waiting for people who are serious about growth. But it won't come easy. You may need to change some habits, do more learning, hire a coach or take some classes.

Case Study 1:

Jim, senior sales rep for company A, had a few named accounts. He was calling on more territory, but his largest account had so much potential that he could easily live off of it; if only he had more business in his primary account. Since his reputation was strong with this one client, the problem was simply gaining exposure to more business outside the area where he was selling. Working with Jim, we put together a plan to go after different areas of this large account, writing up a plan of execution that would eventually require him to give up territory. Our first major milestone would require the addition of a technical presales person – mostly dedicated to Jim.

At first, we just agreed with the management that he would only use one presales person, but that others would also use that person. Our plan was to help this individual become so well known and capable in the account we were working with, that the clients would know him and ask for him by name. Over time we were able to schedule so much of his time that he just wasn't available to anyone else. Of course the sales numbers had to justify using him that much, but they did over time. He became a technical adviser to the vertical we were working on.

As Jim's numbers grew, he proposed a compensation plan change, giving up some percentage of commission for complete control of this resource. It was worth it. As the numbers continued to grow, Jim made far more money, and the engineer took home large commissions as well. From there we expanded the plan to inside sales, and eventually hired an administrator as well. The strategy worked and Jim's business became the envy of the sales team.

Case Study 2:

In another case, working with a reseller of high-end software applications, our plan took a slightly different approach. In this case the administrative aspects of the sales process were crippling my client's production. We made several proposals to get some assistance, but management was not willing to pay. So we agreed to fund a part-time assistant, inside sales person, right out of my client's salary. Still getting permission, but not costing the company anything, my client Tim, contracted part-time to take care of proposals, client interaction, scheduling, renewal business, and more.

By freeing up Tim's time, he was now able to put more effort into selling relationships, while we trained his part-time assistant to do many of the things that previously robbed his selling time. Because Tim was committed to using the extra time he was gaining, additional income was soon coming in and Tim was seeing a good return on his investment. Once in place, we were able to go back to management with a new proposal and justification. The company, seeing the results, agreed to hire this inside rep full time; allowing Tim to continue his growth.

Plan to Grow Your Business

Businesses should have business plans, marketing people should be working from marketing plans and sales people should have an account strategy or plan. The problem is, people have stopped planning. It is rare that I see smaller companies with plans, and while the larger companies tend to have plans, no one at the field level seems to know what they say. Marketing departments are exactly the same. What about you? Do you have an account strategy to work from, or have you just put together some sort of high-level, meaningless plan required by management; one you will never refer to since, after all, it really is pointless.

Your plan should contain some or all of the following:

☐ *Your Strategic Aim or Vision.* This is where you are personally going – include in this section some of what I have covered above and your long term goal to run an account team. Even if you are a hunter, you still want to be running a hunting team. To do otherwise is to set yourself up to start from zero, every quarter for the rest of your life.

☐ *Your Niche.* What will you be the adviser of? I have written much about this topic, but here you want to identify it. So stop and write something down, edit it later. Where is your focus and where do you specialize? What do you really want to be known for?

☐ *Your People Group.* Again, stop and write this down. Who do you love calling on, and where will you focus your growth? You may not have complete control over this right now, but put it in writing and work toward it.

☐ *Identify Your Key Competition.* Often when I ask someone to name their rival, I hear, "We don't really have any competition," or "IT is our primary competition." While that may appear to be correct, it really isn't. Know who is out there and how they are branded.

☐ *Pricing.* Study and understand my section on fee setting, write down some guidelines for yourself about how you will set fees, where you will discount and under what circumstances. Also, have a plan to learn negotiation skills and work through it in the coming months.

☐ *Identify Key Partners.* If you resell, include vendor sales people in your region that you can help; understanding that they will often bring you into deals and promote you as the go to channel partner, once you establish loyalty. If you are on the product side, the same is true with channel partners. Plan to make this model work.

☐ *Plan Out Campaigns and Events.* Encourage your company and partners to join you in setting up events, speak at local business meetings, write articles, do press releases and set up webinars. Have a marketing strategy to take this program forward.

☐ *Put a Plan in Place to Build Your Pipeline.* This should include time with existing customers, past customers, and new prospects. Each should be approached differently, but a plan is needed to balance your time and think through your approach.

Training, Events, and Sales Coaching

Keeping up to date and having your eye on constant improvement, is critical. Covey calls this *sharpening the saw*. Everyone knows this phrase by now, yet few actually do it. Why? For one thing, it is hard to get managers to fund the stuff that really matters, on the other hand, most of us are operating on the principles of the *Tyranny of the Urgent*; another popular book title that is well known, but unheeded. In UNIX we call it memory thrashing – just working as hard as possible without order; bouncing from one thing to the next.

As I began my own business, one piece of advice my father gave me early on has paid off well. He said, "I should have done more of that." He was referring to conferences, training programs and other self improvement programs for sales people. There are so many great books, audio programs and conferences available. I don't recommend you go to them all, or read every book, however, I would endorse the advice given by author John Maxwell's ad that calls people to *turn their car into a university*. Why not? Why should we waste hours each day driving around listening to talk radio, when we could be listening to speakers and audio books on the subject of sales and marketing?

Every quarter I attend a daylong workshop through the National Speakers association. I pay for this out of my own pocket and it is not cheap. But the ideas and motivation that have come from this are far more valuable than the price. I even give up a Saturday each quarter to do this. If it were on a work day, I would still do it. I also take multiple days every quarter for planning, reading, and reflection on my business. Why? It's time to create, come up with new ideas, review the wins and losses and figure out how to improve. You can't really work on your business while working in your business.

Here Are Some Suggestions:

- ☐ Find the best books on sales and marketing. You can't afford the time to just read everything, so ask around and find out what people are reading and how your peers have been helped by certain books. Social media is a great way to discover worthy manuscripts.

- ☐ Invest in audio books that teach marketing, negotiation, and sales.

- ☐ Look for seminars on CD. All sales trainers offer their programs on audio. While the class is better in person, the audio is a great choice for one to continue the learning process.

189

☐ Attend training at least once a year. This might be a one or two day class and is not the free product training delivered by your company or vendor partners. Find the best programs and ask for reimbursement.

☐ Coaching and Mentor Programs. Coaching is kind of a new thing in business, but over the past decade managers, and especially executives, have found great value in it. No different than having a personal trainer, golf instructor, or taking music lessons; there is nothing like one on one input. I have personally hired coaches in my business and have provided coaching to many marketing, sales and management professionals. Most people who have done this agree, the return on this type of input is about the best investment one can make.

Moving On – Trading Up

Finally we come to the most challenging part of growing your business; firing those customers who hold you back. In the early years of my company, I was willing to take on clients with little regard for price and effort. With nothing in my pipeline, I took what I could get. But as business grew and I developed my message, skills and ability to advise, I became worth more in the market. Some of those early customers refused to pay the new fees, and I began to feel irritated when they called. I had to determine which ones could step up to the new programs, and which were better off moving to another provider. This offered some incentive for me because, where there is a vacuum, you will work to fill it.

I recommend reporting annual sales by customer, sorted by gross profit or revenue – whichever you are paid on. The top of this list will show the clients that are really working with you. Likely, after a few years, the list will be long. But, over half of them are usually unprofitable when you consider the time it takes to keep them alive. Free yourself up by moving them off your list.

Don't be afraid of losing these customers. Focus on keeping the important ones healthy, and shed the old ones before they become disgruntled. Better to have them wish they could afford you, than to leave you, irritated at your lack of customer service. It's okay if they tell others you are expensive, as long as they agree your service is excellent and your schedule is busy.

Summary:

☐ Building your business requires you have a brand that draws people. Certifications and great people are not enough – you must specialize in one of the four things buyers buy.

☐ Writing is part of building your brand. Start writing excellent content, providing practical insight for the people your serve. This is your people group – learn their needs and start meeting them through educational content.

☐ Follow up great content with great events. Focus on education, not product, and begin assembling business leaders together to learn and grow.

☐ Leverage social media. This forum provides every one of us with a free platform to create great content and meet the needs of our focus group.

☐ Network – create content, then use it as a way of helping those you meet. Trade cards for content, not cold calls, and begin building your network.

☐ Manage the contacts you meet through CRM by grouping like people and sending out specific content to meet the needs of target groups of people.

☐ Leverage idea emails to attract new meetings, and brainstorm with clients. Be sure to come with great ideas that will open doors for new opportunities around one of the four things buyers buy.

☐ Learn to partner in ways that create new business opportunities. Forget about peer partners. Instead, build a team of subcontractors you can feed business to while collecting referral fees or commissions. Then market your services to companies that provide upstream services, such as application development.

☐ Build your team. Justify to your management that you are worth investing in by showing them you can multiply production with dedicated resources.

11. SETTING FEES

"No budget!" How many times have you heard these words? "No one has budget, there's no money to spend, we have to wait until next quarter..." So just go back to the office and tell your sales manager to hold off on selling until Q1? No problem, I'm sure they'll understand. Meanwhile, can he raise your base so you can pay your bills a few more months?

What if the doctor said, "You're about to have a heart attack?" Would you tell him, "This is a bad time – Christmas is approaching and all my funds are tied up," or maybe, "The economy isn't great so I'll have to hold off on treatment"? No way! You'd be out there, reallocating, taking money from savings or even your 401K, with a penalty, if you needed funds to live on while recovering. Remember, you're on commission, so if you're not selling, you're not getting paid. Insurance might cover some bills, but you are going to need money to live on. But, you still take care of the issue. Why? Because it's urgent! Because budgets lie.

Security is urgent. There is no confining budget parameters when it comes to this area. That is why I am always talking about selling security, or tying risk mitigation to product and project sales. Earlier I mentioned buying Salesforce.com for security reasons. That's right, I was experiencing major problems with Act! and on the verge of losing my contact database. After three "corrupted database" experiences, I moved to a product used by major global companies, Salesforce.com. I reasoned that if Salesforce.com was experiencing problems, John Chambers of Cisco Systems (a forty billion dollar company) would be on the phone pushing them toward a solution. I bought at a time when funds were low, but it didn't matter. I reallocated.

Find the urgency. Every company has urgent issues, they just don't always know it. Be the one who shows them the concerns. However, make sure you present it to those who matter, in a way they can understand. Then show them the solution. If it's as urgent as a heart attack, you're in. For example, if an asset owner is losing 100 million credit card numbers, it borders on having a heart attack.

Establish Value Before you Price

Fee setting is a critical part of your success. Why? Because it seems to be one of the key issues sales people run into on just about every deal. "The price is too high," "We don't have budget," "How much of a discount can we get?" The list goes on with excuses and pleas for you to cut the price. But it always boils down to value. So what do I mean when I say, "Agree on value before quoting a price."?

Earlier in the year I was talking with a prospect about speaking at a marketing event. Through several meetings I finally made my way to the decision maker; the place where we all want to be. When I heard the words, "But we can get a speaker for free." I was ready. Why? Because I've hit this same objection countless times. There are lots of things out there offered for free…free email, free wireless, free Google docs, free teleconference services, free newspapers, and the list goes on. So why should we continue to pay for these services? Because somewhere along the way. we've discovered some value that is not included in the free service. How about free eye surgery? Would you buy it? Not me. I am hiring the best surgeon I can find, regardless of price, even if I do have to reallocate funding from other activities, like eating pizza!

Establishing this kind of value requires spending time with asset owners, learning about their business, their pressures, upcoming decisions, risks, etc. Once you understand, you begin to paint a picture that describes how you might solve the problem. In my case, I know that hiring a speaker is not that big of a problem. Getting a great speaker in the area of technology is a bigger problem, but not insurmountable. Getting a speaker that can move 50 executives to take action is a giant hurdle. Most technology speakers are there to tell you what they know, not move the audience to buy. And finally, who knows how to get 50 executives into a room in the first place? I do. In the case I mentioned above, understanding my client's pain allowed me to explain where his upcoming event was likely to go wrong, and then show how I was going to solve the problem he was about to face. His free speaker can't do that. What's the value? If only ten percent of those executives buy projects or managed services, my client would be up many thousands, hundreds of thousands, maybe even millions of dollars, depending on the kind of event he is hosting. So, what's that worth? A lot! What are your solutions worth? I don't know…what problems are you solving?

Don't Break Out the Pricing

Imagine asking the car dealer to break out the pricing on spark plugs, steering wheels, etc., and then ask them to walk through the process of assembly with you. Ridiculous, right? However, we do it all the time with our customers. The place where this is most out of control, is on the consultancy side.

When you buy the car, you care about the car. You want a car that runs, performs, fits with your lifestyle (I drive a FWD SUV outfitted with bike racks and packed with mountain bike tools, parts and clothing). The assembly process doesn't really matter, but the overall cost must fit in the value budget you've set, based on education.

So why are we walking through the steps and selling methodology; the manufacturing process? Sometimes this matters when explaining a product's unique qualities, but not often. Focus on the result, not the process. Focus on the value, not the price. When people ask how long it will take, find out the required deadline. The amount of time you spend should not be factored into their decision – only the elapsed time. They need something, you have a solution you can deliver...period. Now, how much is this worth to their organization?

Computing Fixed Cost – the Calculus

How do you compute a fixed cost that is sure to be profitable? I should start by admitting that everyone takes a loss at some point, and this is true for all types of pricing models, even straight time & materials. However, the norm should be higher profit margins, not a loss. So how do you do it? This topic deserves an entire book, which I may write one day, but for now a few pointers.

Complete the Discovery Process

This means taking time to analyze the situation, talking with the appropriate people, and really understanding what they have in place and what needs to be done. You can short cut this process, thinking it is too expensive, but you throw away two things by doing this. First, you won't have as much of an opportunity to sell your value across all key influencers and asset owners. Second, you won't have the inside scoop on what the project entails, which later becomes your basis for building justification.

Price Based on Value

Based on your understanding of their need, the perceived value to the client and market rate, come up with a price. Let's say this project is central to protecting their billion dollar secret process. What is it worth to protect it, if the likelihood of a security breach is high? This takes practice and guts. I start with perceived value, consider pricing, then compare it to market rates. I don't mind being the most expensive as long as I can justify my price through experience and testimonies. Most of the time, value far exceeds T&M pricing. Don't be surprised if your project earns you $10,000 in one day vs. your $150/hr rate.

Compute the Time

Once I have a price, I figure out how much time it will take. Notice I did not compute my price based on hours. This is the big deception – the idea that a fixed price is your best guess at T&M. Now, if the cost of doing the job is far more than my calculated value price, I may have a problem. Either I don't understand what it's worth, I don't have an effective way of doing the job (like someone building a house without power tools) or what the client wants is not possible within a reasonable fee. Usually it's number one. I've been beaten down by discount shoppers more than once, but these are not my target clients and they probably aren't yours either. Send them to an online e-tailor where they can cut out the middle man and do most of the engineering and support themselves.

Consider the Options

Finally, I figure out other options. I price out the best option, the least option with phases and a middle option. Options help the client visualize what they are getting, what lower cost options cut out, and they head off requests for discounts. Example; If option one is $100,000 and option two is $75,000, I have already told them what they get for 75,000, so there is no reason to select one and ask for a 25% discount. It's not an option.

Things that Command Higher Fees

What allows a company or individual to command higher fees? I've written various blog posts over the past few years on fees. Recently, I commented on setting higher fixed fees vs. totaling your projected hours and presenting a fixed amount (this generally leads to underestimating and a decrease in project GP). But what allows a company to propose higher fees without the competition coming in to win the deal with lower pricing? Commodity sales compete on price...high-value sales don't. Here is a list of category offerings I use when considering how to go to market.

1. Product
2. Staffing
3. Projects
4. Strategy
5. Vision

The order builds from pure commodity to greater intellectual capital. On the low end, companies like Dell are selling low priced desktop systems online. Nothing unique here, but they are fulfilling a market demand; consumers want inexpensive computers, in fact they demand them. Dell can fulfill this market demand by finding more efficient ways to make cuts in manufacturing and distribution. What was once a $5000 entry point in the early 80's (and 5K back then was something to talk about), is now a few hundred dollars. Netbooks and iPads promise to further change the game here.

Staffing follows with various skills that set apart individuals. Projects help companies move forward with initiatives that change the business. This is where value pricing really starts to make sense.

As we move down my list, start thinking about Accenture or PricewaterhouseCoopers. Strategy commands big dollars. In a prior business, I referred to our growing company, as the *Andersen Alternative* (back before the days of the Accenture brand). The message was clear; we were consultants, working down the model toward higher value consulting, while selling the technology to implement those things we recommended doing.

Finally, we have people who create vision. People like Geoffrey Moore (author of *Inside the Tornado*) come to mind. Moore is consulting at the vision level with large high-tech companies, helping them figure out where to go next. It's visionary work, and its high value work.

Most resellers are not built to reach vision creation; their sweet spot is probably in the project area. Larger integrators are beginning to build business processes, ITIL consulting and other forms of business consulting into their model to offset the commoditization of product. If you don't start thinking about this now, you may find yourself without profits next year, and perhaps out of business in the near future. But let me reiterate, the problem is not with the area you work in, rather it is in the model you've built. Resellers are built to sell projects, Dell was built to sell hardware. Both have high profit potential…but building one model and selling another is destined for failure.

Justifying Your Fee

Until recently my three year old son had never had pizza! Can you believe it? Why have I deprived my son? Because he is allergic to everything. Gluten (which knocks out just about every restaurant bread), wheat, corn, dairy…that is, until recently.

After seeing numerous doctors, some local, some far away, we finally have the problem solved. Our local doctors offered him cortisone to treat skin rashes, which covered his body head to toe when he was an infant. My wife, believing the surface treatment was the wrong answer, began researching it. She soon discovered food allergies can cause these rashes. Well, with a long list of allergy foods in hand, we were able to keep Tiny Tim (as I call him) somewhat free of rashes. The problem is, that means Tiny Tim can only eat a handful of boring foods, while watching the rest of us enjoy pizza and ice cream.

Then a couple of months ago someone referred us to a doctor just three hours from my house. Two visits, three weeks of treatment using natural products (no drugs), and he's free to eat whatever his heart desires. Of course, my insurance doesn't pay for this type of treatment…it's all out of pocket. But do you think I questioned the fee? Did I send out RFQs, collect three bids, push the doc for a 30% discount, count his hours? No! He solved a serious problem using his intellectual capital. He earned the right to advise me, charge me, and then convinced me to call him the next time I have a medical need. This is the essence of becoming the trusted adviser. This is not a commodity.

NOTE. Tiny Tim and I are having pizza tonight!

Fixed Price Dilemma

After several blog posts on proposals and some words about pricing, my readers began responding with all sorts of reasons why they can't give a fixed price. Believe me, I understand the dilemma. If you just don't know what it will take, you don't want the risk…here are the common objections:

1. Client doesn't want to pay more than the hours they see you onsite.
2. You always lose when you fix price.
3. No one knows what it will take to complete the job.
4. What about scope creep?

The list goes on and on. First, let's understand the real issues:

☐ When you do T&M, the client sees it as T&M with a cap. Even if you say, "there is no cap," they expect one. If someone quotes me $500 to fix something in my house and sends me a bill for $2000, we are going to have a problem. Even if I pay the invoice, it's probably the last time I hire them.

☐ When there's a cap, I take all the risk. If we come in early, I make less just because I was efficient. In other words, I sold the $10,000 deal, got the approval, and perhaps a PO was issued for $10,000. And I've even forecasted it! But I only bill $7000, leaving 3K on the table. I just lost commission on 3K and my company lost the balance right off the bottom line.

☐ On the other side, if I go over, the PO is issued, the people I am dealing with have put the funding together, it's all signed off and ready to go, and then three weeks later I am back in their office trying to get the PO increased. What do you do? Put everything on hold while you wait? That would not go over very well with my clients!

☐ Or I could decide to keep going with no further approval. Every hour we go over is a loss in profit if my firm charges me the burden cost of the engineer's time (paying me on actual gross profit of that engineer). Before I know it, there is no GP left in the deal and my commission in zero.

So why do people continue to justify the T&M approach? If you find you are losing on every deal, see if you can trace it back to this method. I had one client who was losing about 25% on every deal. Well, that was simple. Start adding that amount to every new quote and you will be right on. If the price is too high, the T&M quote will also be too high – another issue solved. If the client only wants to pay for hours you can prove you spent, the deal was sold on price, not value. If you just don't know, break it into phases and quote what can be quoted, estimate the rest for phase 2 and stop quoting T&M prices!

The Tech Support Money Hole

When I was growing up my father used to refer to our boat as a money hole. You probably have something like a boat; something that continually eats away at the bottom line. When it comes to selling support work, there are several holes I've identified.

Things to avoid if you want to produce hard dollar profit:

☐ Selling managed services with a contractual agreement to be on site. Make sure your fee is high enough to include the cost of staff augmentation if you do this. In most cases it is unnecessary.

☐ Selling on site support or engineering (staff augmentation) with a commitment to be on site two or three days per week. This is especially bad when the person has to be there every other day – it is nearly impossible to fill the other days. This is break-even at best. Another trap is selling half days. What will they do the other half?

☐ Billing a client for three hours. You'll never recover that 4th hour before lunch or the end of the day.

☐ Support calls with no minimum charge.

☐ A close second is, too small of a minimum charge. Consider two hours…if the engineer has to drive an hour in traffic one way, the support call will be break-even at best.

☐ Not understanding burden cost. If a support engineer drives two hours (there and back) between every two hour minimum time call, the profit is zero in most cases. Move to contracted managed support with annual contracts, spread your risk, and make sure your fees cover your cost with the required profit.

☐ Converting support calls to managed contracts without a clear understanding of your cost and profit. Once converted, good luck increasing prices! You should be making more on managed contracts, not less.

When to Walk

Will you walk? We're talking about fee setting, and no fee setting chapter would be complete without facing the reality of a failed negotiation. If you're not willing to walk away from the business, you have no business negotiating. Once the client perceives your willingness to discount, they'll require it as part of every deal. Set your fees wisely, being honest with yourself about your ability, and be consistent. Everyone knows that car dealers are more willing to negotiate at year end, and that Cisco, HP, Sun, Oracle, (fill in whatever product company you sell to) will do the same (Usually at month or quarter end) for any big deal. Anything to make the numbers work. So what have we trained our customers to do? Wait.

Your job is to be the best. Jim Collins writes, in his book, *Good to Great*, about the hedgehog. Being the best, having the passion, and finally the economic engine. When clients see your value and know your prices are fixed, they'll stop playing games. Remember Michael Bosworth's comment on squeezing the wet washcloth in his book, *Solution Selling*? This is where it happens. They won't stop squeezing until the water stops dripping.

What's the solution. Be great, be willing to walk, and leave the client wanting you. Then, continue to market to them until they realize they do need you. In the long run, you'll waste less time, make more money, and have better clients.

The Discount Trap

Do cars really go on sale? I remember the first car I bought off the lot. I was just graduating from college and I told my father about a big sale they were having at a local dealer. He looked at me...I could see what he was thinking. "Didn't I just pay to put you through college?"

How many people drive away from the car dealer feeling like they got a great deal? It never happens. Why? We don't trust people that sell cars because the entire sales process appears to be dishonest. You drive up, there is always a sale going on with some silly inflated monkey in the parking lot, the sticker price is meaningless and the sale price is a deception. Between *Edmunds* and *Kelley Blue Book* online, we now know that car dealer sales, their "invoice price", and the margins they've claimed are all lies. There was margin in the mystery of car pricing, but that mystery has almost completely disappeared leaving dealerships with one of the worst reputations in sales. Even the line, "Pre-owned" is ridiculous.

Discounting is a trap. No one expects to pay list on Cisco or HP products, and most know what to expect in terms of street price. Well, you can't really control the street price as a rep, but you can help position your firm as one of integrity by dealing with consulting prices properly. Here are some principles to consider when proposing project work:

☐ As I've already stated, fix price all services. T&M (Time & Materials) means "dollars per hour" and is a commodity business. Avoid this trap on high-end tech project work. (These prices should only be used in staff-augmentation work).

☐ Price based on value. Don't deliver prices until both parties know and agree on the value. In other words, don't short cut the discovery process just because the client needs a quote now. If you're wrong, you lose.

☐ Once the price is submitted, stick to it. If you quote $10,000 and then come back with $7000 for the same scope, you just lied. You said it would cost 10K but now you've changed your mind. It really costs 7K. Is 7K really it, or can I get you to cave some more? And what will happen next time you quote? Are you going to say, "This time I am giving you my final price?" Do you see how silly this sounds?

☐ If the price is too high, one of two things happened. The value changed in the mind of the customer (or something else just trumped it), or you didn't gain agreement with the true decision maker before quoting the price. If this happens, now what? You must change the scope! Either do it in phases, change the deliverable, change the person doing the work,…but change something. You can't win by discounting…instead you become their car dealer's peer.

☐ If in the end they can't afford you, leave them wishing they could afford you.

☐ At times customers have said, I can get the same thing for twenty percent less from another firm. In the speaking industry I often hear, "We can get an event or *lunch* & *learn* speaker from the manufacturer for FREE!" But is it the same? Of course not….sell the value.

Tell them, "If you can get the same thing for free or twenty percent less, go for it! But you can't and here's why." Then be ready with your value proposition. If it's great, you will either win or leave them believing they have second best. Both should be seen as acceptable outcomes.

Example: How Big You Lose When you Discount!

The following is a good example of just how much is lost, when you discount services or consulting efforts. Let's assume you quote a job, fixed price, but calculated by estimating your time. Here are some considerations you use in your quotation process:

- *Engineering rate: $150/ Hour. (this could be any rate you normally use).*
- *Companies publish burden rate: $75/ Hr.*
- *Hours estimated to do the job: 8 (one full day)*
- *Total proposed price (Fixed Fee): $1200*
- *Expected burden cost on the deal: $600*
- *Expected gross profit (GP) on the deal: $600*

So you put together your proposal and submit it to the client along with whatever products are to be installed. The client looks at it and figures there's no harm in asking for some discount. "How about if we just go with $1000 even?" Well, that's fair. After all, it's so close.

Assuming your engineer does complete the work in 8 hours, the client get's billed $1000.

Looking at the numbers more closely: That is about 17% off. Not a huge discount, so you're not worried. However, let's look at the GP discount:

Your fee: $1000
Actual burden cost: 8 X $75 = $600 (Same as above)
Realized GP: $400

Whoa, you gave away $200. That's a 33.33% discount which is about twice the discount you thought you were giving! No wonder the numbers don't work at year end…

But let's take this a step further. Let's say the engineer completes the work in six hours rather than eight. He is to be commended for doing a great job, but now the fee is down to $800 based on the discount rate, your burden is still $600 unless the engineer finds two more hours of billable work somewhere without driving. That won't happen. So you end up with $200 in profit, $600 in burden, and your margin is now just 25% on services. You just lost 50% of your profits!

Typical Staffing Example: Losing on Schedule

Here's another example of losing big, this time on schedule. The client asks to have someone on site full time. This is a great deal as it represents recurring revenue. They can't afford a full time IT person (or perhaps project team member), so they contract with you to have the person come three days each week. The obvious way to make this work is to have that person show up on Monday, Wednesday, and Friday for eight hours each day. You agree on a rate and begin work.

In this case, the salesperson wins; at least short term. The rate is $120 per hour, with a burden of $75. This leaves $45 per hour in gross profit, on which the sales rep will be paid. There are 24 hours billed each week, or just under 100 per month.

On the back end, technical services is stuck with a contract that takes their engineer on site three days per week, or 24 out of 40 hours per week. This leaves 16 hours of unused time, which can only be used on Tuesdays and Thursdays. What are the chances that someone will sell a contract using that same person only on Tuesday and Thursday? From my experience, not very good. The engineer's utilization rate is now at 60%, or just over break-even. I'm sure some work will come in, but not enough to get these numbers where they need to be. Take vacation, sick time, and training time out of this person's year and you will be at or below break-even before you know it. Even if they do manage to pull in a few dollars over break-even, it's not a good deal for the company and won't make up for falling margins on product sales. The goal of managed services and value pricing is not to break-even, but to produce stronger profits to make up for the downward trends on product margins.

A final note: If this same contract is sold to have the person on site for two days each week, say Tuesday and Thursday, the loss is much greater. Never agree to that deal!

When More Sales Lead to Less Income

Traditional thinking says that more sales will lead to a higher income. Here is one more example that demonstrates the deception in this type of thinking. I frequently come across sales people working for smaller VARs, selling to small mom & pop companies. They don't spend much, so the deals are smaller. Yet the VAR model was built on high involvement sales, making calls onsite, taking people out to lunch and perhaps performing demos or providing evaluations of the products being represented. The problem is, they are transactional and so volume becomes a focus.

You control pro bono work - discounts control you.

So, let's say each deal is priced in the neighborhood of $1500 and most of the deals are product install. For argument's sake, we'll say the product is two-thirds of the deal, with a half-day install.

- *Total Deal Price: $1500*
- *Margin: $350 (Assuming ten points on product, the balance on services)*
- *Income based on 10% payout: $35*

So how many of these transactions do you need to make a reasonable income? With a 30K base, you would have to do about 166 of these each month to make 100K annually! You can extrapolate from there, but the point is, you don't want more deals, you want larger deals, recurring deals, and margin-rich deals. Stop selling transactions and start solving big problems.

In a recent discussion I had with a young entrepreneur, he asked, "But can this company afford the larger project?" Great question! If it's central to his twenty million dollar business, he can. If it's just some new cool technology, he can't. So once again, you have to ask, "What problems am I solving, and how much are they worth?"

Valid Times to Discount

Is there ever a time to charge less? In fact there is…Remember Crazy Eddie? – funny, but the wrong approach for your company. Try YouTube if you have no idea what I am talking about.

☐ If a company's terms put payment way out there, often a discount for upfront payment is warranted. While speaker's fees generally are prepaid, consulting fees are not. Using a fixed fee model allows you to invoice early, and many companies actually have a policy to accept early teams with a 10% discount (or less). An added benefit comes in that the project is much less likely to be downsized or canceled when fees are prepaid.

☐ Subcontractor work or sales, where you are not the front line seller, can also be discounted since there is little cost of sale, and possibly little or no commission being paid.

☐ Certain referral sales may also be discounted since your prospecting time is low.

Note: Challenging economic times are not justification for discounts. Instead, figure out what value is needed to move people, and find things to do that justify themselves based on value

Finally, should you do something for free? Yes. I'd rather do work at full price, tossing in some *pro bono* work when called for, than discount across the board. As I have mentioned, once you start discounting, your street price goes down and cannot be regained. On the other hand, if a client is in desperation or you have enormous competitive pressure while entering a new market, *pro bono* work can be performed without creating a long-term expectation. The bottom line is, you control *pro bono* work, but discounts control you.

When They Just Can't Afford It?

What happens when the client can't afford something? Naturally, the conversation turns to dollars and discounts. "We don't want to short-cut the solution, yet we can't afford the price." In other words, "It's not in our budget, but we still want it – what can you do?" Earlier I mentioned establishing value prior to price, but now the price has been proposed, and the client can't come up with the money. Or, in another scenario, you have a contract (perhaps recurring revenues through managed services) and the client can no longer afford the level of services originally contracted for. So what do you do? Here's a simple way to get back on track.

"Price aside…." Money can never become the central issue. People don't figure out how much they have to spend and then look for something, anything that will fit the budget. At least they shouldn't. That's how people end up with a lot of junk they just don't need. Instead, set the price aside for a moment and figure out what is really needed. If money is tight, scrutinize what the client legitimately requires. Great consulting means improving the client's condition, not selling more stuff.

If they can't afford you, you can't afford them

So I simply say, "Price aside, let's look at what we are proposing and figure out if this is really what you need." Let the client see the pros and cons, the value and risk, etc. Ask probing questions such as, "If we cut this out, people will be able to send any type of sensitive company information through email unchecked. Is that okay with you?" "If we cut this out your data won't be backed up off site. So if someone forgets to run the backup, the tape fails or the person who takes it home loses it or it gets stolen, your data will be unrecoverable and on the street. Is that okay?"

Force people to look at the situation honestly, considering value, the risks and the opportunities. They may still not have the money, but if it's clearly what they need, at least they will want it. At that point, they may find the money, or start saving for it. Discounting is never the right answer.

No matter how much value you represent, and no matter how well you communicate it, you will find that some prospects/clients, just can't afford you. In this economy, expect that number to grow within your current client base. So what do you do?

Move on! But remember, every past client, every prospect, and those struggling to pay their bills right now, represent spokespeople for your company; expect them to pass on their assessment of working with you. So a couple of points are key here:

☐ First, don't be afraid to lose customers. If it's the economy, no problem, there are more customers out there. On the other hand, if

205

you have a service problem, fix it. Over time, customers come and go, and hopefully your value grows (along with fees); while their business may be shrinking.

☐ If they can't afford you, you can't afford them. Don't compromise to win a client that will continually struggle to make payment. In the end, you lose, even if it's just from the stress of waiting on payments.

☐ Be prepared to refer them to a less expensive solution. You want everyone you consult with to perceive you as helpful, and wish they could do business with you. One day they may be in a position to hire you, right now they are in a position to recommend you. So keep a list of quality partners that target lower end markets.

☐ Finally, don't let your clients get behind in payments. Extending credit may seem like you are doing them a favor, but you are not. Debt creates bondage... it adds stress to the relationship.

With this in mind, plan your solution strategy based on the market you intend to serve. Put brackets around the low and high end of your target, and serve them well. Refer business to partners that fall outside of your parameters, and charge for the value you deliver in your circle. This is good business.

Raising Your Fees

When was the last time you raised your fees? If your business still quotes T&M most of the time, now is the time to make the change. If you set fixed price fees based on estimated time, you might consider moving to value pricing.

If you're looking for justification on fee increases, look at the value you bring to your clients. If your value is low, it's time to upgrade. However, most companies I talk to insist their value is high and their clients are highly satisfied. If this is the case, you have justification to raise your fees. But don't penalize your existing customer contracts. Guarantee pricing to your best clients, while you move new business opportunities to new prices. Consider adding new offerings to your existing programs that deliver more value with a higher price. Then slowly phase out older programs to move older clients up. Figure it will take several months, if not a year to see bottom line impact, so get started now. Those who wait until their income statements are in a crisis will be sorry.

Some Considerations. It's Time to Charge More If:

- You are losing money on existing contracts
- Installations are coming in with lower margins than expected
- Fixed prices are turning into losses
- You are the low price leader in a high-tech market
- Larger companies won't consider you because of amateur pricing levels
- Your business is project oriented
- Your value exceeds your price

Some of My Favorite Ways to Increase Fees

Here are some ways to increase fees without penalizing your clients.

☐ Measure risk – Impact and likelihood of a disaster: jointly place a value on it and set your fee accordingly.

☐ Look for problem areas that consistently show up across the companies you do business with. Come up with solutions and use this material to call higher.

☐ Trade product gross profit for recurring revenue. This builds annuity rather than a one-time transaction.

☐ Use assessments, rather than traditional open-ended questions, to discover larger opportunities.

☐ Be willing to give away assessments in order to reach higher level people in the account. This leads to selling larger value priced deals.

☐ Propose options to build adjacent business in the accounts you are already working in.

☐ Build greater expertise into your consulting group to offer more complex solutions.

☐ Develop presentation skills that appeal to the executive level. You'll find that you are worth more to them, than the next guy's weak attempt (we will discuss this thoroughly, later in the book).

☐ Pass up smaller transactions to create more time for complex deals that offer greater reward.

☐ Develop stronger marketing programs to position your company as the expertise leader, rather than the low price leader.

Making money isn't that difficult when you start pricing things for what they are worth and focusing on clients who can afford what they need.

Summary

☐ There is no budget. Find things that are urgent rather than trying to sell people stuff they don't need.

☐ Establish value before quoting your price. If the value is there, the price won't be your primary obstacle.

☐ Fixed cost should be calculated on value, not the minimum number of hours you think it will take. If you are losing money on fixed price projects, change the way you are calculating your fees.

☐ Higher fees come with higher end expertise and advisement. Focus on the four things buyers buy and start moving your sales from product/install to true project type opportunities.

☐ Avoid quoting deals that use technical resources on scattered days for hours at a time. This is a losing proposition.

☐ Walk away from unprofitable business. It's not worth your time, and in the long run, you'll find better opportunities if you have more hours to find those prospects.

☐ Don't discount. This is a lose for you, win for them, proposition. You always end up on the losing side of this equation. Instead, trade value for cost.

☐ Begin working on a strategy to raise fees. When your wallet starts hurting, it's often too late.

12. CUSTOMER FOCUSED

REI (Recreational Equipment Inc., a membership co-op). is my all time favorite store. It is a cornucopia of items for backpacking, cross country skiing, rock climbing, mountain biking and just about anything you might need to heighten your experience with the great outdoors. REI has been one of the few stores I frequent for this type of purchase.

I joined on the recommendation of a friend when I was eleven years old, and I've never looked back – I am brand loyal. My membership card is older than most of the check-out attendants, so occasionally I enjoy bringing out my I.D. card, just to grab the attention of the staff. During a recent purchase, the checkout person asked to see my card to scan my membership number. I laughed, "Scan it in?" There is no scanning technology on my card. They keyed it in, but admitted it was pretty cool and called my card a collector's item. So, why am I so loyal to this store?

Let's face it, you can buy just about anything online at a cheaper price if you hunt long enough, but at REI, everything is *100% satisfaction guaranteed*. That means that if the equipment does not hold up, they will replace it without a hassle; and I can verify that it's true! While I try not to abuse the system, I have had some equipment fail after years of use and REI always stands behind their slogan, replacing the item with a smile.

On the other hand, there are stores I have shopped at, and then tried to return an item to, who have annoyed me with their ridiculous restocking fees, store credits, and arguments, claiming that I am the problem. It took a few years, but I now have my own shopping policy. I don't buy from proprietors that charge restocking fees, refuse refunds or give me a hard time if something doesn't work out. Customer satisfaction has become a condition of purchase, not just for me, but also for people all over the world. In fact, if your online ratings are bad, you may never see me, because I check them before going to the store.

Travel Experiences

When I fly, they always say, "We know you have a choice." But do I really? I live in a hub city, so choosing another airline usually means connecting. The airline in my city has consistently delivered poor customer service, refused to help if I make a mistake booking online and has their planes set up with less leg room than any other airline I fly. They have removed in-flight entertainment, they charge for Internet access, and have tried charging for soft drinks, even on cross country flights. All of this would be okay, if the tickets were cheap and the flight attendants pleasant to deal with; but they are not. This is an example of customer service at its worst!

On the other hand I have noticed a significant uplift in hotel customer service across the board. The Wall Street Journal recently did a story on travel price increases and customer satisfaction, noting that air travelers are more upset than ever, while hotel satisfaction ratings have risen, despite price increases in a down economy. While they didn't seem to know why, I think I have the answer. It's customer relationship management. As a platinum member of Marriott, they bend over backwards to help me out. They've given me rooms last minute, when all rooms are booked (not sure who they are kicking out). They escort me to the elevator, refund money if I book and miss the cancelation deadline, and when I show up late at night, I've had them give me free food and offer a number of extra services to make sure everything is just right. In addition, as their competition grows, they have been upgrading their brand by putting in nicer bedding, doing lobby renovations and training their staff to be more customer oriented. Being platinum on the airline gets me an occasional upgrade, however, the customer treatment always seems to be the same – mechanical at best, and downright rude at times. They constantly remind me, "We are here for your safety." Customer service is intentionally left out of the equation.

The Internet Changes Everything

When I need something, I go online. Even if I plan to make my purchases at a local store, am considering hiring someone or need to investigate an account I may be working with, the Internet is the place I immediately visit. When I travel to an unknown city, hire a limo or look for somewhere to eat, I go online first. Why? To check ratings and read about customer experiences. The Internet changes everything. With that trusted vehicle, it is easy to rate products and services. And, the more people buy, the more people rate; giving some products a great boost, while others are destined to sink as the truth comes out that, "This product just doesn't work."

I recently commented online concerning an airline experience. I received an automated tweet back, letting me know this airline does not monitor its online reputation, and recommended I contact them directly. Ridiculous! If you plan to succeed, you need to know what people are saying about you and your company. Your company must be serious about online reputation, monitoring it daily, and responding. In another forum, I commented on a security software brand, making a negative comment about a channel marketing program they were using. Within an hour I had a direct message from someone in marketing. They were actively monitoring the net for "mentions" of their brand, and responding back to my negative comments. I was impressed, and told them so.

Both verbally and online, reputation must be a primary concern for you as a representative of your company, and your personal brand. In the context of moving from vendor to adviser, my goal here is to provide some insight about how the adviser must view customer service. Further reading and training for how to deliver excellent customer service is recommended, as you work to build a stronger brand around your own customer service levels.

Vendors Provide a Level of Customer Service

The soda machine is a vendor – or a vending machine. When I put coins in the machine, I expect my selected product to spew from the machine, landing in the trough at the bottom. It had better match the button I am pushing, and the can should not be dented or dirty. The drink should be cold, and the change had better be correct. This is the life of a vending machine. I don't expect counsel on which flavor to buy, ratings on which product has greater value, and I don't really expect a high quality product – mostly it's junk food, and most of my expectation centers around fast, cheap, and reasonably clean. Since most machines can produce this, the only question left is price and location. In most cases, the machine has no competition, it just needs to be placed somewhere convenient; some place where the buyer has little choice, such as a hotel floor. Price elasticity (the ability for that price to fluctuate) is pretty good, but at some point above $2.00, I start questioning how badly I really want whatever is offered.

The vendor has its place, but at some price point, I want more sales involvement. I want advice, service, quality, and a great attitude; I want a relationship. This is the world you sell in. In order for this to work, there are several principles to keep in mind.

Principles of Customer Service

"He who tends the fig tree, eats is fruit"

One of my favorite Proverbs makes the point that if you want a big harvest, you must tend to the one giving the fruit; in this case it is your clients. Like the fig tree, they need to be nurtured and cared for. The biggest problem with annuity revenue sales (the ones that produce the best long term profits) is that the buyer forgets why they made the purchase as the seller moves on to close the next one. A constant reminder of value must be delivered over years if you want to keep this contract from your competition. Tend the fig tree daily.

The Customer Isn't Always Right, But They Think They Are

There are some clients not worth keeping. However, you the sales person, must be the one to eliminate clients that do not fit into your business model. If they make the choice, chances are they will spread the word of dissatisfaction much further than you would like. Be proactive and refer smaller, or larger clients that don't fit your niche, to someone who will give them great service where you cannot. Your reputation will thank you.

Maintain the 100% Satisfaction Guarantee

Your company may not stand behind you on this, but your job is to help them see the light. Keeping your customer satisfied never means giving away the farm, but rather having an attitude that communicates a willingness to resolve any issue. You never win when the client walks away angry. Expect them to tell at least fifteen people what a crummy company you work for, and later, expect to see the same complaints online.

Learn to Say No Correctly

As a sales rep, expect people to place too many demands on you. The *yes* man quickly becomes overwhelmed with tasks that can't be done in the time committed. Stop saying yes, and learn to empathize with your client over having to wait. I find it helps to at least check your calendar in front of them, looking for a way to make it happen. Demonstrating an attitude of availability doesn't mean you can do it; rather it is an attitude that convinces the client of your sincerity and desire to get it done. On the other hand, agreeing to get things done, and failing to do so, demonstrates irresponsibility and soon develops into a source of irritation.

Make Yourself Available on a Predetermined Schedule

You, as the sales rep, must be available. Unfortunately, your family and clients will often compete for time. Balancing the two can be a struggle and has ended many marriages. I find it helps to clearly communicate to my clients upfront, how to best reach me. In my coaching practice, I receive many unscheduled calls; generally with urgent needs. People have proposals due right away and they need input. Or a deal suddenly looks like it is drying up and my client desperately needs input on a strategy to save it. By providing clear guidelines on availability, along with methods of reaching me while traveling, or after hours, I am able to set some expectations, before it is too late. Consistency is helpful here.

Resolve Anger

Anger and sarcasm are the quickest ways to ruin a relationship with your client. That being said, employers report that anger is one of the most detrimental issues among coworkers. Anger usually comes from blocked goals, rights that are insisted upon, expectations, and past bitterness; usually toward someone not involved in the current issue. When working with sales managers, I urge them to learn how to identify angry people and refuse to hire them, regardless of their skill set. Do you feel irritated? If you are struggling in this area, it's time to get help. There are many great resources on anger resolution, but we won't deal with them here. I love what John Maxwell says, "If you seem to have a problem with everyone, the problem is you."

Dishonesty Destroys Customer Relationships

Sales people have earned a reputation of dishonesty over generations of deceptive selling techniques. Solomon wrote numerous Proverbs about dishonest weights and false measures. The practice continues today as companies sell products that don't work, use deceptive pricing practices and hide defects from the buyer. Commit to being honest, no matter what. In the long run, this is the best choice and your integrity will produce long-term customer satisfaction. If you are going to be the adviser, clients must be able to count on you for the truth. This does not mean you disclose your margins, it just means you don't lie about them.

Understanding Win-Win

I have had sales people take the customer's side in such a way that it compromised their own company's financial situation. There are times where refunds are due and hours should not be billed; but giving into unreasonable financial demands and customers who would take advantage of you, is a disservice to you as well as to the client. In the long run, if you are unprofitable, your client will lose. Win-win means the customer understands you need to make a profit, you deliver value that is commensurate with the fees you charge, and when things are going downhill, you respond quickly to fix them. There have been times where I had to refund money, but it's rare. Usually, with clear communication and a quick response, dissatisfaction can be resolved. Make sure you only deal with customers who understand both companies are in business to make a profit. And your profits are given in exchange for value you bring to your client.

Delegate Mismatched Clients

Not every client is a good fit. Learn where you excel and become great at it. Discern, early on, which clients would do better with another provider. Some clients are too big, too complex, too small, too cheap, or perhaps, just have bad character themselves. Before looking to sell something, look for clients who represent a strong match between what you do, how you do it, what they need, and how they need it. Delegate everything else to partners who can meet needs differently than those you meet.

If Your Products Don't Work, Leave

This is hard, especially in a bad economy or a personal economic crisis. I recall conducting a training class in New York one spring. As I went through marketing strategies and worked to help sales people improve the messaging they had been handed, one attendee complained, "But these products don't work!" I simply replied, "Then quit." I was there to help improve messaging, not fix the product. If you can't represent your products and services as excellent, you can't honestly sell for your company. To do so would violate the principles of integrity – you can't become the trusted adviser in this situation.

What to do when things Go Bad

The company that claims, "Every project is a success," is lying. Projects deal with people and technology, and both are unpredictable. With the rate of technology development and testing schedules, software code is going to fail from time to time, and people are going to make mistakes no matter whom you hire, and what companies you do business with. It just happens.

When this occurs, I tell myself and my clients that the person with the problem needs to leave this situation happier than they were before the problem occurred. Even if I end up "firing" my customer (a term I use for customers who are not a good fit), I still want them to leave with a desire to gain me back as their provider. At the same time, learning from this situation is important. When I go to Starbucks, and they make my drink incorrectly (yes, it happens), I politely remind them that while they make millions of these every week, I've been saving all week to buy one and it must be perfect. This is the way the client feels, whether they voice it or not. In fact, we (the provider) should be asking for feedback, wanting to be the first to know if something isn't right. It is better for them to inform us, than spread the word that our work is unacceptable.

When Things Go Wrong:

1. The First Step is to Empathize with the Customer. I'm not the best at understanding another person's pain, but with some effort, I can begin to see how it looks on their side. Apologies do not produce a desirable response if the person on the receiving side doesn't sense a sincere comprehension of their pain. Instead, they view your apology as being sorry you had to hear the complaint; which is unacceptable.

2. Once you Understand the Problem, you need to determine what that person must see and hear, so they are assured resolution is coming. It must communicate that the outcome will remove pain. This is an opportunity to demonstrate some of the character traits mentioned earlier: availability, responsiveness, flexibility, etc. A timely response goes a long way as does making that issue a priority. Of course, most of us schedule so tightly, and are forced to within the T&M billing constraints, that customer issues can't be resolved quickly. Once again, the value-pricing model makes this much easier.

3. Gain an Understanding of Cause and Impact. Often, impact is the first priority, closely followed by cause. The impact to the client gives us a sense of just how urgent the problem is, while the cause provides insight into how it happened, and if it could possibly happen again. Some things happen once in a lifetime, or once in many life times, like winning a lottery. There is no reason to put systems in place to stop something that will never happen again, like a title wave hitting the Mid-Atlantic shores. If there isn't a history of reoccurrence, you may have a problem calling for attention.

4. Looking Into the Future, Will it Continue? My friend Chris Hogan, who counsels couples often asks couples as he counsels with them, "If things don't change, what will the future look like?" This is an important issue to pose, with an eye toward future impact, as it helps us understand and justify any expense required to fix the issue. Often, issues on projects are rooted in the people staffing them. When a personnel decision is constantly postponed, customer satisfaction goes downhill.

5. Related to Number 4, Determine if this is a Personnel Issue. It is Important to Determine if this is a Personnel Issue, technical problem, training issue, character issue, etc. When character issues are involved, clients often see it before you do. If you don't take action, the customer is left feeling uncared for.

6. Get a Plan. Often, the best option is to bring in someone with authority from your company, with a plan to propose to the client. Obviously this means the issue has to be big enough to warrant such a response. Having been to many of these meetings, when working in past management positions, I can attest to the fact that the client appreciates getting top level attention, especially when it include steps of action to rectify the situation. If failure persists, you may be in trouble. In any case, self-control and a gracious response go a long way because the client sees you care about the issue, even if you are unable to affect the outcome. If your company continues to fail in this area, it may be time to move on.

Back to the Mission

In my mentor program, we frequently begin with mission. I'm tenacious about getting people to articulate what their real mission is because it drives so much of their behavior. The truth is, most companies are in business simply to make money, and when customers get in the way of this mission, the company responds by trying to push through. Companies do exist to make money in one sense, but the mission should not be based on profits. The profit is simply payment to receive the mission. A company that provides lawn care should be in business to provide other firms, townships and private landowners, with beautiful lawns and gardens. The mission should be about green grass, not making money. When the company demonstrates expertise in making grass green, the money comes in. Potential success is determined when the company mission and culture is established. What does your company stand for? If you want to be the trusted adviser, make sure you work for a company with integrity and an aspiration for excellent customer service. In the long run you'll have greater success, less stress, and more happy customers; customers who may follow you throughout your career.

Summary

☐ The 100% guarantee makes sense. You can't afford to have customers running around spreading rumors about you.

☐ The Internet is a game changer. With everyone on social media, your reputation is just a few keystrokes away from great or miserable.

☐ Don't be a vending machine. Instead, take steps to build relationships that allow you to truly identify the experience your client is looking for. When things begin to go downhill, have a response plan. This often means getting managers involved with a get-well plan.

☐ Great customer service starts long before you engage clients. It should be written into your mission. Make sure your company is committed to serving the customer and responding when issues arise.

13. LEVERAGING SOCIAL MEDIA

Why do people spend extra money on Apple, buy everything Apple has to offer and convince everyone around them to purchase Apple? It's like a cult…well, not really, but sometimes you wonder what kind of Kool-Aid these people are drinking. I have a Mac, and yes, I constantly proclaim to those around me the virtues of Mac computers, but *why?*

I recently watched a YouTube video on the success of Apple's marketing efforts. The speaker talked about Apple as the company who sells the *why*; the strategic direction and thinking of the Apple company, rather than the features of the product. Their mission is to make computing fun, easy, innovative, etc.; not just creating a group of followers, but rather becoming the thought leader for a group that already exists out there. For instance, there are many homeschoolers with various ideologies, theologies and prejudices surrounding how education should be presented. These subgroups yearn to be organized. When a thought leader emerges (and there are many), followers with similar thinking gravitate to that person. They begin reading the books, articles, and social media produced by the thought leader. They may attend conferences, buy audio programs, and even begin selling that leader's ideas to their friends. This is not a unique response. The group grows as the thought leader gains momentum. Social media provides the forum, or the glue to hold the people group together, as it presents a way for people, literally around the world, to collaborate and motivate each other. The thought leader must be passionate, committed, focused and perhaps controversial, as I have pointed out in other sections of this book. The leader's unwavering opinion, even if his or her opinion is that everyone should have their own opinion, will drive the group forward.

If you really want to build your brand, you must become one of these thought leaders. This can be accomplished by writing or speaking, but first you must figure out what people group you aim to organize. I just came from a strategy meeting today where the company owner decided privacy and private communication are his passions. But, to create a following, he must find the controversy in this area. Then, he needs to find the group(s) of people who really want privacy in their communications and begin writing about it. He should be following privacy acts, government compliance efforts and corporate policy. He must be leading the charge to institute greater privacy and helping people understand their need for it. As Gary Vaynerchuk writes in his book *Crush it!*, if you really care about something, and you start blogging and speaking out with great passion, you'll discover there is a group who wants to know more. Social media is the unique platform for doing this.

Old Marketing

Two scoops of raisins! Wow! And they have added 20% more raisins in this box! How can they keep adding in more raisins? Kellogg's Raisin Bran has been advertising more raisins ever since I was a kid. By now, the box should be filled with so many raisins, the box no longer can contain any cereal. My family knows well, when I make feigned comments after examining an item at the table or in the store, I am usually reading someone's marketing efforts on a package. It's one of my favorite pastimes while waiting for the female side of my family to finish their shopping. But does this entice me to buy more? Rarely.

There is a place for pretty packaging, slogans, and funny advertisements, but not in the world of high-involvement selling. Sending out mailers, invitations to traditional *lunch* & *learns* and cold calling campaigns, in my opinion, are a waste of time and money. They are expensive and reach only a tightly focused audience. The number of impressions required to move your niche audience (usually about five) is just too numerous to make the expense worth it.

Now, I am not saying giant computer companies should abandon TV and print ads, but I am saying that you, as an individual sales rep, can't really expect to build your territory on this type of advertising. In general, people no longer trust advertising as a means of making a decision, and most of us are just inundated with mailers, billboards and radio ads to the point of exasperation. With TiVo and remote control TV changers, I question how many people actually sit though commercials anymore. I can't stand commercials and refuse to watch any program that has them. In my opinion, even the infomercial is no longer compelling. We've heard them, bought into them and have finally realized; anyone can buy time on television to do a thirty minute show – which is actually a long commercial. I've even had people call me up to offer time on radio or television. It is expensive, and people are tired of it.

In a nutshell, advertisements:

- are a one-way broadcast to a target audience
- are an interruption to what people are reading or watching and create congestion at the mailbox
- tend to pitch products or commodity services – many of which we don't really need
- require many impressions before they become effective – meaning I have to get five postcards or print ads in front of you in a reasonable amount of time.
- are expensive and highly restrictive

Social Media and Internet Marketing

When I started my company, the first thing I did was build a website. Within minutes of launching, I was talking to the entire world for about thirty dollars a month. Since then, several innovative tools have become available, allowing me to interact, create content, publish, reach out, collect names... the options to extend my reach continue to emerge. Many of these tools are free to me as an individual. Only when a large corporation chooses to embrace them company wide, does it start to cost money.

By using these tools, I can reach millions of people in countries I have never been to, automate interaction, schedule ahead and broadcast live, worldwide. And the great news is that it is almost free. The key is figuring out exactly who I really want to reach, my people group, and building my program to contact them. As a salesperson, you may be thinking, you don't need to reach the world, you need to reach New York City, or a small county in North Dakota. I could narrow this down by targeting a special group in my region, but I don't see a reason to limit myself. While the entire world can see me, my site's content finds those who are interested in my message through search criteria; which means I can refine my searchability or become *googleable* to a specific people group, simply by setting my sites up with my target market in mind.

New Marketing

New marketing depends on changing your mindset. Forget about old school methods which require having your marketing department write, print, publish and somehow build your brand. Online, it's all about you and the content you push out. You are the thought leader here; the person people buy from or listen to because you solve problems. Online you can promote that single-handedly. This kind of marketing is not putting out HTML and banners, or pop-ups that annoy websurfers, but rather content that is searchable, using key words and phrases that people will find as they research problems online.

Becoming the adviser now means something new. It means:

- Identifying your people group
- Moving from advertising to content relevant to your group
- A willingness to put intellectual content online for free
- Believing content will draw new prospects
- Being real – people want you, not some vanilla website
- Participating in blogs and forums
- Writing things that help your readers – providing real answers

A Word To Corporate

I still hear company management saying, "Marketing does that." But they are wrong. Companies must be willing to embrace this new direction if they are going to take advantage of what works in today's climate. If everyone in your company had a blog, where they answer key business questions in the areas of their expertise, and they all pointed to landing pages on the company's corporate website, Google would be taking more people to your products and services. While I am not intending to get into search engine optimization (SEO) here (there are many books, consultants, and articles on this subject), it is important to understand how Google ranks their inventory and what makes something highly *googleable*.

Educational Marketing

I've talked about educational marketing in almost every chapter of this book, but social marketing is the platform where this concept really shines. People are searching for answers every day, and by now, most have turned to Google for answers. The only remaining question is, whose answers will they find? Several things to keep in mind as you enter the vast world of social media are:

1. Know Your Target Audience

Some have referred to this as the *personas* – those you hope to attract with your messaging. One of my favorite morning activities is checking to see how many people have found my website over the past 24 hours. I write mostly about sales and marketing, with an eye toward technology organizations. I write to both those manufacturing and selling, and those who resell and provide value added services or consulting services. But as an aside, perhaps a hobby, I occasionally post about my various pizza eating experiences around the world. Being the pizza enthusiast I am, I make it a point to try the local pizza in just about every city and country I visit. It's amazing how many people in Mumbai are searching for *pizza delivery*, and land on my site. But of course, that is not my target audience, nor the *persona* I am after. So as you write, consider the buyer you are after.

- ☐ Find out where they struggle. Don't just guess, ask them. In fact, you might ask what kinds of things they are going to google, and how they are going about it. What search word phrases do they use? In my work, I find people are constantly searching for ROI and TCO. I also want people to find me when looking for a "Technology Motivational Speaker" as it might be a phrase meeting planners would use.

- ☐ Understand your buyer's daily habits, schedules, challenges, age group, lingo, social media habits, favorite media tools and how they might use the Internet as part of their workflow process

- ☐ Learn about what they read for business. Are they reading *The Wall Street Journal* or maybe *Good to Great?* Commenting on books and news sources they look to for guidance will drastically change the way you approach social networking. This isn't about adding a bunch of high school buddies to your Facebook page, but rather providing content that fits well with your prospect's current reading habits.

- ☐ Position yourself. How do you want this target audience to view you? Do you want to be super technical because you primarily sell to the technical people, or are you looking to move up to executive ranks over the course of the sales process? Your writing must reflect your sales process and appeal to the people group you seek to connect with.

2. Be a Thought Leader

Your message must come from you. It's your expert opinion. That means you are the one educating and that means you are the expert. If the message is general, high-level and corporate sounding, people won't read it. If you simply put your written brochure online, you'll have no more traction than the person who drops off their company datasheets at the end of a sales call. Be a leader. Take a position, have an opinion, and be bold with it. Not everyone will follow, but those who do will be loyal to you.

3. Be Specific

I recently did some searching to discover how to repair the rear shock absorber on my mountain bike. There are countless posts and articles out there advertising some component, and videos explaining how something works. The guy who wrote the step by step procedures about how to rebuild the shock I own, is the one I read. He even linked me to a video of himself rebuilding the exact shock absorber I use, and he did it in under ten minutes. Not only did I read his article and watch his video, I also bought the parts from his store.

4. Have a Goal

What's your goal in writing or marketing? Before you put anything online, you should have one. Whether you use Facebook, LinkedIn, Twitter or set up a blog, your goal must drive your content, and you must be consistent. Social media, when used correctly, invites people to follow others. Who do you want to follow you? Some people may choose to make Facebook purely social, and LinkedIn purely business. This is not an easy task since those who really use social media will be inviting you from both sites. However you decide to do this, be consistent. I use social media to position myself as a thought leader in the area of high tech sales. This covers security, networking, systems and associated disciplines which might include data center, managed services, etc. I am reaching out to those responsible for sales and marketing, both directly involved and those overseeing these functions. This is my people group – the group I aim to help. That said, my writing must address the issues these groups deal with, providing specific step by step ideas and insights that allow this group to grow their business.

5. Relearning How to Write

Much has been expressed about the subject of writing; specifically, how to excel in journalism, press releases, white papers, and proposals. All that changes when you go online. Blogging, comments, LinkedIn profiles, and tweets – it's all indexed on Google, and that alters everything. Suddenly, key words and phrases are what matter. You write to be found. Everything should be keyed to searchable text, using the words and phrases your prospects would use if they were searching online. This is how you build traffic, this is how you get found. Do this with great content and you will be building a following and organizing your people group.

Blogs

My blog is my new homepage. Yes, I still have a website, but I am much less concerned about keeping it current and beautiful. In your case, you may not have control over the content, look and feel, or messaging delivered via web to your prospects and clients. However, usually there is nothing stopping you from having a blog.

I look at my blog as a place to catch websurfers – people who are trying to solve problems and who are searching for specific answers, speakers, training or tips and strategies on marketing and selling. As they frequent my site, if my subject matter is good, I am hoping they will subscribe. From there, I am offering content, such as a complementary book or white paper that allows me to ask for greater access to that person. Generally, this is in the form of a name, email, phone number, title or perhaps location. Given that information, I am careful not to spam them or start handing out their address to others. They have trusted me, so I work hard to maintain that level of integrity.

I have a client who started setting up his own website, in parallel with his company website, just to have somewhere to direct his clients, other than their boring corporate site. You don't need to do this. Set up a blog. The blog is my most powerful tool for outreach. It attracts twenty times more visitors than my website, and is much easier to change, update, or customize. It's personal and reaches out to the entire world with content I create daily; and best of all, every word is indexed on Google.

Using my blog, I can gather immediate feedback, develop new relationships, express opinions and refine my own thinking. I can position myself in a favorable light, while addressing the specific issues my clients have. Your company may have many verticals, call on enterprises and SMB, have divisions that deal in networks and others that work on enterprise storage and servers, etc. But chances are, you specialize in some area. Having a blog allows you to create the presence you need online, targeting the people you care about.

A quick note on newsletters. I used to have a newsletter with a few thousand subscribers. However, I found that today's web filtering products were stopping the large majority of these letters from getting through. HTML is not a great tool for email type content, which means most newsletters are getting blocked. Companies, like Constant Contact, tout a 20% response rate, meaning 20% of the letters will get through. They say it like that's great, but in my opinion, if 1000 people signed up, 1000 people should get it. I have come to believe that newsletters are old school and not effective in today's market.

People read blogs and comments. If your company has a newsletter, read it and see if you really think your target audience will read it regularly. Better yet, ask them if they actually read the thing. I doubt it.

If you are shy about heading in this direction, a great place to start is commenting on other blogs. Join LinkedIn groups and interact with people. Subscribe to blogs that your clients might be involved with (simply ask them what they read online), and be a contributor. After a while you will be more comfortable speaking out in a public forum and you'll be ready to launch. Blogging has completely changed my life. My first written materials were in the form of newsletters. I recall being shy and intimidated about stating my opinions, or stepping on toes. Over the years I have come to realize that people want to hear my opinion, and the stronger it is, the more they want to hear me. Even if they disagree. At the same time, their feedback validates my thinking and pushes me to research information more fully. A few things to keep in mind:

☐ The blog is yours. Don't make this a corporate thing, but rather a representation of you – online; sharing your thoughts and opinions with the world. If you own the company, you still want this to be personalized. Don't delegate it to your marketing person, and don't put your blog on your website with a generic header. It's you, so it should have your picture, your name, and state your opinions.

☐ Everything is searchable, so use the words and phrases your target audience uses, or they will never find you.

☐ No one cares about your products, therefore, leave them to areas of your website designated as landing pages. If someone wants information on your product, they can access your static web pages as often as they like.

☐ Don't market. This is not the forum for advertising your 20% off sale. People who follow you want answers, insights and opinions. Be open to comments, questions and critique.

☐ This is not about an ROI calculation. It's about building relationships, trust and a following as a thought leader. Don't get hung up on how many leads come through your blog or other social media, but rather believe that having a large readership somehow translates into customer loyalty and new business over time. Don't expect a sudden uptick in business, but believe that your online presence positions you as something more than you were.

225

- ☐ Write great content. You can't sit around and worry that your content is too valuable to share online for free. Today's market demands constant creativity, and those who have the ability to continually come up with new, great content, will stand out. The more you write, the easier this becomes.

- ☐ Use pictures. I have a section just for family pictures I call, *Real Life*. The idea is that I want people to know I am a real person, with a real family. So, frequently I post pictures of us backpacking and traveling. I also write about my homeschooling. This allows people to get to know me as an individual – which I believe builds trust.

Webinars

Every company should be doing webinars, and if yours isn't, there really is no reason you cannot do them yourself. Free webinars tend to attract crowds of people who might not sign up for a fee based training class, but will sit through updates and briefings to stay on top of their field.

Don't expect to attract high-level buyers here, but with the right follow-up program, you can add to your business by developing an annual webinar schedule. The key is to do this with some consistency and with frequent advertising. I personally executed this under the sponsorship of a manufacturer. While I did get paid for the webinars (and you probably won't), the big payoff came from follow-up meetings set up by my inside sales team – which of course is run by one of my four sons.

Several of my clients have put together programs geared to IT people who manage various aspects of their company's technology, including inventory control, asset management, helpdesk, online safety and traditional security trends. In this case, products, technology, jargon, and custodial level audiences are all okay. Technical groups, once out of school, have options for keeping up to date, but most of them are not very good. Speaking from experience, when I was running an IT organization years ago, I found that most of these programs were not very technical, did not get into the depth of a college class and were generally a waste of time. On the other hand, I distinctly recall a few speakers that ran series, often sponsored by a manufacturer, who really knew what they were talking about. There should be no reason why you can't put this type of program together. I am not suggesting that you be the speaker. If you are a sales person, get your high-end technical people involved and then spearhead the follow up program. If you have to, hire a speaker and get a partner to fund it.

Follow up means you have a program in place before you run the webinar. There is something offered when you end the webinar that leads to a next step in the relationship. Perhaps it's some form of more detailed information, an on-sight demonstration or assessment, or some action that allows you to gain access to more people in that company. Remember, you are liable for the specifics you recommend, and this gives you the right to respectfully require access to asset owners as you continue the process.

LinkedIn

LinkedIn is a place to build a network. There are many facets to this tool, far more than I can address here. If you are not harnessing the power of this cloud technology, you might check out a book about social media tools, or specifically LinkedIn. Here are a few key insights I have learned as I've used this tool:

- ☐ Your profile should be complete. I know, you are concerned with privacy, but you are in sales. So don't put your home phone number out there, but do put your picture, vicinity, job history, expertise, and what you do. This is a billboard with your value posted online. Use it!

- ☐ Remember Google. Write with key words and phrases that your prospective buyers might search on. That means you could include products and brands you are associated with, credentials, company names, and industry buzz words. This doesn't have to be as readable as it is findable. Remember googleable, is the key to this online social media thing.

- ☐ Let people see your LinkedIn connections list! This is the most irritating thing about LinkedIn. If people don't want others to know they are connected to you, then they shouldn't connect to you. You want content that people are interested in viewing on your LinkedIn page, and your LinkedIn connection list is one of the most highly sought after content areas you have.

- ☐ Link to everyone – as long as they don't start spamming you. LinkedIn is actually pretty good about spam. If you report someone, the LinkedIn administrators will take action, so don't be shy here. You can always unlink. The phrase *LION* indicates you are a LinkedIn Open Networker. If you search my name, David Stelzl, you will see I am a LION. I want connections, and if you connect to me and I want to meet someone you are connected to, I will likely ask you. That's what LinkedIn is all about; linking!

☐ Write in first person. This is not a formal resume, but rather a reader friendly way of positioning what you do online. Write it in such a way that makes it interesting. Use bulleted lists to record areas of expertise as well. Be clear, to the point, and searchable.

☐ There is no reason to list every job you've ever had, however, the company names may be searchable, so listing them makes sense. If you have a long list of past employers, you may not want to put down all of them. But if you worked for big names in our industry, list them. It's all searchable.

☐ Join groups. You can join up to 50 groups, so join them. You may not interact with these people, however, you can send more *InMail* to people in your groups, and it's easier to connect to people in groups you share. One strategy is to join groups with people you want to connect to.

☐ Add video, Power Point and especially your favorite books. When adding books, choose those that would be interesting to your prospects. There is no reason to let your professional network know you read a certain fiction author. If you have written white papers or books, or your company has, make sure they show up on your profile.

☐ Set your settings to allow *InMail* – make yourself available.

Once all of that is in place, start leveraging this tool. I have an upgraded account because it lets me see the entire profile of anyone I search. That means, if I call on a certain company, and begin a relationship there, I can do a search and map out the entire organization. That is, if they are on LinkedIn; many are, making this a wise investment.

When I return from meetings with business cards I send out LinkedIn invites to those people I've met. The purpose here is two-fold. I am making another connection to them, which will help reinforce our meeting. I also have one more person in my network, and if they move to other companies, I can I keep track of them. I can't tell you how many contacts in my database have changed companies in the past decade, and without LinkedIn, I would have no idea where they went. So, I read the LinkedIn updates that come out weekly, and when I see someone changing jobs, positions, companies, or anything significant, I contact them. This has turned into tens of thousands of dollars in personal income, just in the past half year.

I also reach out to people I don't know. LinkedIn is set up to get introductions, as long as there is some connection such as a shared group, or the person I am reaching out to is part of a company I am working with. So if I am working with a given division of that company, there is no reason not to send an InMail to someone in another division, referencing those I am currently working with, or asking one of my contacts to make an introduction for me. Don't be shy, network.

Finally, since I am connecting with all kinds of people, I need a way to keep track of those that matter. I do this by entering those that are really in my industry into my CRM database (Salesforce.com). I assign them to the group "LinkedIn", a group I have created just for those who have no other connection than this social media. Since these people have not opted in to my blogs, or regular updates, I can't really send them all kinds of email, or it would be considered spam. So instead, I use this LinkedIn group sparingly. I send them occasional idea letters, working slowly to draw them into another group. If they agree, for instance, to buy something or sign up for something, I can change their group status to one I contact more frequently. If you do not have a way to gain further permission with these people, you are wasting your time. It is not likely that your prospects are reading the LinkedIn updates as frequently as you are, so don't count on it.

Twitter

Some have said this is a waste of time, and perhaps it is. However, it is one more connection. I use Twitter sparingly, and I don't normally follow people who constantly update their status and whereabouts. I really don't care if you are eating at McDonalds right now, or landing in Utah. However, I do follow a few key clients with these types of updates, simply to stay in touch with their schedule. My tweets are generally announcing something I have written, a new book I have put out, a great book I am reading or something I believe will help those who read my blogs. If your prospects are on twitter, you should be. Ask them.

Facebook

Some businesses thrive on Facebook. I recently heard of a dentist who posts health information on his Facebook site. He is advertising with education and using Facebook as a knowledge center; collecting friends and fans, as well as feedback. Not a bad idea for this type of business, especially since he caters to a lot of families who have kids who love Facebook and spend all day on it. My prospects are only posting family pictures, keeping up with past classmates and connecting with grandparents to exchange family photos.

Since this has nothing to do with my business, I simply have a profile, picture and a newsfeed coming from my blog. I never sign onto Facebook, and I don't actively recruit friends. LinkedIn is my network of choice, and that is where I spend my time.

Go to your clients and find out what social media they follow or use professionally, and join them out there. Then start providing useful content, build your network, and create an effective process for following up and keeping track of those you want to work with.

Effectively Using Websites and Landing Pages

All of these tools are places to position thought leader type content. Linking back to pages on your website (landing pages) will provide a net out there to capture people's attention, directing them back to your company's website – but not the home page. In fact, the home page is becoming less important as Google becomes more and more powerful.

Most business people are searching for topics or problem solutions, then looking at the top hits and clicking. You want them to find your fresh content – the social media tools you are constantly updating. From there, you will link them to specific solutions. In my business, I might write about presentations and messaging, tag it, which then attracts sales people who want to improve in this area. From there, I will have links to my Value Proposition Workshop, or perhaps this book. These landing pages should be specific, providing a simple way for the reader to contact me, download something, or buy an item right there. No one is going to stumble across my training programs by going to my website, however, many find it by following the steps I have just outlined.

Let's take a look at your website. If you have any control over its content, make sure it is relevant. A few points here:

No one reads lengthy web pages, especially generic ones

☐ Compare your site to others. Does it look homemade? Sites have changed over the past decade. They have become more headline oriented, easier to navigate and employ mobile device-ready pages. Make sure your site is up to date.

☐ In addition, today's sites have more and better pictures. Overused clip art, such as the computer key that says *security* on it, is obvious and boring.

☐ Remove PDF downloads, and replace them with real webpages. Back when graphics required all kinds of programming, people were putting their data sheets online in PDF form. Today, it's better to go with a link and let people pass it around. No one wants to down load PDFs unless it's something they really want to print.

☐ What does your home page say about your company? Generic product reseller? It should have information on it, upcoming events, pictures of your team and a statement about what it is you really do.

☐ Take a look and see if your site really does look interesting and meaningful, then compare it to the innovative company sites in your industry. Web pages are no longer hard to build, so now's the time to make a change.

☐ Landing pages are the most critical part of this site. Make sure they are actionable. The point of a landing page is to provide a place to go once someone is interested in your content. If a page works, it converts the reader to a buyer. If I talk about this book on my blog, I need a landing page on my site that allows the reader to quickly order it. If I fail to convert the reader to a buyer, my page is not doing its job.

No matter what tools you end up using, social media is powerful. If you aren't personally using it, you are missing one of the greatest inventions sales people have seen in at least a decade, or perhaps since the Internet. The key is learning how to use it correctly. Content, searchability, safety, and personal opinionated content, make this the place to build your brand.

Summary

☐ Old marketing relies on print ads, post cards, and interrupting your prospect's day. It assumes your marketing team is doing it all, apart from sales, and is often lacking in relevance and effectiveness. It's time to change all of this.

☐ Social media is available to you – it's free, easy to use, and has the potential to take you global overnight.

☐ Corporations that keep their people from using social media are missing the boat.

- [ ] The key to social media is great content. Become a thought leader, gathering your people group and delivering content that will help them. That means getting out there and talking to people, understanding their needs, and coming up with creative solutions.

- [ ] Blogging is a powerful platform. While there are millions of blogs out there, you have an opportunity to begin writing to your people group. Make it meaningful, relevant, and fresh. Build your brand by giving your opinion. This is the start of becoming an adviser.

- [ ] Webinars are a powerful platform, generally appealing to a more technical crowd. Use them to build loyalty among these clients; with regular, helpful and current content.

- [ ] Start networking with LinkedIn. Update your profile, use first person language, keywords and phrases that your clients will search. Link to interested persons and begin building your people group.

- [ ] Find the tools that work for your people group. That may be Twitter, Facebook, or Google+. Whatever it is, keep it fresh and relevant.

- [ ] Review your website. Make sure it has helpful landing pages that convert readers to buyers. Use simple, actionable content that lead people to take the next step.

14. GETTING STARTED: MOVING FROM VENDOR TO ADVISER

In the first sales training class I ever attended, the instructor, Landy Chase, started off by telling us, there are sales people who put in some level of effort and those who will spend every waking hour pushing for new business. There are those who will study every book, sales class, and published paper on selling, while others disregard all advice, trying to use "brute force" methods to sell their products.

The Learning Chart

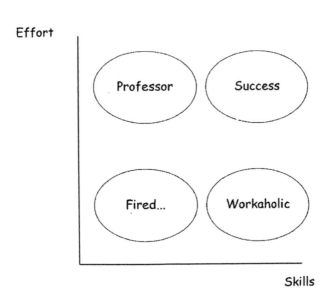

Sales people who put very little time and effort into their business, but spend their hours learning, make great professors; pontificating about the theories and statistics of good and bad sales methodology. However, they never really amount to much in the field of sales. Their numbers are down, so they convince themselves it's not their fault. They remind me of professors I sat under who lectured about the theories of business, but could not actually educate me about the barriers of real-world selling.

Those who put in tremendous efforts at work, but never darken the doors of training classes, never take advantage of coaching, or pick up a book on sales, are the complete opposite. This group ultimately becomes the consummate workaholic; producing, but trading every spare moment, relationship, and hobby for the almighty dollar. They'll end up with failed marriages, rebellious children, and possibly a problem with substance abuse or some major health concern.

Then, there is the person who puts in little effort and also disregards input; this salesman simply washes out. They never sell, never have anything of substance to say, and end up wasting their time until someone fires them.

The person who recognizes the need for hard work, balanced with personal time and family, supported by a constant process of learning and personal development, is the one who will master the sales process. He or she will enjoy audiences with asset owners who have come to appreciate their insights and wise counsel. They will find work to be an enjoyable part of their everyday life. This last group are the ones who will benefit the most from this book.

So where do you fit in and where do you go from here?

Step 1: Personal Discovery

My assumption in writing this book is that, most who read it, will have been selling for some time. You've been in large or small accounts, represented products, services, or both, and have seen successes and failures. Every sales person I meet is unique in his approach to sales, and his ability to interface with people in various positions within a company. My intent is not to change that, but to provide sound advice that can be applied to your personal style and focus, enhancing what you do for your clients.

So the first step here is to evaluate yourself. Utilizing the discovery process I described in this book, assess your own expertise, ability, and comfort level with the consulting process. This will help you understand how to apply what I've shared.

Name Your People Group

Who will you focus your attention on? When I see young people talking about college majors and future careers, I always ask them to describe their future to me. Who are you working for and what are you doing for them. How are they responding? For me, I see my future continuing as an entrepreneurial thinker. When I meet someone who wants to be an accountant working for a large bank, I think to myself: cubical, staring at spreadsheets, with occasional managers peeking over the wall looking for numbers, and no understanding of the companies clients, business strategy, etc. There is no excitement there for me.

Then I think about the young entrepreneur, the technical engineer going off to start his own company, the sales person building a new territory, or a technical expert inventing something and looking for a way to take it to market, I love it! It's my passion, and I get excited about it. Helping these people is what keeps me going each day. If you aren't passionate about helping a certain group of people, you will find yourself frustrated and bored as you try to implement the tools you learn here. Who will you focus your attention on? Who is your people group?

Evaluate Your Talents

You may have God given talents, or skills you have acquired over the years. Then there may be new frontiers you are building or enhancing. In this book, I have covered areas that facilitate strong value proposition, positioning, messaging, and discovery. They require people skills, marketing savvy, presentation skills, and consultative skills (facilitation, creativity, interview skills, writing skills, etc.). Do you have them? If not, I encourage you to study this material, engage with a sales coach, and consider hands on training. This is the difference between the high paid consultant and those who quote products for a living.

Step 2 – Developing Your Vision

In my mentor program I recommend sales people write out a personal plan. Once you have completed your personal assessment, it's time to refine your focus. Consider your direction with your people group and talents in mind.

1. Personal Vision

A personal vision is a strategic aim, or a long-term goal; a place you desire to go with your life, your work, and your individual development. I encourage people to consider this in light of their family, lifestyle, beliefs, and interests, along with their career. It all comes together at some point on your yearly planner. But for the purposes of this book, I will focus mainly on your current career development in sales or marketing.

A vision requires that you be able to picture a concrete scenario, with meaningful work; something you are passionate about, that will drive you from here to the next level. It's the thing that takes you from dreaming about something to actually doing something about it.

Many start with a number – personal income. But money is not the vision, it's the reward for performing well within your vision and mission. Consider your life/work balance, particular passions, expertise, and current position. Write down some bullet points that you really want to aim for over the coming months and years. Is sales your long-term goal or is it consulting or management? Many bring up early retirement at this point, but unless you are really in a position to be retiring, I am looking for something more tangible here. Instead, consider what you do vocationally, and what role you will play in the organization over the coming years.

If your goal is to have your own business, your path will look quite different from the person who aims to run a large sales team that calls on Home Depot or WalMart, or the SMB focused sales person who strives to help small business owners really leverage technology. Any one of the above can be fulfilling when you find yourself providing strong value to that person you work with. If you don't know what you want to be doing (vs. "being an accountant") in the next five years, there is no reason to continue. Now is the time to figure it out.

2. Personal Mission – Refocusing on Your People Group

The vision is internal – something you won't necessarily share with anyone but your closest friend or spouse. It's a long term goal you will hopefully reach one day. Then you will set a new vision. There will be course corrections along the way, but ultimately you hope to reach that refined goal, at some point in the not too distant future.

Your mission on the other hand is what you provide to your people group. I mentioned people groups earlier in the book – this group is important. If you don't know who you enjoy working with, it's hard to know how to move forward. For me the common theme is entrepreneurial. Whether a student, seasoned sales person, small business owner, or someone in the midst of a start-up, that entrepreneurial spirit is what I am after. So when an opportunity comes along to work outside of my focus area, I generally steer away from it.

My mission involves what I do with my people group. I am interested in learning about the challenges, developments, and secrets to success as well as the mistakes that lead to failure and bankruptcy. It is my goal to fully understand the market, marketing principles, trends, and innovative developments; all in an effort to be a resource to those I serve. This drives me to study, read, interview, write, and stay in touch with my people group. If you don't have this, you'll find yourself asking at age 50, "What do I want to do when I grow up?" Don't let this happen.

Step 3: Become an Expert on Your People Group

Once you have identified your people group, your next step is to understand how they conduct business. Find out where about their vision, how they plan to achieve it, and what challenges they will face along the way. As you help them achieve their vision, you will be achieving you own.

Study them. Interview asset owners, and those who work in the trenches of these profit centers to build their businesses. Read their trade magazines, related articles in the *Wall Street Journal*, and other online news sources that will provide clues on key trends and challenges in their industry. Learn their language, their fears, their hopes, and the vision they have for their business and personal career.

This is where the discovery process really matters. This is your group. If you are passionate about this group, you will find greater fulfillment as you see them succeeding. Part of your vision should be to become known as a problem solver and adviser in their business.

Step 4: Establishing Your Plan

With your people group established, a vision to aim for, and a mission to carry out, a plan is now needed. The system you build to benefit this group is important. There is a language they speak, associations they belong to, events they attend, and thought leaders they look to for direction. Begin writing down names of those you need to meet and the problems you need to solve. Make their major problems part of your daily consideration. The adviser is not in business to *just sell product*, but rather to solve business issues; to improve the client's position.

Set goals that will help you get to that point where you really understand their world. Identify those companies you must gain access to as you embrace the issues they are facing.

- Attend their conferences
- Meet key business leaders
- Develop answers to their biggest problems
- Begin a program to educate your people group about how to overcome their biggest challenges

- Develop discovery programs to uncover root problems
- Learn to deliver answers and recommendations in a way that helps your client see the answers – limiting risk or creating efficiencies in their own business

With your overall vision in mind, begin to set goals that will help you achieve your objectives. Goals are measurable things. You can't have a goal to just make $350,000. It's measurable, but it's too far out there. If you want to make a certain annual income, you will need to break it down into monthly increments and measure yourself along the way. However, just hoping to achieve this will not accomplish it. A strategy is needed that will include changes that will affect your daily activities. Goals should be attached to these regular undertakings such as emails, events, and follow up plans. If you intend to put together four marketing events this year; you know you will need close to $100,000 in commissions to come out of each one. This may require millions of dollars in sales.

I recommend establishing five or six key areas of focus to start with, then when they are met, write out some new ones and keep going. You might say, "I need a great message," or "My goal is to put together an educational presentation that can be used whenever I get a high level meeting." Build it, test it, and perfect it. Then mark this goal as complete.

Take each of the chapters I have given you in this book, and set goals to perfect some aspect of each one with something measureable, and begin your move from vendor to adviser. Write down training programs, books to read, messaging to build, events to conduct, other marketing strategies to carry out, etc.

Step 5: Executing Your Plan

Begin the process of educational marketing using the information you have uncovered and the research you've conducted while targeting the asset owners you have connected with. Use social media, webinars, events, email, and phone to attack this market enthusiastically. Plan the balance of your year, wherever you are in your current year, as you read this book. Don't wait until January 1st; start now. Each quarter, plan the quarter, taking on measurable actions to work on and accomplish. As you go through the quarter, consider how to use the month you are in. Plan out activities based on your business cycles, holiday times, etc.

I know people go on vacation in July and the speaking business is generally slow, so I plan other activities during that time. When Fall hits, I know there will be events, especially marketing events as sales teams look to build their pipeline before year end. I know December is not a good time for events, however it is a good time for companies to do some type of strategic planning. It's also a time to set up agreements to speak at national sales meetings that will take place in January and February. So, as I execute my plans, I am looking at the calendar figuring out when to focus on various activities that will build my business.

Finally, course correct. As you move through your plan, expect adjustment. You may find your people group changing slightly, or your message isn't as good as you thought. Find time to correct these things along the way and perfect the system you are building. As you perfect your method, you create and master a system that works to build your vision over time. Success comes when you find, through diligent effort, a group of people that already exist – a group that needs more help than they are currently receiving, in a way they can receive it. As you begin improving their situation, expect your brand to build, your network to increase, and your business to grow. Even an average system, when executed well, will outperform the person who flounders through their day not sure of what to do next.

Conclusion

Building a business is hard. This book is about sales, marketing, messaging, and positioning. I have avoided the sales 101 methodology points on purpose, instead focusing on the value you have and the value you deliver to the people you serve. Some of these things may be skills you have already mastered while others may be difficult to learn. My hope is that by mastering the topics in this book, sales will be fun again. Learning to ask the right questions will allow you to interact with people who run divisions and entire businesses. You will find greater satisfaction in knowing you have solved some of the most difficult challenges your clients face with technology. Then, as these grateful clients see success, they will be inviting you for more input. With this in mind, begin the transition of moving from vendor to adviser. Establish your people group, determine their needs, rework your messaging, reposition yourself as an adviser and begin working with your clients to improve their position. Leaving the "vending" to others.

My hope is that I have provided a handbook that can be used as a guide to build some of the skills lacking in most sales training programs I have seen. Will this book help you grow your business? My hope is that it will.

The challenge as always is in the execution. I often tell my clients and my children, reading is great. Reading many books is great. But it is better to study a few great books with an eye on implementation, than to simply read many books. I would urge you to consider the real value you bring to your clients, and how improvements in communication, positioning, and your ability to deliver, can move you from simply vending to actually advising!

RESOURCES

☐ Find additional insights on David's blog at: www.davidstelzl.com

☐ The *House & the Cloud*; ISBN 1-4196-6618-5. One of the only sales books specifically written on selling high-tech information security and managed services solutions.

☐ *Data@Risk*; ISBN 978-0-9821755-5-2. Takes the concepts of The *House & the Cloud* and puts in them into language you can share with your clients.

☐ For volume orders of this book or for more information, please visit us at www.stelzl.us or contact us at info@stelzl.us